MITES OF THE HONEY BEE

Edited by Thomas C. Webster
Keith S. Delaplane

ABOUT THE COVER

Original cover art by Keith S. Delaplane is modeled from photographs taken by the editors. The front cover represents a tracheal mite in questing posture. The tracheal mite, photographed by Bryan Price and Thomas C. Webster, was part of the first known population of *A. woodi* discovered in Kentucky in 1989. The back cover depicts a honey bee with three Varroa mites on her thorax, an image originally photographed by KSD in the research apiary of the University of Georgia. The art medium is water color montage.

Published by
DADANT & SONS, INC   HAMILTON, ILLINOIS

Dadant & Sons, Inc.,
51 South 2nd St.,
Hamilton, Illinois, 62341
Tel: (217) 847-3324
Fax: (217) 847-3660
Email: dadant@dadant.com
Web Site:http://www.dadant.com

Library of Congress Control Number 00-136403

ISBN 0-915698-11-0

Printed in the U.S.A. By BookMasters, Inc.
Mansfield, Ohio

Typesetting and Pre-press Work By
Sara Kleopfer, Dianne Behnke, April Murphy

Preface

*T*he worldwide dispersal of mites parasitic on honey bees has been one of the most serious problems encountered by modern beekeeping. The devastation of most feral honey bee colonies and many of the colonies kept by beekeepers has completely changed the nature of beekeeping in the affected regions.

The volume of mite research produced during this time, especially the past decade, has become substantial enough to merit a new review. We have attempted to provide this in the form of chapters which synthesize the practical aspects of current knowledge about these parasites. We have also tried to make the book accessible and useful to beekeepers, apiary inspectors and local extension agents as well as scientists.

Shortly after these chapters were compiled, studies of *Varroa* genetics, morphology and distribution have shown that *Varroa jacobsoni* is probably more than one species. Readers should make themselves aware of new nomenclature and the implications of these discoveries.

We thank Etta Thacker for her extensive help in indexing, proofreading and reformatting the manuscripts.

Thomas C. Webster
Land Grant Programs
Kentucky State University

Keith S. Delaplane
Department of Entomology
University of Georgia

February 2000

THE AUTHORS

Otto Boecking
Institut für Landwirtschaftliche Zoologie und Bienenkunde
Universität Melbweg 42 D-53127
Bonn, Germany

D. Michael Burgett
Department of Entomology
Oregon State University
Corvallis, OR 97331-2709   United States

Kerry J. Clark
Ministry of Agriculture and Food
1201 103rd Avenue
Dawson Creek, British Columbia
Canada V1G 4J2

Clarence H. Collison
Department of Entomology and Plant Pathology
Mississippi State University
Mississippi State, MS 39762-9775   United States

Robert Danka
USDA-ARS Honey Bee Breeding, Genetics and Physiology Laboratory
1157 Ben Hur Rd.
Baton Rouge, LA 70820   United States

Keith S. Delaplane
Department of Entomology
The University of Georgia
Athens, GA 30602-4356   United States

Frank A. Eischen
Honey Bee Group
Beneficial Insect Research Unit
USDA-ARS-SARC
2413 E. Highway 83
Weslaco, TX 78596   United States

THE AUTHORS

Marion D. Ellis
Department of Entomology
University of Nebraska
Lincoln, NE 68583-0816   United States

Uri Gerson
Department of Entomology
Faculty of Agricultural, Food and Environmental Quality Sciences
Hebrew University of Jerusalem
Rehovot 76100   Israel

Lilia I. de Guzman
USDA-ARS Honey Bee Breeding, Genetics and Physiology Laboratory
1157 Ben Hur Rd.
Baton Rouge, LA 70820   United States

W. Michael Hood
Department of Entomology
Clemson University
Clemson, SC 29634-0365   United States

Roger Hoopingarner
2712 Fontaine Trail
Holt, MI 48842-9742   United States

Jasna Kralj
Ane Zeherlove 6
1000 Ljubljana
Slovenia

Stephen J. Martin
National Bee Unit
Central Science Laboratory
Sand Hutton
York YO41 1LZ   United Kingdom

THE AUTHORS

Norberto Milani
Dipartmento di Biologia Applicata alla Difesa delle Piante
Instituto de Defesa delle Piante
Universita degli Studi
Udine 33100 Italy

Eric C. Mussen
Department of Entomology
University of California
Davis, CA 95616-8584 United States

Medhat Nasr
Ontario Beekeepers Association
c/o Department of Environmental Biology
University of Guelph
Guelph, Ontario N1G 2W1 Canada

Glen Needham
Acarology Laboratory
Department of Entomology
The Ohio State University
484 West 12th Avenue
Columbus, OH 43210 United States

Don Nelson
Agriculture and Agri-Food Canada
Research Branch
P. O. Box 29
Beaverlodge, Alberta T0H 0C0 Canada

Gard Otis
Department of Environmental Biology
University of Guelph
Guelph, Ontario N1G 2W1 Canada

Jeffery S. Pettis
USDA-ARS Bee Research Laboratory
Beltsville, MD 20705 United States

THE AUTHORS

Thomas E. Rinderer
USDA-ARS Honey Bee Breeding, Genetics and Physiology Laboratory
1157 Ben Hur Rd.
Baton Rouge, LA 70820   United States

Diana Sammataro
Department of Entomology
501 Agricultural Sciences and Industries Building
Pennsylvania State University
University Park, PA 16802   United States

M. T. Sanford
Department of Entomology and Nematology
University of Florida
Gainesville, FL 32611-0620 United States

Marla Spivak
Department of Entomology
219 Hodson Hall
University of Minnesota
St. Paul, MN 55108-6125   United States

Thomas C. Webster
Atwood Research Facility
Kentucky State University
Frankfort, KY 40601   United States

William T. Wilson
Honey Bee Group
Beneficial Insect Research Unit
USDA-ARS-SARC
2413 E. Highway 83
Weslaco, TX 78596   United States

TABLE OF CONTENTS

Part I   Introduction
Chapter 1 . . . . .Page 1
Mite biology
Glen R. Needham, Uri Gerson and
Diana Sammataro

Part II   Tracheal mites and other *Acarapis*
Chapter 2 . . . . .Page 17
Biology and life history of *Acarapis dorsalis*
and *A. externus*
Lilia I. de Guzman, D. Michael Burgett
and Thomas E. Rinderer
Chapter 3 . . . . .Page 29
Biology and life history of tracheal mites
Jeffery S. Pettis
Chapter 4 . . . . .Page 43
Introduction, spread and economic impact of
tracheal mites in North America
Eric C. Mussen
Chapter 5 . . . . .Page 57
Pathological effects of tracheal mite infestations
Clarence H. Collison
Chapter 6 . . . . .Page 73
Methods of sampling and measuring
populations of tracheal mites
Medhat E. Nasr
Chapter 7 . . . . .Page 85
Chemical control of tracheal mites
William T. Wilson, D. L. Nelson and
Kerry J. Clark
Chapter 8 . . . . .Page 105
Cultural and natural control of tracheal mites
Frank A. Eischen
Chapter 9 . . . . .Page 117
Resistance of honey bees to tracheal mites
Robert Danka

TABLE OF CONTENTS

Part III   Varroa mites

Chapter 10 . . . . .Page 131
> Biology and life history of Varroa mites
> Stephen J. Martin

Chapter 11 . . . . .Page 149
> Introduction, spread and economic impact of
>   Varroa mites in North America
> M. T. Sanford

Chapter 12 . . . . .Page 163
> Methods of sampling and measuring
>   populations of Varroa mites
> Thomas C. Webster

Chapter 13 . . . . .Page 179
> Chemical control of Varroa mites
> Marion Ellis

Chapter 14 . . . . .Page 197
> Biotechnical control of Varroa mites
> Roger Hoopingarner

Chapter 15 . . . . .Page 205
> Resistance of honey bees to Varroa mites
> Marla Spivak and Otto Boecking

Chapter 16 . . . . .Page 229
> Treatment thresholds for Varroa mites
> W. Michael Hood and Keith S. Delaplane

Chapter 17 . . . . .Page 241
> Management of the resistance of Varroa mites to
>   acaricides
> Norberto Milani

Part IV Other mite species

Chapter 18 . . . . .Page 251
> Mites of economic importance not present
>   in North America
> Gard Otis and Jasna Kralj

MITE BIOLOGY

Glen R. Needham
Uri Gerson
Diana Sammataro

Mites are a major component of the animal kingdom. Their diminutive size (around 0.5 mm or less) belies the various roles, good, bad and neutral, that they play in nature. The size of an organism is not necessarily correlated with complexity. If not for the negative impact created in the beehive by several specialized mite species, their presence might have been overlooked. The goal in this brief introductory chapter is to supply a perspective on mites as organisms and to provide basic information about certain aspects of mite biology.

Early in the 20th century, the world of the honey bee was threatened by a newly-discovered mite called *Acarapis woodi*. This discovery eliminated what had been a relatively simple life for beekeepers. The mite story became more troublesome when an external parasite, *Varroa jacobsoni*, an introduced species from Asian bees, was detected in Europe, and together they have all but wiped out the casual beekeeper and feral (wild) bees. By the 1980's both of these mites had made their way to North and South America, and have forever changed the way bees are managed.

Both mites are discussed in great detail in the ensuing chapters of this book by experts. A hopeful trend in our fight against these dangerous adversaries is that more collaborative work is being done by researchers around the world. There has been a modest investment by beekeeping industries and government in finding solutions. Unfortunately, efforts to devise means of protection from these parasites are difficult. The complexity and challenge of managing healthy colonies are reflected in the lack of solutions available today, despite many years of struggle. Sole reliance on chemical controls, and abuses of those active ingredients, are bringing about the development of resistance to pesticides by some of these mites. Although some new chemicals show promise, there have not been, nor are there likely to be any quick fixes. Use of vegetable shortening, along with granulated sugar, is the closest thing to a cheap, effective and environmentally friendly control method of tracheal mites[38]. The long-term future of beekeeping now rests in the hands of a few dedicated scientists and beekeepers worldwide, who are striving to gain a better understanding of the basic biology of these mites and their effect on the bee hosts. Many of those individuals are contributors to this book.

Mites (Acari). Mites are invertebrates with four pairs of articulated legs (Arthropods), chelicerate (pincer-like) mouthparts and a fused body. Unlike insects, they lack wings, eyes and antennae. Instead, they have sensory hairs to maneuver in the environment. The existence of *acarology* as a separate discipline (from zoology and entomology) is based almost solely on the problems mites (including ticks) present to humans and to their domestic animals. Homer was probably the first to refer to a mite, a tick on Ulyssus' dog[35].

Even the trained specialists who know arthropods underestimate the wealth and variety of mite species and their importance in nature, although mites have been known as pests since the 9th century B.C. The Acari are the most widely distributed arachnids (which also include the spiders and scorpions), and the number of their species may well rival that of insects (>1 million), but only about 30,000 have been given names[21].

Their biological diversity is impressive; the Acari have colonized just about every habitat that animals can occupy[4]. This includes not only plants and animals, but also the bottom of the oceans[34], hot springs[43], deserts[42], and just about every conceivable habitat in between (sea snake eyes, monkey lungs, parrot feathers). To see for yourself, just pick up a handful of organic soil and examine it under a dissecting microscope or good magnifying glass. You will find mite specimens of different shapes, sizes and activity. Handle a bird nest just after it was abandoned by the nestlings and you may see dozens of small organisms (bird mites) scurrying across your hand. Fresh water streams, ponds, lakes and even hot springs have their own mite faunas. Some, like spider mites, seriously damage host plants, while feeding by others causes unsightly growths (galls).

Some mites hitch rides on other arthropods. Daddy longlegs (Opiliones) often have bright red mites on their legs, which are immatures getting moved about on their mobile, active transport. The Madagascar hissing cockroach, common to zoos, classrooms and laboratories, has a visible mite that exists solely on these hosts, causing them no harm[44]. Most of us adults carry follicle mites (Demodicidae) in our facial pores. Acari were the first animals on the moon, as follicle mites called the skin of Neil Armstrong their home. Mites make us sneeze as about 5% of the population is allergic to dust mite feces and to their cast skins.

Mites invade the internal organs of humans, other vertebrates and invertebrates, where they form various associations with their hosts. These associations include a host and its associate, usually called symbiont. Associations range from commensalism (the symbiont-mite benefits, host not helped or harmed) to parasitism (symbiont benefits at expense of host, either inside or outside of host). The bee mites, *Varroa* and *Acarapis*, are common examples of parasites. Mites living in temporary habitats (including weakened hosts) often use other arthropods (especially winged insects) or vertebrates as vehicles of dispersion, as mites have no wings. For bee mites there is double the dispersal potential: first via the host and then by humans, who move bees on trucks, trailers, boats, airplanes and even in pockets of beekeepers. Eva Crane's overview links the advent of air travel with the global dispersal of bee mites[6].

Another feature that provides many mites with an advantage in life is their reproductive strategy. Many mite species have a system where the female controls which eggs are fertilized, much like honey bees. The fertilized egg becomes a female who has the benefit of genetic material from both parents, whereas the unfertilized egg becomes a male, with only half of the genetic complement (only mother's genes). *Acarapis woodi*, like many other parasitic mites, uses a short-cut for development. Mites typically go through the following stages: egg—larva—protonymph—deutonymph (sometimes a tritonymph)—adult. The tracheal mite, however, has only the egg, larva and adult stages. This greatly shortens the time for development to about two weeks, so that populations of *Acarapis* can grow very quickly.

An abbreviated development time along with a high number of off-spring, allow mites to be very adaptable in changing environments. A major artificial environmental change in beehives was the addition of acaricides for mite control. High reproductive capacity, shortened life cycles and especially the continuous use of the same pesticide may speed up acaricide resistance. Apistan® strips for *Varroa* control are becoming less effective and mite biology explains part of the problem. The other is the overuse of active ingredients by beekeepers, which results in greater selection pressure (killing) being placed on the mites, leaving only resistant individuals to mate and produce more resistant offspring.

Lifestyles and body forms. Mite diversity in lifestyles is especially reflected in acarine body forms and life-history patterns[17]. The body of a mite has an integument that is variously hard and dark, or light in color and very flexible. Mite development is highly variable and may consist of numerous postembryonic instars. However, unlike the lower insects (which undergo gradual metamorphosis, like grasshoppers), immature mites may be very different from the adults. This provides for great plasticity, enabling them to live in different habitats or to colo-nize those that change quickly even during the various stages. A well-known example is the chigger mite, which as a larva feeds on lizards and occasionally bites humans. The subsequent nymphs and adults are bright red, free-living predators. As with other small arthropods, most mites are short lived and development occurs over days or weeks.

Just the size of mites like *Acarapis woodi* is a critical feature. Smallness has its advantages and disadvantages. An obvious advantage is the ability of *A. woodi* to scurry under the flat lobe that covers the bee's first thoracic spiracle, and once there to colonize the main tra-cheal trunk (Chapter 3). Being small allows more mites to occupy the limited space within tracheae, which facilitates reproduction but hastens the bee death.

As a result, these mites cannot be outside the host for very long or they will rapidly desiccate and die. The primary disadvantage of diminutive size is the risk of dehydration, because mites have such a large surface area compared to their internal volume. This limitation necessitates obligate parasitism and/or the acarine must be able to obtain moisture some way other than by feeding (e.g. vapor uptake from subsaturated air, drinking water, producing metabolic water). The problem with drinking in such a small creature is the risk of being entrapped by surface tension of the liquid.

Acarapis has a diminutive size, and beekeepers know that this mite is impossible to visualize while working their bees, and thus diagnose a colony infestation. It is very difficult to reach the mites with a pesticide within the bee's breathing tubes. If a volatile active ingredient (e.g. menthol) is inhaled by a bee, it should be lethal to the parasite but safe for the host. Since both are arthropods, many of their basic physiological processes are similar, making the window of opportunity for finding such toxicants quite narrow. Beekeepers know that bees are extremely sensitive to accidental pesticide poisoning, making the host especially vulnerable to many of the common active ingredients used for agriculture.

The ectoparasite *Varroa* has several key morphological features that make it successful (Fig. 1.1). Dorsoventral compression (rather than lateral compression, like in fleas) of the females allows them to fit snugly beneath structures like the abdominal sclerites (plates). This reduces their vulnerability to grooming or to being knocked off during a bee's active life; also, being in that location probably slows water loss by transpiration across their integument. When the adult mites enter the brood cell this same morphology allows them to fit between the cell wall and brood body surface. *Varroa* are seen with their back (dorsal) surface down, entirely covered in the liquid food being fed to larvae. A special snorkel-like respiratory structure extends through the fluid to the surface, in order to facilitate breathing while submerged. Like tracheal mites, *Varroa* can evade acaricides when the brood cell is capped just prior to pupation. More details of *Varroa* morphology are given in this book.

The hive as a habitat for mites. The biology of parasitic bee mites, and hence control, can best be understood by reference to their hosts. The

▶*Figure 1.1 Size and shape of three arthropods enable them to thrive as highly specialized parasites. They are pictured at approximately the same magnification (65X) for comparative purposes. Photos by Bill Styer, Ohio Agricultural Research and Development Center, Wooster, Ohio. Copyright, Acarology Laboratory, The Ohio State University.*

▲*a) Bilaterally compressed (flat from side-to-side) cat flea,* Ctenophalides felix *moves easily between the vertical hairs of the host.*

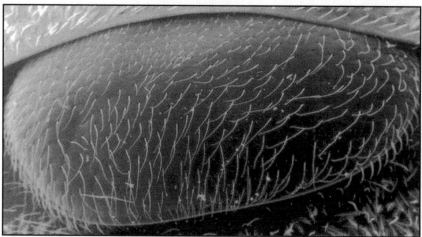

▲*b) Dorsoventrally compressed (flat top to bottom)* Varroa jacobsoni *female lays partially hidden beneath an abdominal tergite of a honey bee and this shape allows her to fit between the immature bee and the brood cell wall.*

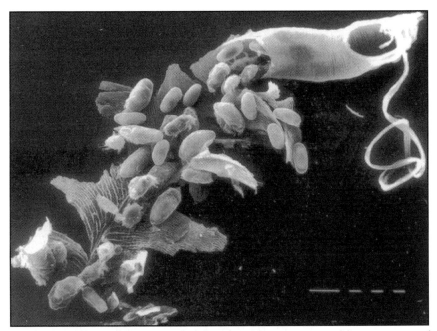

▲*c) Numerous minute tracheal mites* (Acarapis woodi) *are exposed from a single dissected thoracic tracheal trunk.*

honey bee, *Apis mellifera*, is a social insect that lives in colonies. Each colony has two female castes: one queen and workers, which may number 20,000-50,000 per colony. Colony life is regulated by an array of pheromones, emitted mainly by the queen. The colony also has males, called drones, which serve mainly to inseminate the queen during her mating flight.

Characteristic of social insects, there is a division of labor in the colony. Young workers nurse and groom the queen and brood; older workers forage for pollen, nectar, propolis and water, and defend the colony. Nest homeostasis is maintained by the workers, who keep the temperature and humidity nearly constant despite external conditions. An abundance of proteinaceous foods (pollen) and carbohydrates (honey) are usually available. Total development of the queen requires about 16 days, that of workers 21 days, and the drones 24 days. The queen can survive for several years, but workers and drones usually live only a few weeks. During cold periods the workers, which may then survive for several months, cluster around the queen to incubate any eggs laid during this time.

Non-bee invaders that can circumvent colony defenses will thus benefit from the favorable conditions of the hive environment for their own development and reproduction. Most of the successful invaders are mites, and they make up the largest and most diverse group of honey bee associates. Different honey bee species have varied nesting habitats, and their relationships with acarine parasites are discussed below.

Mites are common inhabitants of the bee colony. Some 86 mite species have been recorded in association with *Apis* and their nests[15,16], but most are neutral or benign in nature. De Jong[10] provides a detailed list of most mites known from honey bees. Eickwort[16] breaks the "hive" mites into four ecological categories: 1) mites scavenging on hive debris; 2) predatory mites that eat the scavengers; 3) mites that "hitch" a ride to flowers and other hives on foraging honey bees; and, 4) honey bee parasites.

Non-parasitic bee mites. Three common groups of mites associated with bees are the Astigmata, Prostigmata and the Mesostigmata[38]. Many astigmatic mites live on the hive's floor, feeding on bee debris, dead insects and fungi growing thereon. *Forcellinia faini* (Astigmata), a common, whitish, slow-moving scavenger initially described in Puerto Rico, was abundantly collected in hive debris in northern and southern Thailand[18]. A representative of the Prostigmata is the tarsonemid *Pseudacarapis indoapis* (Lindquist), a tentative pollen feeder, apparently restricted to *Apis cerana*[27].

Melichares dentriticus (Mesostigmata), a cosmopolitan predator on scavenger mites, is common to stored products[20], while members of *Neocypholaelaps* and *Afrocypholaelaps* live in flowers. They feed on the pollen of subtropical and tropical trees and are phoretic on bees. Several dozen *Afrocypholaelaps africana* were found on individual bees visiting mangrove umbels in Queensland[40]. Mites dispersing on *A. mellifera*, mostly as egg-bearing females, board and depart the bees via the tongue. The bees did not appear to be annoyed by these mites, nor were their foraging activities disrupted. Ramanan and Ghai[36] reported that 1-400 *A. africana* occurred on individuals of *A. cerana* in India. As bees return to the hive, mites disembark, roam on the combs and subsist on the pollen. *Melittiphis alvearius* has been found in hives and on bees in various parts of the world[14]. Serological procedures demonstrated that, contrary to formerly-held views, this mite is not a predator, but feeds on stored pollen[19].

Table 1.1 Mesostigmatic mites parasitizing bees, arranged
according to host bee species[22]. An asterisk denotes
mites believed to be originally associated with the
particular bee species.

Species of *Apis*	Mites
andreniformis	*Euvarroa sinhai*[13]
	*Euvarroa wongsirii** [25]
cerana	*Tropilaelaps clareae* (?)[13]
	*Varroa jacobsoni**
	*Varroa underwoodi** [13]
dorsata	*Tropilaelaps clareae** [12]
	*Tropilaelaps koenigerum** [13]
florea	*Euvarroa sinhai**
	Tropilaelaps clareae[13]
koschevnikovi	*Varroa rindereri** [8]
	Varroa jacobsoni[13]
laboriosa	*Tropilaelaps clareae*
	Tropilaelaps koenigerum[13]
mellifera	*Euvarroa sinhai*[22]
	Tropilaelaps clareae[13]
	Varroa jacobsoni[13]
nigrocincta	*Varroa underwoodi*[3]
nuluensis	*Varroa jacobsoni*[13]
	Varroa near underwoodi[7]

Other parasitic bee mites. Most parasitic bee mites (with the exception of *Acarapis*) were in the tribe Varroini (or Group V) in the family Laelapidae[5] (Table 1.1).

Euvarroa. *Euvarroa sinhai* is a parasite of *A. florea*, occurring in Asia from Iran through India to Sri Lanka. The mite develops naturally on the capped drone brood[32], but has been reared in the laboratory on *A. mellifera* worker brood[33]. Development requires less than one week, and each female produces 4-5 offspring. Drones as well as workers are used for dispersal. The female mite overwinters in the colony, probably feeding on the clustering bees. Colony infestation by *E. sinhai* is somehow hindered by the construction of queen cells[1] and its population growth is inhibited in the presence of *T. clareae* and of *V. jacobsoni*[41]. Transfer experiments[23] confirmed that *E. sinhai* may survive on *A. mellifera* and *A. cerana*, emphasizing their ability to cross-infest exotic hosts.

    Euvarroa wongsirii parasitizes drone brood of *A. andreniformis* in Thailand and Malaysia. Its biology appears similar to *E. sinhai* and it can live for at least 50 days on worker bees outside the nest[31].

Tropilaelaps clareae. This mite belongs in the mesostigmatic family Laelapidae, which has members that are mammalian parasites. *Tropilaelaps clareae*, originally obtained from a field rat[11] from the Philippines, normally occurs on *A. dorsata*; this mite also parasitizes *A. mellifera*[25]. Currently, *T. clareae* is restricted to Asia, from Iran in the northwest, to Papua New Guinea in the southeast[29]. A single, alarming report of this mite in Kenya[24,30] has not been repeated.

    The sudden global emergence of bee mites prompted initial research on detection, monitoring population levels and controlling mites. An animated map of the spread of *Varroa* is found on the world wide web at *http://www.CSFNET.ORG/image/animap2.gif.*

    Recent molecular techniques have demonstrated that *V.jacobsoni* most likely is a complex of species represented by at least 5 sibling species[2], only one of which has spread from *A. cerana* to *A. mellifera*, causing the enormous bee losses. Morphological differences have been recorded between these species and the species appear to be reproductively isolated from one another. Hence the varroa on *A.mellifera* could soon be renamed. The name *Varroa destructor* has been proposed (D.Anderson, pers.comm.), and if several species and strains are masquerading under the name *V. jacobsoni*, and they possess different levels of virulence, the survival of untreated bee colonies despite the varroa mite's presence in South America may be explained[9]. Martin and Ball[28] reported differences in mite virulence and virus associations on honey bee survival in the UK.

In the meantime, basic mite studies have been lagging. Several areas of research need to be addressed if bees are to remain a viable segment of agriculture. For example, it is not clear how particular bee mites actually damage their hosts, and what the role various disease organisms play in the ensuing colony decline. The presence of viruses is a special challenge and controlling these mites would almost certainly diminish viral effects. Next, the emerging recognition of new bee species and their mite parasites makes continued research a high priority. We need to determine whether any of these 'new' mites will also cross-infest the dominant domesticated honey bee, *A. mellifera*, should they ever be introduced. More parasitic mites would be disaster to the bee industry. Then, the development of chemicals or other modes of controlling bee mites would be facilitated by rearing them apart from bees. Much more work on *in vitro* culture of all parasitic bee mites is needed, although laboratory methods for culturing varroa and *T. clareae* were developed by Rath[37].

Finally, the most pressing problem remains control, preferably without synthetic chemicals. Thus we conclude by advocating the vigorous testing of various active ingredients, such as "botanicals", the breeding of bees for resistance to both mites and exploring other biological or cultural techniques. The challenges ahead include attracting mites away from bees, killing mites without contaminating hive products or injuring bees, and keeping the controls economic, effortless and easy for both the hobbyist and commercial beekeeper. Another problem is to determine an economic injury level of mite infestation and a threshold to indicate treatment times; this would take the guesswork out of when to medicate. The long-term solution to parasitic bee mites is in developing an integrated pest management program, to manage mites by multiple means, not relying on any one or two chemical treatments.

Summary. Mites are one of the most numerous and species-rich groups of organisms on the planet. Most are beneficial or neutral from man's perspective, but a few have managed to invade the complex arena of the honey bee hive. Here they are making the life of the beekeeper very difficult while eliminating most of the feral bees. The tracheal mite,

Acarapis woodi, and the varroa mite, *Varroa jacobsoni*, are primary pests of the honey bee in many parts of the world. These mites are especially adapted to 'fit' into the bee colony, finding security in either the tracheal system (tracheal mite); or for varroa within a capped comb cell and under the tergite or wing of a host bee. Each spends very little time away from these harborages, which makes control very difficult. Both mites are eyeless, but still somehow manage to find sites for feeding and reproduction where most invaders would be detected and killed. The challenge facing today's beekeeping world is to detect these parasites, and then to control them within the fragile and pristine colony without contaminating honey or adversely impacting the host bees.

References cited.
1. **Aggarwal, K. & R. P. Kapil. 1988.** Observations on the effect of queen cell construction on *Euvarroa sinhai* infestation in drone brood of *Apis florea*. pp. 404-408. *In* G. R. Needham, R. E. Page Jr, M. Delfinado-Baker and C. E. Bowman, [eds.], Africanized honey bees and bee mites. Halsted Press, New York.

2. **Anderson, D. L. 1999.** Are there different species of *Varroa jacobsoni*? *In*: Proceedings Apimondia 99, Congress XXXVI, Vancouver, BC Canada. Sept 1999, pp. 59-62

3. **Anderson, D. L., R. B. Halliday & G. W. Otis. 1997.** The occurrence of *Varroa underwoodi* (Acarina: Varroidae) in Papua New Guinea and Indonesia. Apidologie. 28: 143-47.

4. **Baker, E. W. & G. W. Wharton. 1952.** An Introduction to Acarology. MacMillan Co., NY.

5. **Casanueva, M. E. 1993.** Phylogenetic studies of the free-living and arthropod associated Laelapidae (Acari: Mesostigmata). Gayana Zool. 57: 21-46.

6. **Crane, E. 1988.** Africanized bee, and mites parasitic on bees, in relation to world beekeeping. Needham, G. R., R. E. Page, Jr., M. Delfinado-Baker & C. E. Bowman, Eds, *In*: Africanized honey bees and bee mites. Ellis Horwood, Chichester, pp. 1-9.

7. **de Guzman, L. I. & M. Delfinado-Baker. 1996.** A new species of

Varroa (Acari: Varroidae) associated with *Apis koschevnikovi* (Apidae: Hymenoptera) in Borneo. Int. J. Acar. 22: 23-7.

8. de Guzman, L. I. & M. Delfinado-Baker. 1996. A scientific note on the occurrence of *Varroa* mites on adult worker bees of *Apis nuluensis* in Borneo. Apidologie. 27: 329-30.

9. de Guzman, L. I., T. E. Rinderer, J. A. Stelzer & D. Anderson. 1998. Congruence of RAPD and mitochondrial DNA markers in assessing *Varroa jacobsoni* genotypes. J. Apic. Res. 37: 49-51.

10. De Jong, D., R. Morse & G. C. Eickwort. 1982. Mites pests of honey bees. Annual Review of Entomology. 27: 229-252.

11. Delfinado, M. & E. W. Baker. 1961. *Tropilaelaps*, a new genus of mites from the Philippines (Laelapidae s. lat.) Acarina. Fieldiana: Zool. 44: 53-56

12. Delfinado-Baker, M., B. A. Underwood & E. W. Baker. 1985. The occurrence of *Tropilaelaps* mites in brood nests of *Apis dorsata* and *A. laboriosa* in Nepal, with description of the nymphal stages. Am. Bee J. 125: 703-6.

13. Delfinado-Baker, M., E. W. Baker & A. C. G. Phoon. 1989. Mites (Acari) associated with bees (Apidae) in Asia, with description of a new species. Am. Bee. J. 122: 416-17.

14. Delfinado-Baker, M. 1994. A harmless mite found on honey bees— *Melittiphis alvearius*: from Italy to New Zealand. Am. Bee. J. 134: 199

15. Eickwort, G. 1988. The origins of mites associated with honey bees, pp. 327-338. *In* G. R.Needham, R. E. Page, Jr., M. Delfinado-Baker & C. E. Bowman, [eds.], Africanized honey bees and bee mites. Halsted Press, New York.

16. Eickwort, G. 1997. Mites: An overview. *In: Honey Bee Pests, Predators, and Diseases*, 3rd Edition. A.I. Root Co., Medina, OH, pp. 241-250.

17. Evans, G. O. 1992. Principles of Acarology. CAB International, Wallingford, UK, 563 pp.

18. Fain, A. & U. Gerson. 1990. Notes on two astigmatic mites (Acari) living in beehives in Thailand. Acarologia. 31: 381-4

19. Gibbins, B. L. & R. F. van Toor. 1990. Investigation of the para-

sitic status of *Melittiphis alvearius* (Berlese) on honeybees, *Apis mellifera* L., by immunoassay. J. Apic. Res. 29: 46-52).

20. **Hughes, A. M. 1976.** *The Mites of Stored Food and Houses.* Her Majesty's Stationary Office. 400 pp.),

21. **Johnston, D. E. 1982.** *Synopsis and Classification of Living Organisms* 2, McGraw-Hill, New York, pp. 111-117.

22. **Koeniger, N. 1996.** The 1996 special issue of Apidologie on Asian honeybee species. Apidologie. 27: 329-330.

23. **Koeniger, N., G. Koeniger, L. I. de Guzman & C. Lekprayoon. 1993.** Survival of *Euvarroa sinhai* Delfinado and Baker (Acari, Varroidae) on workers of *Apis cerana* Fabr, *Apis florea* Fabr and *Apis mellifera* L in cages. Apidologie. 24: 403-10.

24. **Kumar, N. R. & R. W. Kumar. 1993.** *Tropilaelaps clareae* found on *Apis mellifera* in Africa. Bee World. 74: 101-2.

25. **Laigo, F. M. & R. A. Morse. 1968.** The mite *Tropilaelaps clareae* in *Apis dorsata* colonies in the Philippines. Bee World. 49: 116-18.

26. **Lekprayoon, C. & P. Tangkanasing. 1991.** *Euvarroa wongsirii,* a new species of bee mite from Thailand. Inter. J. Acarol. 17: 255-58.

27. **Lindquist, E. E. 1986.** The world genera of Tarsonemidae (Acari: Heterostigmata): a morphological, phylogenetic, and systematic revision, with a reclassification of family-group taxa in the Heterostigmata. Mem. Entom. Soc. Canada. 136: 1-517.

28. **Martin, S. J. & B. Ball. 1999.** Variations in the virulence of *Varroa* infestations. IN: *Proc. XIII In. Congr. IUSSI;* Adelaide, p. 303.

29. **Mattheson, A. 1993.** World bee health report. Bee World. 74: 176-212

30. **Mattheson, A. 1997.** Country records for honey bee diseases, parasites and pests. *In:* Honey Bee Pests, Predators, and Diseases. R. M Morse & P. K Flottum, ed. 2: 13-31. Medina OH: A.I. Root. 3rd ed pp. 587-602.

31. **Morin, C. E. & G. W. Otis. 1993.** Observations on the morphology and biology of *Euvarroa wongsirii* (Mesostigmata: Varroidae), a par-asite of *Apis andreniformis* (Hymenoptera: Apidae. Inter. J. Acar. 19: 167-72.

32. **Mossadegh, M. S. & B. A. Komeili. 1986.** *Euvarroa sinhai*

Delfinado & Baker (Acarina: Mesostigmata): a parasitic mite on *Apis florea* F. in Iran. Am. Bee J. 126: 684-5.

33. **Mossadegh, M. S. 1990.** Development of *Euvarroa sinhai* (Acarina: Mesostigmata), a parasitic mite of *Apis florea,* on *A. mellifera* worker brood. Exp. Appl. Acar. 9: 73-8.

34. **Newell, I. M. 1967.** Abyssal Halacaridae (Acari) from the Southeast Pacific insects. Pacific Insects 9:693-708.

35. **Obenchain, F. D. & R. Galun. 1982.** Physiology of Ticks. Pergamon Press, Oxford, 509pp.

36. **Ramanan, V. R. & S. Ghai. 1984.** Observations on the mite *Neocypholaelaps indica* Evans and its relationship with the honey bee *Apis cerana indica* Fabricius and the flowering of Eucalyptus trees. Entomon. 9: 291-92.

37. **Rath, W. 1995.** The laboratory culture of the mites *Varroa jacobsoni* and *Tropilaelaps clareae* . Exp. Appl. Acarol. 10: 289-93.

38. **Sammataro, D., S. Cobey, H. Smith & G. R. Needham 1994.** Controlling tracheal mites (Acari: Tarsomemidae) in honey bees (Hymenoptera: Apidae) with vegetable oil. J. Econ. Entomology 87: 910-16.

39. **Sammataro, D., U. Gerson & G. R. Needham 2000.** Parasitic Mites of Honey Bees: Life History, Implications and Impact. Annual Review of Entomology. In press.

40. **Seeman, O. D. & D. E. Walter. 1995.** Life history of *Afrocypholaelaps africana* (Evans) (Acari: Ameroseiidae), a mite inhabiting mangrove flowers and phoretic on honeybees. J. Austral. Entom. Soc. 34: 45-50).

41. **Sihag, R. C. 1988.** Incidence of *Varroa, Euvarroa* and *Tropilaelaps* mites in the colonies of honey bees *Apis mellifera* L. in Haryana (India). Am. Bee J. 128: 212-13.

42. **Wallwork, J. A., B. W. Kamill & R. Whitford. 1985.** Distribution and diversity patterns of soils mites and other microcarthropods in a Chihuahuan desert site. J. Arid Environ. 9: 215-31.

43. **Wiegert, R. G. & R. D. Mitchell. 1973.** Ecology of Yellowstone thermal effluent systems: intersects of blue-green algae, grazing flies

(Paracoenia, Ephydridae) and water mites (Partnuniella, Hydrachnellae). Hydrobiolgica 41: 251-71.

44. **Yoder, J. A. & J. C. Barcelona. 1995.** Food and water resources used by the Madagascan hissing-cockroach mite, *Gromphadorholaelaps schaeferi*. Exp. Applied Acarol. 19: 259-73.

Chapter 2

BIOLOGY AND LIFE HISTORY OF *ACARAPIS DORSALIS* AND *ACARAPIS EXTERNUS*

Lilia I. de Guzman
D. Michael Burgett
Thomas E. Rinderer

There are three mites in the genus *Acarapis* that are specific to the western honey bee (*Apis mellifera* L.). One of them is an internal parasite, *Acarapis woodi* (Rennie). The other two are external parasites, *Acarapis dorsalis* Morgenthaler and *Acarapis externus* Morgenthaler.

An external mite, which was morphologically different from *A. woodi*, was reported as early as 1926, five years after *A. woodi* was described by Rennie[31]. Morgenthaler proposed the name *A. externus* and later observed that this mite breeds on the underside and sides of the neck of a host bee[23]. Morison[27] detected external mites on the bee thorax that differed from Morgenthaler's, and these were designated *A. dorsalis*. However, both external *Acarapis* were not described until 1934 by Morgenthaler[26].

The two external *Acarapis*, like *A. woodi*, are blood feeders[29]. They have been reported to cause no visible symptoms of injury to bee hosts[14,16], and Shaw & others[33] believed that there was no relationship between the prevalence of external *Acarapis* and colony performance. Both external *Acarapis* are generally considered harmless parasites of honey bees, although *A. externus* may cause wing loss or malfunction[12]. Ibay[24] also reported mortality of experimental colonies in Oregon that were highly infested with both external *Acarapis*. Thus, these mites may be more troublesome for honey bees than generally believed. However, the pest status of these two species has never been thoroughly investigated.

Identification and detection. Morphological characteristics separating the three *Acarapis* species are meager and confined to the adult females[14]. Eckert[16] and Delfinado-Baker and Baker[14] found only a few morphological differences between the three *Acarapis* species. *A. externus* has a larger body and longer terminal segments of leg IV compared to *A. woodi* and *A. dorsalis*. The distance between the two spiracles is shorter in *A. woodi* than it is for *A. dorsalis* and *A. externus*. The shape of the posterior margin of the coxal plate between leg IV is different between the three species. The coxal plate in *A. dorsalis* has a posterior margin that is more deeply cleaved than it is in *A. woodi,* while *A. externus* has a nearly straight posterior margin. Eckert suggested that the characteristic of *A. externus* of excreting and using gummy substances, presumably secreted by the female before laying eggs to fasten them together, can be used to separate it from *A. dorsalis* which lays eggs singly in the dorsal scutoscutellar groove of the bee thorax.

Due to their small size and morphological similarities, the three *Acarapis* species are most usually identified by location on the bee host (Fig. 2.1). *A. externus* is found on the underside of the neck, the membranous area between the head and thorax, and in the tentorial pits of the head. *A. dorsalis* uses the dorsal groove of the thorax between the scutum and scutellum, while *A. woodi* infests the tracheae. Like *A. woodi,* both external *Acarapis* are migratory and have been collected from other parts of the honey bee such as wings, propodeum, thorax near the bases of the wings, and on the first segment of the abdomen[5,16,24,32,33] (Fig. 2.2). Their ability to use the same areas for aggregation or reproduction further complicates the identification of external *Acarapis* species.

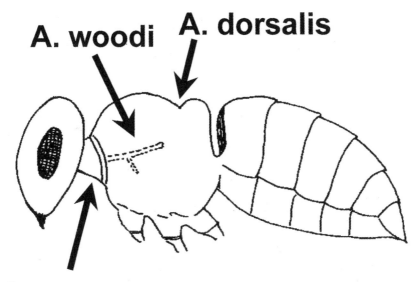

A. woodi A. dorsalis

A. externus

▲ *Fig. 2.1 Location of the three species of* Acarapis *on an adult honey bee.*

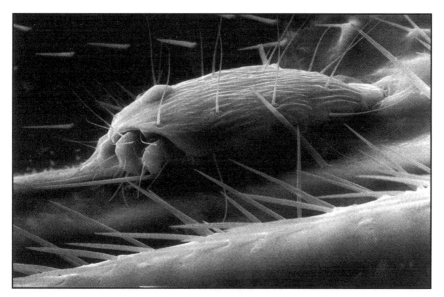

▲ *Fig. 2.2 Adult female of* Acarapis dorsalis *on the wing vein of a honey bee.*

Life history. Because the adults of external *Acarapis* are migratory, limited information on their life history is available. Several attempts have been made to culture *Acarapis* in the laboratory, but none has been successful[16,18,24]. *Acarapis* mites undergo all life stages (egg, larva, nymph, and adult) on a single bee host. The eggs are unusually large, being about the same size as the adult female that lays them. The larva has six legs of which one pair is well developed and two pairs underdeveloped. The larva is an active feeder, while the nymph is a non-feeding stage[14,16,27]. Like *A. woodi*, males are distinguished from females based on body size and the number of hairs on the tibia of leg IV. Males are usually smaller with one long hair on tibia IV, while females are bigger with two tibial hairs[14]. Like the larvae, adult *Acarapis* mites are parasitic on honey bee hosts. They have long cheliceral stylets with which they feed on the host bee[13].

Life cycle comparisons. Marked, newly emerged bees were introduced into mite-infested colonies to determine the life cycle periods of external *Acarapis*. They have been estimated to be 8-10 days[16,24,32], which is about four days less than that of tracheal mites[3,6,18,25,32]. The developmental time of *A. externus* is similar to that of *A. dorsalis*. However, differences in the length of egg and larval/nymphal stages are noted (Table 2.1). Egg incubation takes only three days in *A. externus* as compared to four days in *A. dorsalis*. The larval stages, however, require one day longer (5-6 days). Males emerge earlier than females.

The female to male ratio is 1.9:1 to 3:1 for *A. dorsalis*[7,20] and 1:1 to 2.1:1 for *A. externus*[6,20]. The highest numbers of females are observed during fall months. The apparent abundance of females in both species suggests that males are shorter-lived than females, and thus observed ratios may be influenced by the life history or behavior of the mites.

The longevity of external *Acarapis* has not been studied. However, studies of *A. woodi* show that adult mites can live about 40 days[18,30]. Longevity of external *Acarapis* may be less than that of *A. woodi*, considering that the external species exploit less-protected microhabitats outside the bee's body. When the host bee dies, all life stages of *A. dorsalis* die by about 72 hours[27].

Age preferences. Like *A. woodi*, *A. dorsalis* prefers young worker bees 1-15 days of age[24,27,32,33]. However, preference studies reveal that *A. externus* can maintain its population on older bees[24]. Prevalence of *A.*

externus remains relatively high on bees 35 days of age. Thus, *A. externus* is more capable than *A. dorsalis* of surviving on older bees. This behavior may be advantageous for mite dispersal by allowing them to relocate on older drifting forager bees. Queens are rarely infested with external *Acarapis*[7,16].

Distribution. Morgenthaler found *A. externus* throughout Switzerland in 1930. Infestation by *A. externus* has also been observed in *Apis cerana* F. in Japan[4,15]. External *Acarapis* have been recorded in Scandinavia, Australia, New Zealand, Europe, the former USSR, North and South America, and Africa[4]. Both external *Acarapis* were found infesting *A. mellifera* in Iran[28]. In the United States, the first external *Acarapis* detected was *A. dorsalis* in New York in 1930. *A. dorsalis* or *A. externus* were later found in 24 other states[7,16,19,32,33].

   A. dorsalis is reported to be more prevalent than *A. externus* in Italy[17], Britain[4], Washington[7], and Oregon[24]. However, surveys done in Switzerland[27], New Zealand[9], British Columbia[8], and Iran[28] show that *A. externus* is the more common species. Delfinado-Baker and Baker[14] believe that the world distribution of the two external *Acarapis* is similar. However, *A. externus* has a higher population density and thus has been more frequently observed and collected than *A. dorsalis*[4]. The reasons for differences in regional interspecific prevalences are unclear.

Table 2.1 Life cycle comparison of the three *Acarapis* species.

life stage	duration (hours)		
	A. dorsalis[†]	*A. externus*[†]	*A. woodi*[††]
egg	96	72	72
immature	96-120	120-144	264
egg-laying to adult	192-216	192-216	336

[†]After Ibay[24]
[††]After Royce & others[32]

However, they could be due to sampling methods or to regional environmental conditions that favor one species over the other.

Population dynamics. The seasonal population fluctuations of the two external *Acarapis* vary. In California, *A. dorsalis* is found to have peaks of infestation during the spring and fall[16]. Clinch[9] observed that external *Acarapis* populations in honey bee colonies in New Zealand are highest in fall and spring and lowest in summer. In Massachusetts[33] and in western Canada[8], the highest external *Acarapis* infestations are observed in spring and summer. The highest *A. dorsalis* infestations in Oregon are recorded in spring months (March to June) and late summer (August to September)[20] (Fig. 2.3). For *A. externus*, the highest prevalences are observed in October and November. The lowest prevalences for *A. dorsalis* are observed in January and July. *A. externus* also has a low infestation rate in July.

Because of the ubiquity of the three *Acarapis* species, multiple infestation of a colony is common. *A. dorsalis* is reported to be more common than *A. externus*[4,7,24]. A similar observation was noted when noninfested nuclei were inoculated with known *Acarapis* populations.

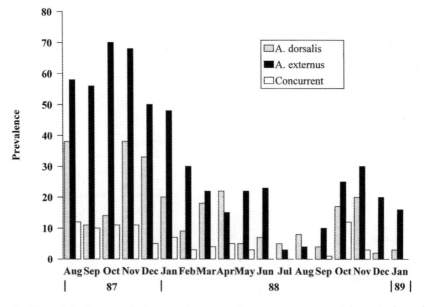

▲ *Fig. 2.3 Seasonal fluctuations in the percentage of bees infested (prevalence) with Acarapis dorsalis. A. externus, or both mites (concurrent) (after de Guzman & Burgett[20]).*

A. dorsalis showed a higher rate of infestation than *A. externus*[24]. This observation suggests that a critical population must be attained by *A. externus* to establish itself in a colony. Unless this critical population is reached prior to invasion by *A. dorsalis*, *A. externus* appears unable to maintain its population in the colony. Natural infestation of colonies showed that *A. externus* seems to be more predominant than *A. dorsalis*[19,20]. When the three *Acarapis* species are present, *A. woodi* seems to be the predominant species both at the colony and individual host bee levels[7,19]. This may be attributed to the ability of *A. woodi* to reproduce faster as indicated by the higher number of mites observed inside the tracheae[19]. This ability may also explain the comparatively high virulence of tracheal mites; more mites per bee means more feeding sites which are instrumental in secondary infections. A smaller proportion of bees was infested with all three *Acarapis* species at the same time[6,7,20]. The reasons for one species becoming more prevalent than others need to be studied, but they probably include differences in mite colonizing abilities, reproductive rates, or genetic differences in the host bees.

De Guzman[19] compared natural prevalences of the three *Acarapis* species in three stocks of honey bees and one of their hybrids that were used primarily for varroa mite research[21]. A commercial Italian stock from Louisiana had low *A. dorsalis* prevalences, but high prevalences of both *A. woodi* and *A. externus*. Colonies of the Hastings stock had high levels of both *A. woodi* and *A. dorsalis*. The susceptibility of Hastings to *A. externus* is unclear since results of two trials were not consistent. The ARS-Y-C-1 honey bee stock and an F_1 hybrid between Hastings and ARS-Y-C-1 were resistant to *A. woodi*[22] and *A. dorsalis*, but had high levels of *A. externus*. The longevities of these colonies harboring four species of mites were similar. However, their resistance levels to varroa mites differed[21]. The authors reported that the Louisiana stock which had lower levels of varroa died earlier than Hastings, F_1 hybrid, and ARS-Y-C-1, which had higher varroa mite infestations. However, this early death of the Louisiana stock colonies may have been influenced by the high levels of *A. woodi* and *A. externus* in the colonies. *A. woodi* is known to reduce longevity of infested bees[2]. Likewise, mortality had been observed in colonies free from *A. woodi* and varroa mites, but with high infestations of *A. dorsalis* (64%), *A. externus* (62%) and both species (49%) in Oregon[24]. The concurrent parasitism of the three *Acarapis* species and varroa mites in a honey bee colony may accelerate the decline of colony health. Thus, high infestations of the external *Acarapis* in addition to the presence of two major honey bee parasites (varroa and tracheal mites) in the colonies could be a co-factor in precipitating colony mortalities.

Control. External *Acarapis* mites are believed to be unimportant economically[3]. Their presence causes no measurable loss in the population or production of honey bee colonies[16]. But because they feed on their hosts' blood, it is possible that they have negative effects on infested bees. A few chemicals have been tested for the control of external *Acarapis*. However, none of these chemicals is registered for use in the United States. In New Zealand, Clinch and Faulke[11] obtained an 85% reduction in the number of infested bees when a single dose of 40 mg endosulfan per colony was fed in 2:1 sugar syrup. A second treatment applied after 19 days resulted in 98% decrease in infested bees. Subsequent study showed that fenbutatin oxide and trichlohexyltin hydroxide were more effective than endosulfan and safer than amitraz[10]. Sulfur dioxide vapors also decrease the number of external *Acarapis*[1]. The efficacy of menthol and Apistan (used to control tracheal and varroa mites, respectively) for the control of external *Acarapis* has not been studied. However, these two *Acarapis* mites are external parasites, thus they should be easier to control than tracheal mites which are protected inside the tracheae.

Summary. External *Acarapis* mites appear to be largely innocuous parasites of the western honey bee *Apis mellifera*. Unusual environmental conditions may trigger high infestation rates that could diminish the health of the colonies, but in most beekeeping circumstances treatment for the control of external *Acarapis* species is not necessary.

References cited.
  1. **Anonymous. 1932.** The bee laboratory. *Bee World* 13: 35-36.

  2. **Bailey, L. 1958.** The epidemiology of the infestation of the honey bee, *Apis mellifera* L., by the mite *Acarapis woodi* (Rennie) and the mortality of infested bees. Parasitol. 48: 493-506.

  3. **Bailey, L. 1963.** Infectious diseases of honey bees. Land Books Ltd.,

London, England.

4. **Bailey, L. & B.V. Ball. 1991.** Honey bee pathology. Academic Press, London.

5. **Borchert, A. 1934.** On the breeding places of the external mite (*Acarapis*) on the honey bees. Bee World 15: 43-44.

6. **Brügger, A. 1936.** Zur Kenntnis der äusserlichen *Acarapis*-milben. Arch. Bienenk 17: 113-142.

7. **Burgett. D.M., L.A. Royce & L.A. Ibay. 1989.** The concurrence of the *Acarapis* species complex (Acari: Tarsonemidae) in a commercial honey bee apiary in the Pacific Northwest. Exp. Appl. Acarol. 7:251-255.

8. **Clark, K.J. 1985.** Mites (Acari) associated with the honey bee *Apis mellifera* L. (Hymenoptera: Apidae), with emphasis on British Columbia. MS thesis, Simon Fraser University, Vancouver.

9. **Clinch, P.G. 1976.** Observations on the seasonal incidence of external *Acarapis* spp. on honey bees. N.Z. J. Exp. Agric. 4: 257-258.

10. **Clinch, P.G. 1979.** Control of *Acarapis externus* M: further tests to determine the efficacy of pesticides fed in sugar syrup to infested honey bee colonies. N.Z. J. Exp. Agric. 7: 407-409.

11. **Clinch, P.G. & J. Faulke. 1977.** Toxicity of the external mite (*Acarapis externus* M.) of pesticides fed in sugar syrup to infested honey bees. N.Z. J. Exp. Agric. 5: 185-188.

12. **De Jong. D., R.A. Morse & G.A. Eickwort. 1982.** Mite pests of honey bees. Ann. Rev. Entomol. 27: 229-252.

13. **Delfinado-Baker, M. 1988.** The tracheal mite of honey bees: a crisis in beekeeping, pp. 493-497. *In* G.R. Needham, R.E. Page Jr., M. Delfinado-Baker & C.E. Bowman [eds.], Africanized honey bees and bee mites. Halstread Press, New York.

14. **Delfinado-Baker, M. & E.W. Baker. 1982.** Notes on honey bee mites of the genus *Acarapis* Hirst (Acari: Tarsonemidae). Int. J. Acarol. 8: 211-226.

15. **Delfinado-Baker, M., E.W. Baker & A.C.G. Phoon. 1989.** Mites (Acari) associated with bees (Apidae) in Asia, with description of

a new species. Am. Bee. J. 129: 609-610, 612-613.

16. **Eckert, J.E. 1961.** *Acarapis* mites of the honey bee, *Apis mellifera* L. J. Insect Pathol. 3: 409-425.

17. **Giordani, G. 1965.** Laboratory research on *Acarapis woodi* Rennie, the causative agent of Acarine disease of honeybees (*Apis mellifera* L.). Note 2. Bull. Apicole 6: 185-203.

18. **Giordani, G. 1967.** Laboratory research on *Acarapis woodi* Rennie, the causative agent of Acarine disease of the honey bee. Note 5. J. Apic. Res. 6: 147-157.

19. **Guzman, L.I. de. 1994.** Tolerance potential and defense mechanisms of honey bees (*Apis mellifera* L.) to *Varroa jacobsoni* Oud. (Acari: Varroidae) and *Acarapis* species (Acari: Tarsonemidae). Ph.D. dissertation, Louisiana State University, Baton Rouge.

20. **Guzman, L.I. de & D.M. Burgett. 1991.** Seasonal abundance of the *Apis mellifera* L. ectoparasites *Acarapis dorsalis* Morgenthaler and *Acarapis externus* Morgenthaler (Acari: Tarsonemidae) in Oregon. BeeScience 1: 219-224.

21. **Guzman, L.I. de, T.E. Rinderer, G.T. Delatte & R.E. Macchiavelli. 1996.** *Varroa jacobsoni* Oudemans tolerance in selected stocks of *Apis mellifera* L. Apidologie 27: 193-210.

22 **Guzman, L.I. de, T.E. Rinderer & G.T. Delatte. 1998.** Comparative resistance of four honey bee (Hymenoptera: Apidae) stocks to infestation by *Acarapis woodi* (Rennie) (Acari: Tarsonemidae). J. Econ. Entomol. 91:1078-1083.

23. **Homann, H. 1933.** Die Milben in gesunden Bienenstöcken. Z. Parasitenkunde 6: 350-415.

24. **Ibay, L. A. 1989.** Biology of the two external *Acarapis* species of honey bees: *Acarapis dorsalis* Morgenthaler and *Acarapis externus* Morgenthaler (Acari: Tarsonemidae). MS thesis, Oregon State University, Corvallis.

25. **Morgenthaler, O. 1931.** Ein Versuchs-Bienenstand für Milbenkrankheit im Berner Seeland und einige dort gewonnene Ergebnisse. Schweizerische Bienen-Zeitung 53: 538-545.

26. **Morgenthaler, O. 1934.** Krankheitserregende und harmlose Arten -

der Bienenmilbe *Acarapis*, zugleich ein Beitrag zum species-problem. Rev. Suisse Zool. 41: 429-446.

27. **Morison, G.D. 1931.** Observations on the number of mites, *Acarapis woodi* (Rennie) found in the tracheae of the honey bee. Bee World 12: 74-76.

28. **Mossadegh, M.S. & R. Bahreini. 1994.** *Acarapis* mites of honeybee, *Apis mellifera* in Iran. Exp. Appl. Acarol. 18: 503-506.

29. **Örösi-Pal, Z. 1934.** Experiments on the feeding habits of the *Acarapis* mites. Bee World 15: 93-94.

30. **Pettis, J.S. 1991.** Tracheal mite, *Acarapis woodi* (Rennie) biology and ecology in the honey bee (*Apis mellifera* L.). Ph.D. dissertation, Texas A&M University, College Station.

31. **Rennie, J. 1921.** Isle of Wight disease in hive beesBacarine disease: the organism associated with the disease-*Tarsonemus woodi*, n. sp. Trans. R. Soc. Edinburgh 52: 768-779.

32. **Royce, L.A., G.W. Krantz, L.A. Ibay & D.M. Burgett. 1988.** Some observations on the biology and behavior of *Acarapis woodi* and *Acarapis dorsalis* in Oregon, pp. 498-505. *In* G.R. Needham, R.E. Page Jr., M. Delfinado-Baker & C.E. Bowman [eds], Africanized honey bees and bee mites. Halstread Press, New York.

33. **Shaw, F.R., W.J. Fischang, E.R. Balboni & J.W. Eversole. 1961.** External mites on honey bees in the U.S. Glean. Bee Cult. 89: 402-403, 447.

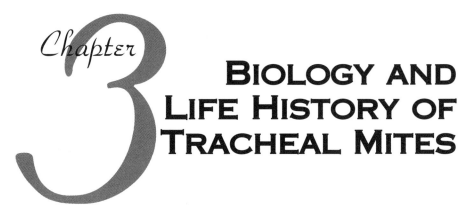

Chapter 3
BIOLOGY AND LIFE HISTORY OF TRACHEAL MITES

Jeffery S. Pettis

T he honey bee tracheal mite lives within a unique environment, that of the tracheal, or respiratory, system of adult honey bees. The mite's life cycle is such that it reproduces within individual bees, but its survival depends upon the survival of the honey bee colony as a whole. For the mite to survive it must adapt to the seasonal changes within honey bee colonies, such as the broodless period in winter with a prolonged absence of new young host bees. Although the mite depends on the survival of its host, in North America we see numerous colony deaths associated with tracheal mites. Thus, the host-parasite relationship appears to be in an unsteady state. However, we can select for bees that are tolerant or resistant to tracheal mites, and thus encourage a more stable host-parasite relationship. This parasite has been known and studied for over 70 years. This chapter will explore the biology of the parasite and its effects on adult honey bees.

Background. The honey bee tracheal mite, *Acarapis woodi* (Rennie), is an internal obligate parasite of adult honey bees. The mite was first described by Rennie[43], who named it *Tarsonemus woodi*; the name was later changed to *Acarapis woodi*. Rennie found tracheal mites in bees from colonies with the so-called Isle of Wight disease, and he believed the mites were the causative agent. This disease was first noted around 1905 on the Isle of Wight, in the United Kingdom, and in following years was reported throughout Great Britain and continental Europe[5,7]. The exact cause of Isle of Wight disease is still debated. The history of the infestation and the discovery of tracheal mites are reviewed by Phillips[41,42].

Distribution and other *Acarapis* species. The tracheal mite appears to have had a long association with the European honey bee, *A. mellifera*. However, other host species are reported, the Asian honey bee, *Apis cerana*[28,2,12] and possibly the giant honey bee, *Apis dorsata*. Reports from India indicate that tracheal mites have caused losses in *A. cerana* colonies similar to the North American experiences with European colonies[51,3,1,50]. Lehnert & others[21] established that Africanized honey bees in Brazil harbor the tracheal mite. A more complete search of other honey bees within the genus *Apis* could help determine the host specificity of this parasite.

    Acarapis woodi is present on every continent except Australia[8,27]. There are at least three species of *Acarapis* mites, including *A. dorsalis* and *A. externus*. The species closely resemble each other and are differentiated largely by observing where they occur on the bee's body (see Chapter 2).

Life cycle. Adult male and female mites, larvae, and eggs are all found in the honey bee respiratory system of the thorax and head. This system is composed of ten *spiracles* (external openings to the air) and internal branched tubes called *tracheae*. Tracheal tubes nearest the spiracles are large, but get progressively narrower in diameter as they branch[55]. It is in the large tracheal trunks branching from the spiracles of the first thoracic section (*prothorax*) that all stages of *A. woodi* are found (Fig 3.1). Occasionally, mites are found in the air sacks of the head and thorax. Female mites enter the thoracic spiracles of an adult bee generally less than three days of age[20,15], but older bees may become infested[53] especially in the winter cluster.

    Why do mites choose to infest young bees? It was initially believed

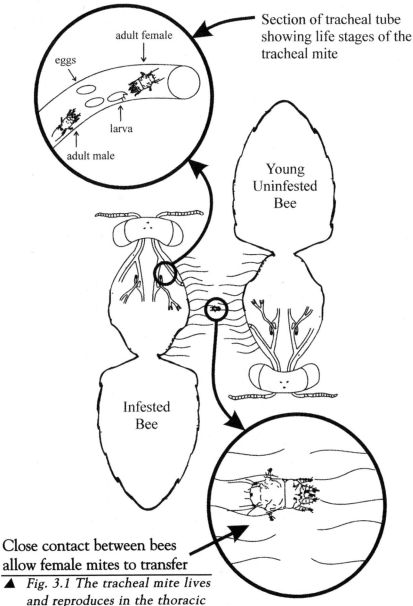

Section of tracheal tube showing life stages of the tracheal mite

eggs

adult female

larva

adult male

Young Uninfested Bee

Infested Bee

Close contact between bees allow female mites to transfer

▲ *Fig. 3.1 The tracheal mite lives and reproduces in the thoracic tracheal tubes of adult honey bees. All life stages can be found in the tubes and only mated females move outside to find a new host. The female climbs onto the tip of a bee hair and will transfer to any passing bee, but eventually finds her way to a young bee (artwork by Kenneth Wilzer, portions redrawn from Snodgrass[57]).*

that the stiffening of the thoracic hairs in aging bees prevented mites from entering the spiracles[32,47]. However, it was shown that even old bees that had been experimentally shaven were not as readily infested as young bees[20]. A second hypothesis is that the spiracular closing mechanism and grooming behavior become more efficient in older bees, thus more effectively excluding the mites from the tracheae. In grooming, bees comb their pleural hairs with their second pair of legs and may dislodge mites. However, Lee[20] tested this by removing the second pair of legs from bees exposed to mites, and found that young bees were still more readily infested than older ones. Recent evidence shows that grooming behavior can be a resistance mechanism to tracheal mites[9,37]. Bees that readily groomed themselves (autogrooming) had lower mite levels than bees that groomed infrequently[37] and removing the middle leg of bees resulted in increased mite levels[9]. Female mites locate young hosts efficiently and probably make a choice once they are on the new host[48]. Female mites appear to use cuticular hydrocarbons to discriminate between old and young bees[40]. Additionally, they are attracted to the current of expired air coming from the first thoracic spiracle and seem to ignore the second and third spiracles[17]. Mites that select older hosts have insufficient time to reproduce. By infesting younger bees, mites have time to complete their life cycle before the bee dies (Fig. 3.1).

After a female locates a new bee, and once inside the host, she begins to lay eggs in 1-2 days. Morgenthaler[29] reported that females lay from 5 to 7 eggs over a period of 3 to 4 days and after 3 to 4 days the eggs hatch. Similar results on oviposition were obtained by Pettis & Wilson[36] who reported 0.85 eggs per day over the initial 12 days of oviposition. As many as 21 offspring per female mite have been proposed[35]. One generation of mites per host is common, but a second generation is possible in longer-lived bees in the fall and winter[36]. The mite goes through a six-legged larval stage, followed by a pharate nymphal stage[22], and finally develops into an adult male in 11-12 days or an adult female in 14-15 days[12,45,36]. Female mites lay almost one egg a day, each of which is about two-thirds the weight of the female herself[48]. This would be equivalent to a 150 pound woman having a 100 pound baby! The females have an unlimited supply of bee blood to feed upon and produce such large eggs. Adult males are slightly smaller than females and generally emerge one day in advance of the females.

Mating occurs inside the tracheal tubes shortly after females emerge. Brother-sister matings are common when mite levels are low. Mated females move to new host bees by exiting the prothoracic trachea through the spiracular opening (Fig. 3.1). Adult males apparently do not leave the host in which they are born[22]. There is debate about the sex ratio in *A. woodi*. According to Delfinado-Baker & Baker[12], the female:male ratio has been reported as 3:1 or 4:1, yet males sometimes outnumber females. Lozano & others[26] reported the ratio at 2.4:1 after examining more than 40,000 adult bees. The observed ratio can vary widely because newly-mated females migrate out of a tracheae while males do not migrate; thus, a large or disproportionate number of males are often counted in most studies[22].

Tracheal mites will infest all three types of bees in a colony, including young queens, drones, and workers[7,30,38]. Drones have larger tracheal trunks and there is evidence that they are preferentially infested over workers[44,10]. Drifting drones may be important in mite dispersal between bee colonies. Workers, however, being much more numerous, are of prime importance when examining the effects of tracheal mites on bee colonies. Queens, due to their longevity, may serve as a reservoir for mites, but more than two mite generations within a queen seem unlikely as infested tracheae become increasingly damaged with mite feeding over time[38]. The effects of mite parasitism on queen performance or supersedure are unknown and need to be studied.

Tracheal mites live in an enclosed air-filled tube with their food supply literally flowing by just outside in the bee's thorax. Insects have a open circulatory system where the blood is not contained in blood vessels, but flows freely inside the body. Mites feed by piercing the bee's tracheal wall with *stylets*, sharp needle-like mouthparts. Once the wall is pierced, the mite places its mouth opening near the puncture, and sucks up bee blood or hemolymph. This was demonstrated by using Congo Red stain solution which when injected into host bees was subsequently found in mites in the tracheae of those bees[31]. Larval mites also feed in the same manner as adults, but are less mobile within the tracheae[17].

The repeated puncturing of the tracheal wall has damaging effects. Infested tracheae will often show brown blotches with brown scabs or even appear entirely blackened with dark bands, depending on the number of mites infesting the host[36,24]. In comparison, healthy tracheae are clear, translucent, and show no signs of stains. Liu & others[24] showed that a film forms on the inside walls of tracheal tubes as mites feed, but the nature and composition of this film are unknown. Bailey[6] states that spraying infested bees with suspensions of pathogenic bacteria did not increase the susceptibility to disease, but more data would be necessary to confirm this. Mite feeding may also affect the surrounding flight muscles and hypopharyngeal glands[23,25].

If we could artificially rear tracheal mites it would help in our study of mite biology and in screening potential mite control compounds. To date, attempts to rear *A. woodi* in the laboratory have been only partially successful and no complete generations have been reared[16]. Studies on the other two species of *A. dorsalis* and *A. externus* have shed some light on reproductive patterns. However, these two species are external on bees and may differ from the internal *A. woodi*[12,22,18]. Most of our knowledge about the mite's biology have come from manipulating the host bees in some way and then seeing how these changes affect mite dispersal, reproduction, or longevity.

Bee to bee dispersal. Tracheal mites must reproduce and then leave a bee before the bee dies. In short-lived summer bees there is a race between how fast the mite can reproduce and how soon the bee dies, especially during nectar flows when foraging is heavy. When a bee dies those mites still within that bee will die, except perhaps for the occasional mite which is able to "jump ship" from a dead bee to a live bee. We have no evidence that this really occurs. Normally, a mated adult female mite will leave an older host and go to a young host bee < 3 days of age[20,15]. This transfer to a younger host is an essential component in the life cycle of *A. woodi*. It is the only period when mites are known to be outside of the tracheal system. Female mites transfer to a new host by climbing to the tip of a bee hair, anchoring itself with its hind legs in the hair, and then using the forelegs to grasp the hair of a passing bee[17,48] (Fig. 3.1). Only the female tracheal mites leave the host, and they begin doing so at approximately 13 days old[36]. No cues have been identified which initiate dispersal behavior from a bee; perhaps mating may serve as a cue to disperse. On the colony level, a *diurnal* (daily) cycle in mite dispersal has been demonstrated. Approximately 85 percent of all mite transfers to young bees occurs at night[39]. A reduction in overall host activity was associated with the increased nocturnal dispersal of mites[39]. From these findings, the authors proposed that mites may detect host motion and wait until the host is motionless before initiating dispersal.

Many factors are probably involved in the stimulation and dispersal of mites from older to younger bees. By examining the rate of mite dispersal between host bees, researchers have determined some factors that influence the dispersal process. Bailey[4] demonstrated that increasing temperatures resulted in increased numbers of mite transfers among bees held in an incubator. Pettis & others[38] found that mites can disperse to young bees across a screen barrier. Presumably, close contact occurs between the older infested bees and young confined bees as they feed each other through the screen. Hirschfelder & Sachs[17] observed that mites do not readily leave bees to go onto wax foundation, but rather transfer to another bee directly. The authors feel that this is not a common form of transmission, although "under natural conditions inside the hive, any mite which happens to get on to the comb surface may reach a new host." Hirschfelder & Sachs[17] examined mite responses to puffs of air, vibrations, and other stimuli that might serve as cues to host location. Intermittent air puffs and vibration were both positive stimuli. The authors believed that vibration would stimulate mites to move to the wing bases; this idea has been supported by Royce & others[45] who showed that mites move first to the wing base of a new host and then into the tracheal system. Gary & Page[14,34] demonstrated phenotypic and genotypic variation in susceptibility of young bees to mite infestation. Recent work has shown that dispersing mites use cuticular hydrocarbons as cues in host location[40]. Mites in a laboratory bioassay responded positively to extracts of young bee cuticle as opposed to controls and old bee extract[52].

Mite transfer is perhaps a vulnerable period in the mite's life cycle, as it is the only time mites are external on the bees. Eischen & others[13] showed that amitraz applied topically to young queens prevented mite transfer. Smith & others[54] have shown that a light film of vegetable oil on young bees will inhibit mite transfer. Several researchers have used this knowledge to show that an oil-based extender patty can be used as a control method[11,49]. Grooming behavior by worker bees has also been shown to limit mite dispersal to young bees[37] and known resistant lines of bees (Buckfast) exhibit high levels of self-grooming[9]. Grooming behavior is heritable and is the first resistance mechanism to be identified against tracheal mites.

Colony to colony dispersal. The tracheal mite is an obligate parasite and cannot survive for more than a few hours away from its host, the honey bee. As such, the mite must rely on the host bee to move it between colonies. In nature, feral colonies are more widely dispersed than those in apiaries maintained by beekeepers. Three phenomena are probably responsible for movement of the parasite from colony to colony: robbing, drifting of individual workers and drones, and swarming. Robbing could play a role in mite dispersal, but this seems unlikely as the increased activity associated with robbing is probably not conducive to successful mite transfer to new hosts; Pettis & others[39] hypothesize that mite dispersal between bees occurs when bees are calm with little motion. If robbing is involved, then infested workers most likely join the robbers and return to the non-infested colony. Infested drones and workers, by drifting, could easily serve as vectors to move mites to new colonies. Moreover, it is possible that mite parasitism alters bee behavior such that they drift more readily. This speculation has not been demonstrated experimentally. Swarming bees move mites to new areas, as the parasite is harbored inside infested workers within the swarm[56]. Although swarming certainly disperses tracheal mites, it has also been proposed as a natural regulatory mechanism that limits mite population growth within a colony[46]. Mite levels in individual colonies can vary widely, but generally increase in the late summer and fall, are lowest in the late spring and summer, and are most easily detected in winter[19,33]. Often spring decline in mite prevalence is associated with nectar flows and rapidly expanding bee populations.

Summary. The honey bee tracheal mite, *Acarapis woodi* (Rennie), is an internal obligate parasite that lives within the tracheal system of adult honey bees. The mite was first described by Rennie who believed it to be the cause of Isle of Wight disease. The mite's life cycle is such that it reproduces within individual bees, but its survival depends on the survival of the honey bee colony as a whole. For the mite to survive, it must adapt to seasonal changes within the honey bee colony such as broodless winter periods characterized by a prolonged absence of new young bee hosts. This chapter reviews the biology of the parasite and its effects on adult honey bees.

References cited.
1. Adlakha, R.L. 1976. Acarine disease of the honey bees in India. Am. Bee J. 116: 324-344.

2. Atwal, A.S. 1971. Acarine disease problem of the Indian honey bee, *Apis indica* F. Am. Bee J. 111: 134-5.

3. Atwal, A.S. & O.P. Sharma. 1970. Acarine disease of adult honey bees: prevention and control. Indian Farming. 20: 39-40.

4. Bailey, L. 1958. The epidemiology of the infestation of the honey bee, *Apis mellifera*, by the mite *Acarapis woodi* Rennie and the mortality of infested bees. Parasitol. 48: 493-506.

5. Bailey, L. 1963. Infectious diseases of the honey-bee. Land Books, London.

6. Bailey, L. 1965. Susceptibility of honey bees, *Apis mellifera* Linnaeus, infested with *Acarapis woodi* (Rennie) to infection by airborne pathogens. J. Invertebr. Pathol. 7: 141-143.

7. Bailey, L. 1981. Honey Bee Pathology, Academic, London.

8. Bradbear, N. 1988. World distribution of major honey bee diseases and pests. Bee World 69: 15-39.

9. Danka, R.G. & J.D. Villa. 1998. Evidence of autogrooming as a mechanism of honey bee resistance to tracheal mite infestation. J. Apic. Res. 37: 39-46.

10. Dawicke, B.L. 1991. A comparison of the migration of the honey bee tracheal mite (*Acarapis woodi* (Rennie)) in drone and worker honey bees (*Apis mellifera* L.) MS thesis, University of Guelph, Guelph, Ontario.

11. Delaplane, K.S. 1992. Controlling tracheal mites (Acari: Tarsonemidae) in colonies of honey bees (Hymenoptera: Apidae) with vegetable oil and menthol. J. Econ. Entomol. 85: 2118-2124.

12. Delfinado-Baker, M. & E.W. Baker 1982. Notes on honey bee mites of the genus *Acarapis* Hirst (Acari: Tarsonemidae). Int. J. Acarol. 8: 211-226.

13. Eischen, F.A., J.S. Pettis & A. Dietz. 1986. Prevention of *Acarapis woodi* infestation in queen honey bees with amitraz. Am. Bee J.

126: 498-500.

14. **Gary, N.E. & R.E. Page. 1987.** Phenotypic variation in susceptibility of honey bees, *Apis mellifera*, to infestation by tracheal mites *Acarapis woodi*. J. Exp. Appl. Acarol. 3: 291-305.

15. **Gary, N.E., R.E. Page & K. Lorenzen. 1989.** Effects of age of worker honey bees (*Apis mellifera* L.) on tracheal mite (*Acarapis woodi* Rennie) infestation. J. Exp. Appl. Acarol. 7: 153-160.

16. **Giordani, G. 1967.** Laboratory research on *Acarapis woodi* Rennie, the causative agent of acarine disease of honey bee. Note 5. J. Apic. Res. 6: 147-157.

17. **Hirschfelder, H. & H. Sachs. 1952.** Recent research on acarine disease. Bee World 33: 201-209.

18. **Ibay, L.A. & D.M. Burgett. 1989.** Biology of the two external *Acarapis* species of honey bees: *Acarapis dorsalis* Morgenthaler and *Acarapis externus* Morgenthaler. Am. Bee J. 129: 816.

19. **Killion, E.E. & L.A. Lindenfelser. 1988.** Observations on the honey bee tracheal mite in Illinois, pp. 518-525 *In* G.R. Needham, R.E. Page Jr., M. Delfinado-Baker & C.E. Bowman [eds.], Africanized honey bees and bee mites. Halsted Press, New York.

20. **Lee, D.C. 1963.** The susceptibility of honey bees of different ages to infestation by *Acarapis woodi* (Rennie). J. Insect Pathol. 5: 11-15.

21. **Lehnert, T., A.S. Michael & M.D. Levin. 1974.** Disease survey of South American africanized bees. Am. Bee J. 114: 338.

22. **Lindquist, E.E. 1986.** The world genera of Tarsonemidae. Memoirs Entomol. Soc. Can., No. 136.

23. **Liu, T.P. 1990.** Ultrastructure of the flight muscle of worker honey bees heavily infested by the tracheal mite *Acarapis woodi*. Apidologie 21: 537-540.

24. **Liu, T.P., Mobus B., Braybrook, G. 1989a.** A scanning electron microscope study on the prothoracic tracheae of honey bees, *Apis mellifera* L. infested by the mite *Acarapis woodi*. J. Apic. Res. 28: 85-93.

25. **Liu, T.P., Mobus B., Braybrook, G. 1989b.** Fine structure of hypopharyngeal glands from honey bees with and without infesta-

tion by the tracheal mite *Acarapis woodi.* J. Apic. Res. 28: 81-84.

26. **Lozano, L.G., J.O. Moffett, B. Campos-P., M. Guillen-M., O.N. Perez-E., D.L. Maki & W.T. Wilson. 1989.** Tracheal mite *Acarapis woodi* (Rennie) (Acari: Tarsonemidae) infestations in the honey bee, *Apis mellifera* L. (Hymenoptera: Apidae) in Tamaulipas, Mexico. J. Entomol. Sci. 24: 40-46.

27. **Matheson, A. 1993.** World bee health report. Bee World 74: 176-212.

28. **Milne, P.S. 1957.** Acarine disease in *Apis indica.* Bee World 38: 156.

29. **Morgenthaler, O. 1931.** An acarine disease experimental apiary in the Bernese Lake-District and some results obtained there. Bee World 12: 8-10.

30. **Morgenthaler, O. 1933.** *Acarapis woodi* in queens. Bee World 14: 81.

31. **Örösi-Pal, Z. 1934.** Experiments on the feeding habits of the *Acarapis* mites. Bee World 15: 93-94.

32. **Örösi-Pal, Z. 1935.** Die altersimmunitat der honigbiene gegen die milbe (*Acarapis woodi*) Z. Parasitenkunde 7: 401-407.

33. **Otis, G.W., J.B. Bath, D.L. Randall & G.M. Grant. 1987.** Studies on the honey bee tracheal mite (*Acarapis woodi*) (Acari: Tarsonemidae) during winter. Can. J. Zool. 66: 2122-2127.

34. **Page, R.E., Jr. & N.E. Gary. 1989.** Genotypic variation in susceptibility of honey bees (*Apis mellifera*) to infestation by tracheal mites (*Acarapis woodi*). Exp. Appl. Acarol. 8: 275-283.

35. **Pettis, J.S. 1991.** Biology and dispersal behavior of the honey bee tracheal mite *Acarapis woodi.* Ph.D. dissertation, Texas A&M University, College Station.

36. **Pettis, J.S. & W.T. Wilson. 1995.** Life history of the honey bee tracheal mite (Acari: Tarsonemidae). Ann. Entomol. Soc. Am. 89: 368-374.

37. **Pettis, J.S. & T. Pankiw. 1998.** Grooming behavior by *Apis mellifera* L. in the presence of *Acarapis woodi* (Rennie) (Acari: Tarsonemidae). Apidologie 29:223-235.

38. Pettis, J.S., A. Dietz & F.A. Eischen. 1989. Incidence rates of *Acarapis woodi* (Rennie) in queen honey bees of various ages. Apidologie 20: 69-75.

39. Pettis, J.S., W.T. Wilson & F.A. Eischen. 1992. Nocturnal dispersal by female *Acarapis woodi* in honey bee (*Apis mellifera*) colonies. Exp. Appl. Acarol. 15:99-108.

40. Phelan, L.P., A.W. Smith & G.R. Needham. 1991. Mediation of host selection by cuticular hydrocarbons in the honeybee tracheal mite *Acarapis woodi* (Rennie). J. Chem Ecol. 17: 463-473.

41. Phillips, E.F. 1922. The occurrence of diseases of adult bees. U.S. Dept. Agric. circular 218.

42. Phillips, E.F. 1923. The occurrence of diseases of adult bees II. U.S. Dept. Agric. circular 287.

43. Rennie, J. 1921. Isle of Wight disease in hive bees-acarine disease: the organism associated with the disease-*Tarsonemus woodi*, n. sp. Trans. R. Soc. Edinburgh 52: 768-779.

44. Royce, L.A. & P.A. Rossignol. 1991. Sex bias in tracheal mite [*Acarapis woodi* (Rennie)] infestation of honey bees (*Apis mellifera* L.). Bee Sci. 1: 159-161.

45. Royce, L.A., G.W. Krantz, L.A. Ibay & D.M. Burgett. 1988. Some observations on the biology and behavior of *Acarapis woodi* and *Acarapis dorsalis* in Oregon, pp. 498-505. *In* G.R. Needham, R.E. Page Jr., M. Delfinado-Baker & C.E. Bowman [eds], Africanized honey bees and bee mites. Halsted Press, New York.

46. Royce, L.A., P.A Rossignol, D.M. Burgett & B.A. Stringer. 1991. Reduction of tracheal mite parasitism of honey bees by swarming. Phil. Trans. R. Soc. Lond. B. 331: 123-129.

47. Sachs, H. 1952. Uber das verhalten und die Orientierung der tra cheenmilbe *Acarapis woodi* (Rennie 1921) auf bienen. Z. Bienenforschung 1: 148-170.

48. Sammataro, D. & G.R. Needham. 1996. Host-seeking behavior of tracheal mites (Acari: Tarsonemidae) on honey bees (Hymenoptera: Apidae). Exp. Appl. Acarol. 20: 121-136.

49. Sammataro, D., S. Cobey, B.H. Smith & G.R. Needham. 1994.

Controlling tracheal mites (Acari: Tarsonemidae) in honey bees (Hymenoptera: Apidae) with vegetable oil. J. Econ. Entomol. 87: 910-916.

50. **Shah, F.A. 1987.** 20 years of acarine mite in India. Glean. Bee Cult. 115: 517.

51. **Singh, S. 1957.** Acarine disease in the Indian honey bee (*Apis indica* F.) Indian Bee J. 19: 27-28.

52. **Smith, A.W. 1990.** Population dynamics and chemical ecology of the honey bee tracheal mite (Acari: Tarsonemidae), in Ohio. Ph.D. dissertation. Ohio State University, Columbus.

53. **Smith, A.W., G.R. Needham, R.E. Page, Jr. & M.K. Fondrk. 1991a.** Dispersal of the honey bee tracheal mite *Acarapis woodi* (Acari: Tarsonemidae) to old winter bees. Bee Sci. 1: 95-99.

54. **Smith, A.W., R.E. Page, Jr. & G.R. Needham. 1991b.** Vegetable oil disrupts the dispersal of tracheal mite *Acarapis woodi* (Rennie) to young host bees. Am. Bee J. 131: 44-46.

55. **Snodgrass, R.E. 1956.** Anatomy of the honey bee. Cornell University Press. Ithaca, New York.

56. **Wilson, W.T., D.L. Maki, J. Vargas C., R.L. Cox & W.L. Rubink. 1988.** Honey bee swarm frequency and tracheal mite infestation levels in bait hives along the US/Mexico border. Am. Bee J. 128: 811-812.

Chapter 4

INTRODUCTION, SPREAD, AND ECONOMIC IMPACT OF TRACHEAL MITES IN NORTH AMERICA

Eric C. Mussen

*A*n analysis of the impacts of honey bee tracheal mites on the USA and Canadian beekeeping industries must include both direct injury inflicted on infested bee colonies and indirect injuries caused by consequences of the introduction of the parasite. Estimates of those losses by state and provincial apiarists were solicited for this review. Controlled laboratory and field studies describing the direct damages to individual honey bees and honey bee colonies are relatively few. The first indirect effect of tracheal mite infestation, a USA quarantine, was implemented over 70 years ago. It is not known whether the original quarantine caused direct financial losses to beekeepers, but it does appear that the protection was warranted.

The honey bee tracheal mite was discovered, studied, and named *Tarsonemus woodi* by J. Rennie[25], and renamed *Acarapis woodi* by Hirst[13]. Rennie was examining honey bees that showed signs of "Isle of Wight Disease". Semi-paralyzed bees, some with "disjointed wings" (unhooked hind wings spread wide to give a "K-wing" appearance [Fig.

4.1]), had scarred or solid black thoracic tracheae. Examination of tracheae in worker, queen, and drone honey bees revealed the presence of microscopic mites. The coincidental occurrence of the mites and disease signs led Rennie to believe that the mites were implicated in the problem. Both the mites and the disease spread through western Europe, and colony losses were severe[1,2.]

Due to the high correlation between mites and disease conditions, the United States government passed a federal law, the Honeybee Act of 1922, which prohibited further importation of honey bees into that country. It is surprising that the tracheal mite was not found in the

▲ *Figure 4.1 A worker bee displaying the "K-wing" symptom. The hind wing unhooks from the fore wing, giving the wings an appearance of the letter K. This symptom is sometimes associated with tracheal mites.*

USA much earlier because individuals for decades have made anecdotal references to queens being sent by relatives and friends from foreign countries.

Legal and illegal movement of tracheal mite-infested honey bees led to the gradual spread of the mite around most of the world[20]. It still came as a surprise when USA Department of Agriculture (USDA) researchers found tracheal mites in Colombia in 1980[21], southern Mexico in 1980, and northern Mexico in 1982[29]. The discovery of tracheal mites in southern Texas in 1984 was anticipated because of their presence just the other side of the border. What wasn't expected was the finding that the mite had been moved around Texas by migratory beekeepers and, through the sale of bees, into other states. Within months, tracheal mites were found in bee samples from Texas, Louisiana, Florida, New York, North Dakota, and South Dakota.

Tracheal mites are thought to be able to expand their range "naturally" by being transported between colonies by drifting or robbing bees. Subsequent finds of tracheal mites throughout the USA suggest that they were either already well established or were assisted in their rapid spread by beekeeping practices: trucking hives around the country and sending queens and packaged bees through the mail. Results of surveys conducted in the 1960s and the early 1980s on 200,000 specimens from 400 apiaries in USA and Canada demonstrated that the mite was not established before 1984[22,26].

Survey results obtained from cooperating state (Tables 4.1, 4.3) and provincial (Tables 4.2, 4.4) apiarists in 1995 chronicle the spread and impact of tracheal mites throughout North America. It took less than five years for the mite to spread to most of the major beekeeping states in the USA (Table 4.3). State and provincial quarantines may have slowed the distribution of the mite, but only a very few areas that are isolated from migratory beekeepers and that have not imported queens or bees remain free of infestation.

The discovery of tracheal mites in the USA (July 1984) led immediately to efforts to identify their range and limit their spread. Regulatory agencies at the federal, state, provincial, and county levels are empowered to act in order to prevent damage by an introduced pest. Containment of the pest, usually by quarantine and attempts to eradicate it, are often used when a pest first arrives in hopes of eliminating the problem.

The United States and Canadian federal governments had neither

Table 4.1 Indirect losses in the USA attributed to tracheal mites as indicated by state apiary inspectors in 1995

State	Colonies Depopulated	Movement Prohibited?	Purchase Prohibited?	Sales Prohibited?
AK	15	y	y	n
CA	6,881	y	y	y
CO	0	n	n	n
DE	63	y	n	n
FL	300	y	n	y
HI	0	y	y	n
ID	0	y	n	n
IL	82	y	n	n
IN	0	n	n	n
IA	0	y	n	y
KS	0	y	n	n
KY	0	n	n	n
LA	725	n	n	y
MD	0	n	n	n
MA	0	n	n	n
MI	0	y	n	n
MN	yes	y	y	n
MS	300	y	n	y
MO	0	n	n	n
MT	0	n	n	n
NE	901	y	n	n
NV	0	y	n	n
NH	0	n	n	n
NJ	0	y	n	n
NM	5	y	n	n
NY	300	n	n	n
ND	2,400	y	n	n
OH	0	n	y	n
OR	1,500	y	n	n
PA	0	y	n	n

Table 4.1 *(continued)* Indirect losses in the USA attributed to tracheal mites as indicated by state apiary inspectors in 1995

State	Colonies Depopulated	Movement Prohibited?	Purchase Prohibited?	Sales Prohibited?
SC	0	n	n	y
TN	15,000	n	n	y
TX	2,690	?	?	?
UT	2,000	y	n	n
VT	50	n	n	n
VA	33	n	y	n
WA	100	y	n	n
WI	0	n	n	n
WY	0	n	n	n
Total	33,345			

Table 4.2 Indirect losses in Canada attributed to tracheal mites as indicated by provincial apiary inspectors in 1995

Province	Colonies Depopulated	Movement Prohibited?	Purchase Prohibited?	Sales Prohibited?
AB	0	n	n	n
BC	400	y	n	y
MB	2,000	y	y	y
NB	0	y	n	n
NS	17	y	y	n
ON	3,000	n	y	n
PEI	0	y	y	n
PQ	1,045	n	n	n
SK	3,560	y	y	n
Total	10,022			

Table 4.3 Direct losses in the USA attributed to tracheal mites as indicated by state apiary inspectors in 1995

State	Yrs. to 100% Infestation	Peak Annual Colony Losses	Colony Losses, 1994	$ Losses Since 1984
AK	na	15	0	750
CA	5	100,000	25,000	12,500,000
CO	na	na	na	na
DE	2	1,000	500	156,250
FL	1	na	na	na
HI	na	0	0	0
ID	na	na	na	na
IL	8-10	100	na	na
IN	3-4	10,000	100	1,500,000
IA	2-3	18,000	8,000	2,098,750
KS	3	1,000	150	1,000,000
KY	2	na	na	na
LA	3.5	13,500	9,000	1,575,00
MD	3	2,500	500	400,000
MA	7	4,000	500	400,000
MI	3	35,000	na	2,500,000
MN	4-5	16,000	10,000	2,500,00
MS	5	32,000	16,000	4,800,00
MO	4-5	7,500	5,000	995,000
MT	7	na	na	na
NE	6	39,000	9,000	4,500,000
NV	7	na	na	na
NH	4-5	na	na	na
NJ	na	na	na	na
NM	4	50	50	9,000
NY	3-5	.	.	.
ND	3	na	na	na
OH	6	8,000	4,000	1,600,000
OR	2	6,000	7,000	2,500,000
PA	3	12,000	1,000	1,000,000

Table 4.3 *(continued)* Direct losses in the USA attributed to tracheal mites as indicated by state apiary inspectors in 1995

State	Yrs. to 100% Infestation	Peak Annual Colony Losses	Colony Losses, 1994	$ Losses Since 1984
SC	4-5	10,000	2,000	1,500,000
TN	11	30,000	12,000	5,125,000
TX	na	na	na	na
UT	5	na	na	na
VT	5	500	500	100,000
VA	3	29,000	5,800	42,900,000
WA	6	11,200	11,200	1,265,000
WI	na	15,000	15,000	3,000,000
WY	na	0	0	0
Total		401,365	142,300	93,924,750

Table 4.4 Direct losses in Canada attributed to tracheal mites as indicated by provincial apiary inspectors in 1995

Province	Yrs. to 100% Infestation	Peak Annual Colony Losses	Colony losses, 1994	$ Losses Since 1984
AB	still in progress	50	50	2,500
BC	still in progress	na	3,000	150,000
MB	still in progress	2,000-3,000	2,000-3,000	200,000
NB	na	na	na	na
NS	still in progress	11	0	850
ON	still in progress	na	na	na
PEI	na	na	na	na
PQ	still in progress	na	na	na
SK	still in progress	18,000	2,000	2,000,000
Total		20,500	7,550	2,353,350

the necessary personnel nor funding to implement federal surveys of approximately four million colonies. The task of delimiting the spread of the mite was left to the states and provinces. In August of 1984 the USDA Animal Plant Health Inspection Service (APHIS) informed regulatory agencies that infested colonies were to be held in place and the colonies depopulated. Information from 39 state and nine provincial surveys shows that in excess of 43,367 colonies were voluntarily or involuntarily depopulated. Many states and provinces imposed "interior quarantines" that prohibited the movement of colonies from areas of known infestation to areas believed to be mite-free. More states and provinces imposed "external quarantines" on infested areas and required mite-free certification for incoming bees. Certification and delimitation sample analysis cost hundreds of thousands of dollars[23]. The restrictions on colony movement and on sales of queens and packages from infested regions resulted in serious financial losses for many beekeepers and a reduction in numbers of bee breeders from 42 to 5 in Florida and from 37 to 6 in Louisiana. Less than a year later, USDA described plans to lift the national quarantine and each state had to decide what to do. A review of the history of tracheal mite regulations can be found in Henderson & Morse[12].

Regulatory programs are supposed to be based on scientific premises about pests and their potential consequences to the protected industry. However, the involvement of industry members usually brings political considerations into the decision making process. The way California dealt with the infestation will serve as a good example.

The California Department of Food and Agriculture (CDFA) has a list of many types of agricultural pests. Most are exotic pests that have never arrived. Some have been found and eradicated, and a few have become established and are being controlled. The pests are ranked by their potential "danger" and most of the pests have an "exotic pest profile" written by scientists and used to assist with regulatory decision making, should the pest be found. The pest profile on *Acarapis woodi* contained a number of references that linked the mite to a severe disease condition. It also contained references that stated that the mite currently is not much of a problem in Great Britain[5].

Based on the information in the pest profile, CDFA administrators decided that the destructive potential of tracheal mites was high enough to warrant attempts at control and eradication. The regulation was written and implemented in January of 1985. In the months that followed, many loads of bees were forced to leave the state, and a total of 8,619 colonies of honey bees were scheduled for depopulation. Many of the beekeepers whose bees were eliminated never returned to the profession.

California beekeepers became divided into two opposing camps concerning the mite. One side, including the northern California bee breeders, wished to have mite-infested colonies quarantined and eradicated. This was especially important to protect their sales of more than 250,000 packages of bees annually to Canadian provinces.

Migratory beekeepers were equally adamant about protecting their right to transport hives of bees around the country in order to make their living by providing pollination services and producing honey.

Despite the dissension, CDFA intended to continue the quarantine and eradication program. However, it was apparent that the program would be more acceptable if it had industry backing. The California State Beekeepers Association (CSBA) requested that they be allowed to hold a special membership meeting before CDFA made its final decision. The meeting was to culminate in a vote to support or oppose the continuance of quarantine regulations. Only dues-paying members of CSBA were allowed to vote. In the days preceding the meeting, membership in CSBA doubled to over 500 voting members.

The meeting was held in Fresno, California, in the format of a panel discussion followed by questions. Panel members included experts obtained by proponents on both sides of the issue. The question was, "Is this pest serious enough to try to keep it out of California by regulation, including 'depopulations' of infested colonies?" Depopulation for mites meant killing the bees with no compensation since no legal mite control treatments were available at the time. Those opposed to such an approach said that the mites were not a serious threat and that they would spread all over the country regardless of attempts to stop them.

Following a long and heated debate, CSBA members voted, by secret ballot, to support the following regulatory options, 303 to 49: (1) infested colonies could be eradicated, or (2) infested colonies could be moved to an "open" state, or (3) infested colonies could be moved to a temporary quarantine site, then out of state[6].

The members of the California Apiary Advisory Board (five beekeepers from different geographic regions of the state) met and concurred with the decision and reported such to the Director of CDFA.

Tracheal mites did eventually spread throughout California and across the country. When the central and southern portions of the state had too many infested colonies to justify depopulations, the California regulatory program was reduced to a regional program in 1986 designed to protect only the northern California bee breeders. The protection of northern interests lasted only two years. The discovery of tracheal mites in bee breeder territory in late 1987, coinciding with discovery of *Varroa jacobsoni* in the USA, marked the end of shipping bees to Canada and the end of California's tracheal mite regulations.

Most of the early North American studies on tracheal mites and their control were conducted in Florida. Data showed that even high levels of tracheal mite infestation (percentage of bees infested in the population) did not seem to have detrimental effects on honey bee population sizes, honey yields, or overwintering success[10,27]. The picture began to change after mites moved into cooler climates. Alarming abnormalities and losses occurred during the falls and winters of 1986-1989[12]. Large numbers of worker bees would leave the colonies. They crawled out the entrances and walked away, climbing up on vegetation or just wandering off[28]. Some of the bees had disjointed wings, but many did not. Some of the bees had demonstrable mite infestations, but many did not. Most of the walking bees had distended abdomens due to rectums full of feces.

Inside a hive, there would be only a handful of workers (some infested, most not) and the queen. Stored food was ample, and if the phenomenon occurred in the spring there might be a few eggs, but no larvae or older brood. When hives were opened, the workers remained immobile and gave the appearance of bees that were starving. Colonies in this condition perished in cooler climates, but in California many of them were able to survive. Interestingly, given a frame of emerging brood and a pound or two of bulk bees, the queen would begin laying and the colony would build back to normal levels. Most of those colonies became infested again before the end of the year. The colony did not necessarily become overwhelmed by mites again, even though the genetic stock of the bees was unchanged. This suggests that highly pathogenic mites eliminated themselves by killing their host colonies, and only mildly- to non-pathogenic mites remained.

Until the late 1980s, direct cause and effect relationships between the presence of mites and the health of adult bees had never been demonstrated. With time, studies were conducted that determined that tracheal mite infestations reduced life expectancy of infested worker bees[19], damaged their tracheal tubes[15,17], decimated their brood-food producing glands[18], and destroyed their vertical flight muscles[15,16]. Tracheal mites were shown to be detrimental to overwintering colonies in cold climates. Studies by Gruszka[11], Furgala & others[8,9], Komeili & Ambrose[14] and Otis & Scott-Dupree[24] demonstrated that the presence of mites increased wintering mortality by as much as 50%. At the 1994 winter meeting of the Minnesota Honey Producers Association, beekeepers reported 25-40% losses of Minnesota hives wintered in Minnesota. Similar colonies trucked to Texas for the winter had 5-10% losses. Obviously, tracheal mites are harder on bees that are forced to remain in a tight cluster for many months without rearing brood than on bees that are free to fly, forage, and rear brood throughout the year.

Data from a survey I conducted in 1995 indicate that beekeepers and regulatory personnel believe that mite infestation continues to cause significant losses of wintering colonies (Tables 4.3, 4.4). Using a replacement value of $50 USA per colony, over $7 million in colonies were lost in 1994, and over $90 million worth of colonies have been lost over the past decade (Table 4.3). The number of beekeepers in Massachusetts has decreased by 40% since the arrival of tracheal mites, while the number declined by more than 25% in California.

We are still unable to predict which colonies or apiaries will have these problems. Tracheal mite populations are able to increase rapidly in an apiary, leading to colony losses in spite of widespread use of remedial oil extender patties[7]. At a California Bee Breeders' meeting, one commercial beekeeper stated that tracheal mites increase substantially in some yards for no known reason, increasing winter losses from the previously expected range of 5-10% to 20-25%. Also, since tracheal mites infested his operation, this beekeeper has been able to produce only about six pounds of bulk bees from colonies that used to provide 10-12 pounds.

In spite of optimistic speculations from Europe on the effects of *A. woodi* in North America[3,4], it is apparent that tracheal mites have been worse than expected: "These [North American] losses lend credence to the conclusion that *A. woodi* was indeed the cause of the serious problems experienced by British beekeepers in the years following 1905"[12]. With the introduction of *Varroa jacobsoni*, it has become difficult to differentiate between colony losses due solely to either mite. But tracheal mites are unquestionably a key factor among many causing serious hardship in North American beekeeping.

Summary: Tracheal mites were responsible for passage of the federal Honey Bee Act in 1922. That legislation prohibited importation of living honey bees into the USA in an effort to prevent infesting new world bees with tracheal mites. Despite the law, tracheal mites arrived in the USA in 1984. Stringent quarantine and eradication programs forced some beekeepers out of business and did little to slow the spread of the mites. Initially, opinions were mixed concerning the potential pathogenicity of the parasite. However, infested colonies often were severely weakened or lost over winter despite beekeepers' best efforts to keep them alive. Tabular information is presented from surveys sent to state and provincial apiarists. At their worst, tracheal mites were estimated to cause the loss of over 400,000 colonies of bees annually in the USA and 20,000 in Canada. The cumulative dollar losses to tracheal mites over the first decade of their presence in North America are estimated at $103,325,000, and the mites still are problematic.

References cited.

1. **Adam, Bro. 1985.** The acarine disease menace: short-term and long-term countermeasures. Am. Bee J. 125: 163-164.

2. **Adam, Bro. 1987.** The honey-bee tracheal mite: fact or fiction? Am. Bee J. 127: 36-38.

3. **Bailey, L. 1985.** Bailey comments on tracheal mite (letter to editor). Am. Bee J. 125: 151, 161.

4. **Bailey, L. 1986.** The mite that roared. Am. Bee J. 126: 469.

5. **Bailey, L. & J.N. Perry. 1982.** The diminished incidence of *Acarapis woodi* (Rennie) (Acari: Tarsonemidae) in honeybees, *Apis mellifera* L. (Hymenoptera: Apidae) in Britain. Bull. Entomol. Res. 72: 655-662.

6. **Cobey, S. & T. Lawrence. 1986.** More tracheal mites found in California. Am. Bee J. 126: 87-90.

7. **Delaplane, K.S. 1992.** Controlling tracheal mites (Acari: Tarsonemidae) in colonies of honey bees (Hymenoptera: Apidae) with vegetable oil and menthol. J. Econ. Entomol. 85: 2118-2124.

8. Furgala, B., S.R. Duff, S. Aboulfaraj, D.W. Ragsdale & R.A. Hyser. 1988. Some effects of the honey bee tracheal mite (*Acarapis woodi* Rennie) on non-migratory honey bee colonies in east central Minnesota. Am. Bee J. 128: 802-803.

9. Furgala, B., S. Duff, S. Aboulfaraj, D. Ragsdale & R.A. Hyser. 1989. Some effects of the honey bee tracheal mite (*Acarapis woodi* Rennie) on non-migratory, wintering honey bee (*Apis mellifera*) colonies in east central Minnesota. Am. Bee J. 129: 195-197.

10. Gary, N. & R. Page. 1989. Tracheal mite (Acari: Tarsonemidae) infestation: effects on foraging and survivorship of honey bees (Hymenoptera: Apidae). J. Econ. Entomol. 82: 734-739.

11. Gruszka, J. 1987. Honey-bee tracheal mites: are they harmful? Am. Bee J. 127: 653-654.

12. Henderson, C.E. & R.A. Morse. 1990. Tracheal mites, pp. 219-234. *In* R.A. Morse & R. Nowogrodzki [eds.], Honey bee pests, predators, and diseases, 2d ed. Cornell University Press, Ithaca, New York.

13. Hirst, S. 1921. On some new or little-known acari, mostly parasitic in habit. Proc. Zool. Soc. London. 1921: 357-378.

14. Komeili, A.B. & J.T. Ambrose. 1990. Biology, ecology and damage of tracheal mites on honey bees (*Apis mellifera*). Am. Bee J. 130: 193-199.

15. Komeili, A.B. & J.T. Ambrose. 1991. Electron microscope studies of the tracheae and flight muscles of non-infested, *Acarapis woodi* infested, and crawling honey bees (*Apis mellifera*). Am. Bee J. 131: 253-257.

16. Liu, T.P. 1990. Ultrastructure of the flight muscle of worker honey bees heavily infested by the tracheal mite *Acarapis woodi*. Apidologie 21: 537-540.

17. Liu, T.P., B. Mobus & G. Braybook. 1989. A scanning electron microscope study on the prothoracic tracheae of the honey bee, *Apis mellifera* L., infested by the mite *Acarapis woodi* (Rennie). J. Apic. Res. 28: 81-84.

18. Liu, T.P., B. Mobus & G. Braybook. 1989. Fine structure of hypopharyngeal glands from honeybees with and without infesta-

tion by the tracheal mite, *Acarapis woodi* (Rennie). J. Apic. Res. 28:85-92.

19. **Maki, D.L., W.T. Wilson & R.L. Cox. 1986.** Infestation by *Acarapis woodi* and its effects on honey bee longevity in laboratory cage studies. Am. Bee J. 126: 832.

20. **Matheson, A. 1995.** World bee health update. Bee World 76: 31-39.

21. **Menapace, D.M. & W.T. Wilson. 1980.** *Acarapis woodi* mites found in honey bees from Colombia, South America. Am. Bee J. 12: 761-762, 765.

22. **Otis, G. 1986.** Summary of Canadian mite surveys. Am. Bee J. 126: 567-568.

23. **Otis, G. 1990.** Results of a survey of the economic impact of tracheal mites. Am. Bee J. 130: 28-31.

24. **Otis, G.W. & C.O. Scott-Dupree. 1992.** Effects of *Acarapis woodi* on overwintered colonies of honey bees (Hymenoptera: Apidae) in New York. J. Econ. Entomol. 85: 40-46.

25. **Rennie, J. 1921.** Isle of Wight disease in hive bees Cacarine disease: the organism associated with the disease *Tarsonemus woodi*, n. sp. Trans. R. Soc. Edinburgh 52: 768-779.

26. **Shimanuki, H. & D.A. Knox. 1989.** Tracheal mite surveys. Am. Bee J. 129: 671-672.

27. **Taber, S. 1986.** First research report of acarine effects in the United States. Am. Bee J. 126: 343-345.

28. **Thoenes, S.C. & S.L. Buchmann. 1990.** Tracheal mite induced colony mortality monitored by an electronic scale. Am. Bee J. 130: 816.

29. **Wilson, W.T. & R. Nunamaker. 1982.** The infestation of honey bees in Mexico with *Acarapis woodi*. Am. Bee J. 122: 503-505, 508.

THE PATHOLOGICAL EFFECTS OF THE TRACHEAL MITE ON ITS HOST

Clarence H. Collison

*T*he honey bee tracheal mite, *Acarapis woodi* (Rennie), is an endoparasite that infests the respiratory system of adult honey bees. In the past, symptoms of infestation were sometimes called acarine disease or acariosis. The western honey bee (*Apis mellifera* L.), including Africanized honey bees (*A. m. scutellata*), the giant honey bee (*A. dorsata*), and eastern honey bee (*A. cerana*) are the only known hosts of this parasite[10, 11]. Drones, workers, and queens may be infested.

The entire life cycle of the mite, except for brief migratory periods, is usually spent within the tracheae or breathing tubes in the thorax of adult honey bees. Mites are most commonly found in the main tracheal trunk leading from the first pair of thoracic spiracles[1]. They are also found in all branches large enough to accommodate their size, such as the tracheae leading to the ventral part of the prothorax, those leading to the head and to the thoracic salivary glands, and those passing over the indirect flight muscles. Mites also are occasionally found in air sacs in the head, thorax, and abdomen. Giordani[16] found adult mites with eggs and larvae in the air sacs of the head even when the tracheae were almost empty and soon after the infestation occurred. It was confirmed that the tendency to disperse within the respiratory system is not related to mite population density or length of time the tracheae have been infested.

Mites reproduce and feed within the tracheae. Adults and larvae penetrate the walls of breathing tubes with their mouth parts and feed on hemolymph (blood). Occasionally, migratory mites may feed on the exterior of the bee by piercing the soft membranes primarily around wing bases[28].

The tracheal mite has had a devastating impact on the North American beekeeping industry. Problems began soon after its initial discovery in the United States and Canada in 1984 and 1986, respectively. In Europe, however, the mite has had a long association with *A. mellifera*, and the host-parasite relationship appears to be stable. Under European conditions, mites can persist in a colony for years while causing only little damage. In a situation where there is environmental stress, mite infestations can cause biological problems that eventually lead to economic loss[8]. When combined with other diseases, unfavorable environmental conditions, a poor queen, scarcity of pollen or a poor foraging season, the disease can contribute to the death of a colony.

Economic damage from the mite is normally manifested as increased winter mortality. Colonies with higher mite prevalence normally experience greater mortality[27]. Infested bees have been shown to have shortened life spans [3, 24]. Losses are also seen in the form of decreased honey yields[12] and reduced brood areas in the spring[17, 27]. The build-up of colonies initiated from mite-infested packages in Saskatchewan was so severely reduced that the mite-infested colonies failed to produce a honey crop[26].

Detection of a tracheal mite infestation is difficult since there are no specific outward signs of the disease. Infested individuals usually behave normally and forage actively for nectar and pollen. One observable, non-exclusive symptom of a tracheal mite infestation has been the presence of crawling bees (K-wing bees) on the ground outside a hive (Fig. 5.1). These crawling bees have their wings partially opened as if dislocated. They do not fly when released from an elevated position and are presumably incapable of flight[19]. Numerous causes have been sug-

▲*Figure 5.1 In the terminal phase of colony decline, bees crawl away from the colony in large numbers. Note the foreground bee perched on the blade of grass. In the background are disorganized clumps of bees on the hive entrance (photo: K.S. Delaplane).*

gested to explain the detrimental effects of the mite on the host. The honey bee tracheae become plugged with mites and mite debris, and the flight muscles may be deprived of oxygen. Toxic substances from the mites or mite feces may also be involved. In addition, the mites may act as carriers of viruses or other disease pathogens.

The histopathological effects of the mite upon the honey bee are believed to result from: (1) active injury to the bee by the mite feeding on host hemolymph with a possible toxic action on the host; (2) the passive role of the mite in hindering or inhibiting the normal functions of the infested organs[1]; and (3) possible effects associated with viral, or bacterial inoculations. The known effects on various honey bee systems are described below.

Respiratory system (tracheae). Noninfested thoracic tracheae are clear, colorless or pale amber in color. Mite-infested tracheae deteriorate progressively and show patchy discoloration, a process described as *sclerotization* resulting from polyphenol oxidase reactions. Tracheae that are normally elastic and flexible become stiff and brittle. In a slight infestation, one or both tracheal tubes contain a few adult mites and eggs which can be detected near the spiracular openings. At this stage, the tracheae may appear clear, cloudy or slightly discolored. The tracheae of severely infested bees have brown blotches with brown scabs or crust-like lesions, or may appear completely black and are obstructed by mite debris and numerous mites in all stages of development[9]. The brown blotches on the tracheal wall are made up of closely packed globular bodies. Fluid resembling pus may be present within the tracheae[18]. Blockage and discoloration are most complete in those branches of the anterior tracheal system which pass between the longitudinal and vertical flight muscles and where the salivary glands surround the tracheae. Giordani[15] studied the brown spots characteristic of heavily-infested tracheae and determined by histochemical methods that the pigment was melanin. Insect hemolymph contains a high level of phenol oxidase activity and the amino acid tyrosine and tyrosine's metabolic products[14]. Hemolymph phenol oxidase may be activated once the hemolymph has leaked into the tracheal lumen, thus leading to the formation of melanins[22] or other oxidized phenolic products characteristic of the wound response in insects.

The deterioration of the tracheae may affect the respiratory activity of the honey bee. The mites and debris may also physically obstruct the tracheae, therefore decreasing the oxygen supply to the tissues. A lack of oxygen in the bee flight muscles would render the bees unable to fly and would explain the crawling symptoms of mite-infested bees. A second type of damage results from the mechanical puncturing of the tissues surrounding the infested tracheae when the mite extends its mouth parts through the tracheal walls while feeding. Anderson[2] observed that flight muscles adjacent to infested tracheae were darkened and shrunk. Punctured nerve ganglia appeared watery in color rather than the opaque white of normal tissue. Surplus hemolymph may be seen inside the tracheae at the point where the mite is feeding, thus a third type of damage is possible with the loss of hemolymph.

Two scanning electron microscope studies of the prothoracic tracheae of healthy and infested honey bees indicated that the tracheal condition was in dramatic contrast. In the first study by Liu & others[22], healthy and mite-infested honey bees were collected from Scotland in the summer and fall of 1985. The surface of the outer layer of the tracheae was smooth, and the tracheal intima was ribbed with taenidia in noninfested bees. In mite-infested bees the outer membrane of tracheae appeared to be very brittle, and the surface of the cuticular intima within the trachea often was obscured by a thick layer of unidentified material which was not observed in the tracheae of healthy bees. Numerous porous round globules, together with the mites themselves, often completely blocked some of the tracheal branches. The nature of these globules is not known. They could be secretions or excretions of *A. woodi* since they were often associated with the mite. In addition to the mites, two kinds of debris were found in the tracheae: one kind was solid and the other was porous. This porous material might be hemolymph that had leaked into the tracheal lumen via the feeding wounds.

In the second study, Komeili & Ambrose[19] compared noninfested bees, mite-infested bees that did not exhibit crawling behavior outside the hive, and infested crawling bees. Samples were collected in December and January in North Carolina, USA when the mite load was high and reddish brown spots in infested tracheae became prevalent and conspicuous. The prothoracic tracheal trunks and branches of infested bees and infested crawler bees contained numerous mites and different kinds of debris (globules and mite exuviae). As the infestation increased, parts of the tracheal intima became coated with a thick layer of coated material which is responsible for the reddish-brown spots seen with the light microscope. Tracheal trunks and secondary branches of crawling bees had cracks along their entire length. These cracks might be due to wounds inflicted by the mites and subsequent destruction of the cells or to deposition of debris in the tracheal lumen and the subsequent loss of elasticity. This type of injury could have severe adverse effects on respiration and gas exchange and may even rupture the body cavity. Irregular whitish spots were visible on the surface of infested tracheae. The tracheae of crawling bees had more whitish spots than infested non-crawlers, and the shape and pattern of these spots differed from non-crawlers. No clear evidence of any scar damage corresponding to mite mouth parts was seen.

Mite populations can seriously retard the flow of oxygen to the tissues. Immobilized healthy workers and infested workers were studied at $21°$ and $35°C$[30]. In the initial stages of mite infestations, no differences in the rate of oxygen consumption were observed between healthy and infested bees. At a heavier infestation, the metabolic rate increased in comparison with that of healthy bees, particularly at the higher temperature presumably due to a reduced oxygen supply. In heavily-infested and dying bees, the metabolic rate dropped sharply at 35°.

Flight muscles. The muscle tissues of some mite-infested bees were found to be abnormal near the more heavily-infested areas of the tracheae[1]. The affected tissue was brownish instead of white in color and was somewhat brittle. Killick[18] observed a fiber of a flight muscle which had a very dark brown spindle-shaped swelling with rounded projections passing into the substance of adjacent fibers. Such a condition may have been caused by a mite passing its proboscis through a tracheal wall into the flight muscle. Killick[18] postulated that the toxic action of a "poison" (digestive and toxic fluid associated with mite feeding) is the chief factor in bringing about the death of the bee by paralyzing the flight muscles and rendering the bee unable to keep up its own heat.

Discoloration and atrophy of flight muscles may also occur from a decreasing oxygen supply. The vertical flight muscles of infested crawling bees were degenerated (muscle fibers broken along their entire length), whereas those of noninfested and infested non-crawling bees appeared normal (muscle fiber surface smooth and undamaged)[19]. The longitudinal flight muscles of noninfested, infested and crawler bees with infestations were similar. Komeili and Ambrose[19] clearly showed that the flight muscles of mite-infested crawler bees were degenerated, which affects the ability to fly. Crawling was not observed in all infested bees or colonies, but all crawlers had mites. Crawling may be due to genetic disposition of the bees, duration or severity of infestation, or age of the infested bees. Komeili and Ambrose[19] concluded that tracheal mites are a significant contributor to the occurrence of crawling bees. Even though crawling behavior has been associated with nosema and viral bee diseases, earlier North Carolina tests found crawler bees to be free of any viral disease or nosema spores.

Liu[20] used transmission electron microscopy to study the dorsal longitudinal indirect flight muscles of both healthy and heavily-infested worker honey bees. In the flight muscle of healthy honey bees, the mitochondria were large and arranged in rows between the myofibrils. Glycogen particles were embedded in the myofibrils and accumulated in the sarcoplasm. In the flight muscles of six heavily mite-infested honey bee workers, glycogen particles were completely depleted, and the cristae, inner and outer membranes of the mitochondria, and the myofibrils were electron-dense. The sarcoplasm of the flight muscle was electron-lucid. These changes may indicate that the flight muscle of heavily-infested bees was in the process of degeneration and may also indicate that this degeneration is due to either lack of oxygen or lack of energy reserves. Honey bees use carbohydrates as fuel for flight. It has been shown that the total duration of flight in some insects is closely related to the amount of their glycogen reserves. The lack of glycogen in the flight muscle of heavily-infested honey bees may indicate that a large population of mites in the tracheal system consumed all the energy reserves or retarded the mechanisms that allowed the reserves to be built up. Consequently, honey bees may not be able to fly due to lack of fuel. This too may explain why mite-infested honey bees often crawl.

Nerve ganglia. Anderson[1] observed that the large nerve passing to the base of the wing comes in close contact with one of the large tracheae frequently infested with mites. In several infested bees this nerve appeared watery instead of evenly white as in non-infested bees. The damaged nerve ganglia, in conjunction with muscle damage, may further account for the crawling condition and disjointed wings of many infested bees.

Hypopharyngeal (brood-food) glands. The hypopharyngeal glands from honey bees with and without heavy tracheal mite infestation were examined by electron microscopy[23]. In healthy bees, the individual saccules of the glands were much larger than those observed in the infested bees. Saccules of healthy bees were round and consisted of numerous acinar cells. The nuclei of the acinar cells were large and rich in euchromatin. The cytoplasm contained well-developed endoplasmic reticulum. Numerous membrane-bound, electron-dense granules and large masses of less dense membrane-bound material were observed in the acinar cells of healthy bees. In heavily-infested bees, the nuclei of the acinar cells contained dispersed euchromatin, the endoplasmic reticulum had short, dilated cisternae, and numerous lysosome bodies were observed. Electron-dense secretory granules were lacking. The secretory materials in the extracellular ducts were much more electron-dense than the same materials observed in healthy honey bees. These observations were interpreted as pathological, degenerative changes, associated with heavy mite infestations, not as a consequence of aging.

Hemolymph (blood). As a result of mite feeding, the hemolymph of infested bees has a higher than normal bacterial count[25]. Fekl[13] isolated bacteria from the insides of the tracheae and the hemolymph of honey bees. Bacteria were found in the main thoracic tracheae of 83 out of 100 normal honey bees of which four simultaneously had bacteria in the hemolymph. One honey bee had bacteria in the hemolymph but not in the tracheae. Four species of bacteria were found in the hemolymph and 15 in the tracheae (Table 5.1). Infested honey bees had more bacteria in the hemolymph. In bees infested with *A. woodi* but otherwise normal, 83 out of 100 had bacteria in the tracheae. Of these infested bees, 16 had bacteria in the hemolymph. Thirteen species of bacteria were found in the hemolymph and 17 in the tracheae (Table 5.1). An evaluation was also made on 50 bees with disjointed wings, but in which no mites were observed in the tracheae. These bees came from infested hives. Bacteria in the tracheae were found 43 times; three of these infected bees also had bacteria in the hemolymph.

In general, those species of bacteria found in the tracheae were also found in the hemolymph. The bacteria in the hemolymph were different from those found in the gut and elsewhere in the honey bee. Bacteria were rare in the hemolymph of healthy bees. These results suggest that bacteria enter the hemolymph by way of puncture holes in the tracheae. When the tracheae are injured, hemolymph penetrates into the tracheae, coagulates, and often forms with the mite feces an extended crust. Not all of the bees infested with mites had bacterial infections in their hemolymph. The bacterial infection in the tracheae of infested bees was always significantly greater than in healthy bees. The species composition of the tracheal flora also shifted with mite infestation. Bacteria found in the tracheae were primarily protein-using types, or putrefactive bacteria (to some extent pure fecal bacteria). A few were types severely pathogenic to bees. The composition of the hemolymph flora shifted in the same direction as that of the tracheal flora. The bacterial content of tracheae and hemolymph rose upon the infestation of the tracheae with parasitic mites.

Other pathogens associated with the mites and host. Pathogens in addition to the various types of bacteria isolated from tracheae and hemolymph have also been found. White masses found in tracheae of bees from Mexico were identified as yeast that grew on and killed tracheal mites. The identification was made by Dr. Lavie of France in 1955[31]. From 1963-66, Wille[32] found that many bees with an acarine

Table 5.1 Bacteria isolated from the tracheae and hemolymph of healthy honey bees and bees infested by *Acarapis woodi* (Rennie) as determined by Fekl[13].

Bacteria	Healthy Bees	A. woodi-Infested Bees
Actinomyces spp.	+	+
Aerobacter cloacae	-	+
Bacillus alvei	+	+
Bacillus mesentericus	-	+
Bacillus mycoides	+	+
Bacillus subtilis	+	+
Bacterium prodigiosum	+	+
Escherichia coli	-	+
Micrococcus flavus	+	+
Micrococcus luteus	+	+
Micrococcus pyogenes var. *albus*	+	-
Micrococcus radiatus	+	-
Proteus mirabilis	+	+
Pseudomones fluorescens	+	+
Sarcina aurantiaca	+	+
Sarcina flava	+	+
Sarcina lutes	+	+
Streptococcus faecalis	-	+
Streptococcus liquefaciens	+	+

infestation also had other disorders such as bacterial septicemia, amoeba cysts, and disintegration of the thoracic muscles, but little nosema.

Virus-like particles have been isolated from *A. woodi* and mite-infested bees. Mite-infested honey bees were collected from Buckham, Scotland during the summer of 1985 and from Vacaville, California, USA during 1988-1989[21]. The cells of the body cavity of tracheal mites in the honey bees collected from Scotland harbored numerous isometric virus-like particles. These virus-like particles were formed in a crystalline array and were arranged in a hexagonal pattern. No virus-like particles were observed in the tracheal mites of the honey bees collected from California. In all of the tracheal mites from which virus-like particles were detected, tissues were extensively lysed and the mites appeared to be dead before fixation.

These virus-like particles found only in the tracheal mites bear a close resemblance to some of the honey bee viruses. The large number of virus crystals found in the tracheal mites was always associated with cellular debris which is an indication that these particles replicated themselves within the cells of tracheal mites. Therefore, it is unlikely that these particles are honey bee viruses ingested by the tracheal mites.

Because these virus-like particles were found in the extensively lysed cells, it could indicate that they are lethal to tracheal mites. It is possible that some British honey bees are more resistant to tracheal mite infestation due to the presence of a viral disease in the tracheal mite population.

While attempting to feed mites through a synthetic membrane, Bruce & others[6] determined that tracheal mites can take up spiroplasmas (helical, wall-less bacteria of the class Mollicutes) known to be pathogenic to honey bees. This microbe was used as an indicator to determine whether *A. woodi* had actually penetrated the synthetic membrane and fed. During routine sampling of honey bee colonies for spiroplasmas, the filamentous virus (F virus) was identified from both honey bee hemolymph and from tracheal mites that were present. In addition, the F virus of honey bees was found in *A. woodi*. This is the first report of spiroplasmas and F viruses in this mite. Thus, tracheal mites may act as vectors for at least one bacterium (*Spiroplasma melliferum*) and one virus known to be pathogenic to honey bees.

Normally, *S. melliferum* can be isolated from nectar and honey bees from early spring to mid-July. The disease incidence in bees varied from about 25% to 100% through May and June, then dwindled and reached zero by July 15[7]. Mites collected from honey bees with *S. melliferum*-infected hemolymph during late July to early August were all carrying *S. melliferum*[6]. During August the infestation level of *A. woodi* in the infested colonies dropped from over 50% to about 5%. Perhaps there is a correlation between the seemingly simultaneous decline in the populations of *S. melliferum* and *A. woodi* in the summer.

Microorganisms in insects exposed to stresses such as the tracheal mite can multiply extensively in the tissues of weakened hosts and thus cause disease that may be severe or even fatal[29]. There is a tradition associating *A. woodi* with outbreaks of acute disease[4] and these associations could be valid if there are airborne pathogens that readily infect and soon kill mite-infested bees, but are harmless to non-infested bees. Pathogens of this kind constantly encountered by bees could conceivably eradicate *A. woodi* because this mite needs at least 14 days to complete its life cycle. Artificially applied pathogens might be used to control infestation by the mite[5]. Experiments were conducted to determine if bees infested with *A. woodi* were more easily killed than normal bees when sprayed with suspensions of the bacterium *Pseudomonas apiseptica*, acute bee paralysis virus (ABPV), and chronic bee paralysis virus (CBPV)[5]. Most bees were killed two days after they had been sprayed with *P. apiseptica* and about six days after they had been sprayed with ABPV or CBPV. Significant numbers of bees were killed by each pathogen, but there was little or no difference between the death rates of bees infested or not infested with *A. woodi*. Thus *A. woodi* does not cause any striking effect by enabling airborne pathogens to invade the hemolymph of bees. The additional bacteria found by Fekl[13] in the hemolymph of mite-infested bees are perhaps introduced only in small intermittent doses during the long period mites take to mature, possibly only at the moments when newly-hatched larvae and newly-formed adults pierce the tracheal wall to start feeding. If this is so, then persistent, highly virulent and ubiquitous airborne pathogens could conceivably prevent *A. woodi* from becoming established, but airborne pathogens to which bees are only occasionally exposed seem unlikely to cause outbreaks of acute disease in infested colonies; nor will they serve as a convenient means of eradicating established infestations.

Summary. It is not known exactly why bees infested with tracheal mites die[33]. Studies have shown, however, that tracheal mites cause degenerative changes in the honey bee tracheae, flight muscles, nerve ganglia, and hypopharyngeal glands. These histopathological changes are directly related to damage associated with mite feeding, loss of blood, and partial blockage of the respiratory system with mites and associated debris. A reduced supply of oxygen to the adjacent tissues and depletion of energy reserves are believed to explain why heavily-infested bees often exhibit crawling behavior and lose the ability to fly. The bacteria that have been found in the hemolymph of mite-infested bees presumably invade via wounds made by mites in the tracheae. There is evidence that there are associations of tracheal mites, pathogens (i.e. viruses, yeasts, spiroplasmas), and the honey bee, but the significance of these relationships is unclear at this time, warranting further investigation.

References cited.

1. **Anderson, E.J. 1928.** The pathological changes in honeybees infested with the Isle of Wight Disease. J. Econ. Entomol. 21: 404-407.

2. **Anderson, E.J. 1959.** Acarine disease. Am. Bee J. 99: 288-289.

3. **Bailey, L. 1958.** The epidemiology of the infestation of the honey bee, *Apis mellifera* L., by the mite *Acarapis woodi* (Rennie) and the mortality of infested bees. Parasitology 48: 493-506.

4. **Bailey, L. 1963.** Infectious diseases of the honey-bee. Land Books, London.

5. **Bailey, L. 1965.** Susceptibility of the honey bee *Apis mellifera* Linnaeus, infested with *Acarapis woodi* (Rennie) to infection by airborne pathogens. J. Invertebr. Pathol. 7: 141-143.

6. **Bruce, W.A., K.J. Hackett, H. Shimanuki & R.B. Henegar. 1991.** Bee mites: vectors of honey bee pathogens?, pp.180-182. *In* W. Ritter [ed.], Proceedings, Apimondia Symposium on Recent Research on Honey Bee Pathology, 5-7 September 1990. Janssen Pharmaceutica, Beerse, Belgium.

7. **Clark, T.B. 1977.** *Spiroplasma* sp., a new pathogen in honey bees. J. Invertebr. Pathol. 29: 112-113.

8. **Cox, R.L., J.O. Moffett, W.T. Wilson & M. Ellis. 1989.** Effects of

late spring and summer menthol treatment on colony strength, honey production and tracheal mite infestation levels. Am. Bee J. 129: 547-549.

9. **Delfinado-Baker, M. 1984.** *Acarapis woodi* in the United States. Am. Bee J. 124: 805-806.

10. **Delfinado-Baker, M. 1988.** The tracheal mite of honey bees: a crisis in beekeeping, pp. 493-497. *In* G.R. Needham, R.E. Page Jr., M. Delfinado-Baker & C.E. Bowman [eds.], Africanized honey bees and bee mites. Halstread Press, New York.

11. **Delfinado-Baker, M. & E.W. Baker. 1982.** Notes on honey bee mites of the genus *Acarapis* Hirst (Acari: Tarsonemidae). Int. J. Acarol. 8: 211-226.

12. **Eischen, F.A., D. Cardoso-Tamez, W.T. Wilson & A. Dietz. 1989.** Honey production of honey bee colonies infested with *Acarapis woodi*. (Rennie). Apidologie 20: 1-8.

13. **Fekl, W. 1956.** The bacterial flora of the tracheae and blood of some insects. Z. Morphol. Oekol. Tiere. 44: 442-458.

14. **Gilmour, D. 1965.** The metabolism of insects. W.H. Freeman and Co., San Francisco.

15. **Giordani, G. 1964.** Laboratory research on *Acarapis woodi*. Note 3. Bull. Apic. Inform. 7: 43-60.

16. **Giordani, G. 1977.** Facts about Acarine mites, pp. 459-467. *In* V. Harnaj [ed.], Proceedings, 26th International Congress of Apiculture, 13-19 October 13-19 1977. Adelaide, Australia.

17. **Gruszka, J. & D. Peer. 1986.** Saskatchewan Beekeepers Association tracheal mite project at La Ronge, Saskatchewan, pp. 14-21. *In* Proceedings, Honey bee tracheal mite (*Acarapis woodi*) scientific symposium, 8-9 July 1986. Saint Paul, Minnesota, USA.

18. **Killick, C.R. 1923.** Some aspects of the pathology of Acarine disease. Bee World 4: 169-171.

19. **Komeili, A.B. & J.T. Ambrose. 1991.** Electron microscope studies of the tracheae and flight muscles of noninfested, *Acarapis woodi* infested and crawling honey bees (*Apis mellifera*) Am. Bee J. 131: 253-257.

20. **Liu, T.P. 1990.** Ultrastructure of the flight muscle of worker honey bees heavily infested by the tracheal mite *Acarapis woodi.* Apidologie 21: 537-540.

21. **Liu, T.P. 1991.** Virus-like particles in the tracheal mite *Acarapis woodi* (Rennie). Apidologie 22: 213-219.

22. **Liu, T.P., B. Mobus & G. Braybrook. 1989a.** A scanning electron microscope study on the prothoracic tracheae of the honeybee, *Apis mellifera* L., infested by the mite *Acarapis woodi* (Rennie). J. Apic. Res. 28: 81-84.

23. **Liu, T.P., B. Mobus & G. Braybrook. 1989b.** Fine structure of hypopharyngeal glands from honeybees with and without infestation by the tracheal mite, *Acarapis woodi* (Rennie). J. Apic. Res. 28: 85-92.

24. **Maki, D.L., W.T. Wilson & R.L. Cox. 1986.** Infestation by *Acarapis woodi* and its effect on honey bee longevity in laboratory cage studies. Am. Bee J. 126: 832.

25. **Morse, R.A. 1981.** Acarine mites in Mexico-What does it mean? Glean. Bee Cult. 109: 256,265.

26. **Otis, G.W. 1990.** Results of a survey on the economic impact of tracheal mites. Am. Bee J. 130: 28-31.

27. **Otis, G.W. & C.D. Scott-Dupree. 1992.** Effects of *Acarapis woodi* on overwintered colonies of honey bees (Hymenoptera: Apidae) in New York. J. Econ. Entomol. 85: 40-46.

28. **Pettis, J.S. & W.T. Wilson. 1990.** Life cycle comparisons between *Varroa jacobsoni* and *Acarapis woodi*. Am. Bee J. 130: 597-599.

29. **Sikorowski, P.P. & A.M. Lawrence. 1994.** Microbial contamination and insect rearing. Am. Entomol. 40: 240-253.

30. **Skrobal, D. 1965.** Factors affecting the respiratory metabolism of acarine-infested honeybees. Bull. Apic. Inform. 8: 177-180.

31. **Taber, S. 1984.** Breeding bees resistant to the *Acarapis* mite. Glean. Bee Cult. 112: 514.

32. **Wille, H. 1966.** The acarine mite in relation to other causative organisms of bee diseases. Sudwestdt. Imker. 18: 322-324.

33. **Wilson, W.T. 1990.** Tracheal mites (*Acarapis woodi*): an overview. Am. Bee J. 130: 185.

Chapter 6

SAMPLING METHODS AND ECONOMIC THRESHOLDS FOR TRACHEAL MITES

Medhat E. Nasr

Sampling is central to monitoring tracheal mite infestations in honey bee colonies. A good understanding of sampling is essential for research on the biology and control of these mites. Efficient and accurate sampling techniques are important for forecasting mite population outbreaks and for providing good control recommendations.

Collecting bee samples. In sampling for tracheal mites, live honey bees should be collected. Honey bees that have been dead for a while begin decaying and that makes accurate diagnoses more difficult. A quart Mason® jar can be filled with 70% ethanol or isopropanol (rubbing alcohol) and used to collect bee samples. The jar is used to scoop bees from the inner cover or a frame placed on end. Bees are collected until the jar is one third full. Bees can be stored in alcohol at room temperature for several months without damage before dissection and examination. A bee vacuum device can also be used for collecting bee samples. The bees are killed and stored in alcohol in Mason jars as they are collected. The use of the vacuum device simplifies collecting bees from the surface of combs or other places. In the case of collecting bees for detecting mites with the enzyme-linked immunosorbent assay (ELISA), bees should be frozen as they are collected and stored in a freezer at -20°C until they are extracted for analysis.

Individual honey bee colony sampling. Sampling methods used to estimate tracheal mite infestation rates in honey bee colonies vary widely with respect to sample size, the location within the bee hive from which the bees are sampled, and time of the year.

Many factors affect the spatial and temporal distribution of tracheal mite-infested bees in honey bee colonies. These include: (1) age distribution of worker honey bees, (2) available space in the bee hive through the season, (3) colony activity, (4) time of the year, (5) colony infestation and re-infestation history, and (6) reproductive rate of mites. Calderone and Shimanuki[5] showed that estimates of tracheal mite infestation levels varied significantly between bee samples collected from the brood nest area and the honey storage area. Honey bees sampled from brood areas tend to have lower mite infestation rates than do bees sampled from honey combs. The bee colony activities during the sampling period affect the rate of mite infestation in sampled honey bees[12,17]. In late spring and summer, the percentage of bees infested with mites is reduced when the bee population is approaching its maximum. However, the percentage of honey bees infested with tracheal mites increases in fall, winter and early spring specially when there are no outdoor bee activities[17].

To increase the accuracy of sampling, the effects of non-random distribution of infested bees in a colony can, and should, be minimized. Collecting bees from the brood nest in early morning when foraging is minimal will result in a random sample with representative bees of different ages[5]. To collect honey bees, a vacuum device is moved across the surface of the comb at a constant speed to collect bees in proportion to the number of bees on the comb. The honey bees in this collected sample are considered a representative random sample from the sampled colony. On the other hand, collecting bees from the entrance, inner cover, or top bars will result in a larger portion of older foragers and bias the sample[22]. Mite infestations will appear higher in these biased bee samples than in the random bee samples.

Sampling unit size. A common question is, how many bees, taken at random, should be examined in order to confirm that a bee colony is mite free? The answer lies in the use of mathematical probability. There are several variables that affect the calculations: honey bee colony size, degree of infestation, sample size, probability of detecting mites in the sample, and selection of sample (random vs. biased). In 1922, Betts[3] attempted to calculate the required sample size based on mathematical probabilities. She suggested that examining 33 bees randomly sampled from a colony of 30,000 bees gives even odds (i.e. chance of failure is 50%) that a 2% infestation is missed. Therefore, the examination of more than 33 bees was suggested. In a similar attempt, Bradbury[4] used different assumptions for calculating the required sample size. He suggested that in order to detect a 10 % infestation with 90% certainty; 20 bees must be examined. Generally, most researchers use a sample of 50 randomly collected bees per colony. This sample size gives 90% certainty of detecting a 5% colony infestation level. If the sample size is increased to 100 bees, the level of certainty increases to 95% for detecting the same level of infestation (5%).

Sequential sampling. Sequential sampling is a method for rapidly classifying populations into two broad categories, such as low or high infestation and treat or not treat. Tomasko & others[23] developed a scheme for sequential sampling. Decision parameters are presented in Figure 6.1. In this procedure, samples of 50 bees per colony are collected.

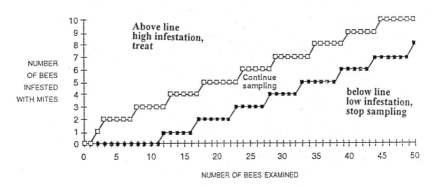

▲ *Figure 6.1 Sequential sampling of honey bees for classification of the infestation proportions using treat, no treat, and continuation boundaries (modified from Tomasko & others[23]).*

Individual bees are then taken in sequence and examined for the presence of mites with decisions made after each bee. One of two possible decisions is made based on the cumulative number of infested bees examined: (1) if the plotted number of infested bees is above the upper limit (30%), the infestation is considered high, treatment is required, and further dissection is not required, or (2) if the number of infested bees is below the lower limit (10%) or between the two limits, the infestation is considered low and continued examination of bees is required. If after examining 50 bees the number of infested bees is still below the lower limit category, one can stop examining bees and declare the colony mite population below economic threshold. On average, sequential sampling requires fewer bees (less than 50 bees per colony) to reach a decision compared to using fixed sample sizes (e.g. 50 bees per colony).

Pooled apiary sampling. This method involves sampling all bee colonies in an apiary to determine if mites are present at levels that warrant treating the entire apiary[1]. For apiaries that have three colonies or less, individual samples (50 bees per colony) can be used for determining mite infestation levels in each sampled colony. However, for apiaries with 4-25 hives, pooled samples from all bee colonies in the apiary can be used. An equal number of bees (5-40) is collected from each bee colony and is pooled together in a jar to make a composite sample (200-300 bees) representing the apiary. If the number of colonies in an apiary exceeds 25, it is suggested that one pooled sample be taken for every 25 hives. All bees are collected from the entrance of hives, from inner covers, or from honey storage areas to increase the proportion of forager bees and the likelihood of finding mites[13]. For the pooled samples, infestation rates are determined from a subsample of 150 bees per apiary. All bees are examined only for the presence of mites in the tracheae. The percentage of infestation is then calculated based on the number of infested bees in 150 bees. This method of sampling apiaries is inexpensive and rapid. In practice, it is an acceptable method for determining mite levels in an apiary since all colonies must be treated at the same time to avoid robbing and drifting caused by the treatment. However, this method of sampling is less sensitive to lower infestation levels and does not resolve variations among individual colonies in the apiary.

Detecting tracheal mites. No reliable visual symptoms characterize bees infested with tracheal mites. Reliable diagnosis can only be made by microscopic examination of the tracheae. Tracheal mites live in the tracheae of the honey bee and possess needle-like mouthparts that are used to puncture the tracheal tissues and feed on the bee's hemolymph (blood). Numerous punctures result in yellow to dark brown scars in the tracheae that show up well under magnification.

Honey bees stored in 70% alcohol can be sent to bee disease diagnostic laboratories or beekeeping extension specialists for dissection and examination for tracheal mites.

Dissection techniques. Several techniques are described for dissecting and examining bees for tracheal mites. The most common method is to pin a bee on its back onto a cork or paraffin[14]. The head and the first pair of legs are removed by pushing them off with a scalpel or razor blade in a forward and downward motion. Under a dissecting microscope, the first thoracic ring (collar) is removed with forceps to expose the main tracheal trunks. The tracheae of healthy bees appear as clear cream or white tissues (Fig. 6.2A). When the infestation is heavy, dark tracheae with scars and numerous mites can be seen (Fig. 6.2B). In the case of light infestation, the tracheae can be carefully removed and placed on a microscopic glass slide in a drop of 85% lactic acid or glycerol and covered with a glass cover. The tracheae are examined with a compound microscope (40-80 X) for the presence of mite adults, nymphs, and eggs. Tracheae may contain mites at different developmental stages and may or may not be discolored. The presence of mites in the tracheae is the only certain indicator of tracheal mite infestation.

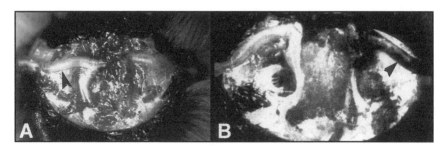

▲*Figure 6.2 After removing the head, first pair of legs and the collar, the thoracic tracheae appear transparent in healthy bees (A) while in infested bees (B) the tracheae appear dark and may have visible mites.*

For examining a large number of bees, the head and the first pair of legs are removed as described above. With a scalpel, a thin transverse section (disc) is cut from the anterior part of the thorax that contains the main tracheal trunks (Fig. 6.3). After cutting discs from the thoraces of 50 or more bees, the discs are placed in a 5-8% potassium hydroxide (KOH) solution and incubated at 37° C overnight (12-16 hours)[7]. The KOH dissolves most of the muscle and fat tissues, exposing transparent tracheal tissues. The discs are then examined under the dissecting microscope for the presence of mites and discoloration. Suspicious looking tracheae with mites can be further examined using the compound microscope (40-80 X).

An easier way to examine mites in discs is to stain the mites in the tracheae[18]. Discs are first cleared of muscle and fat using KOH solution, then placed in a beaker and gently washed with water to remove the remaining KOH. Washed discs are placed in an aqueous methylene blue stain (1% in saline solution) for 5 minutes to stain the mites. Stained discs are washed in water for 2-5 minutes and rinsed with 70% ethyl

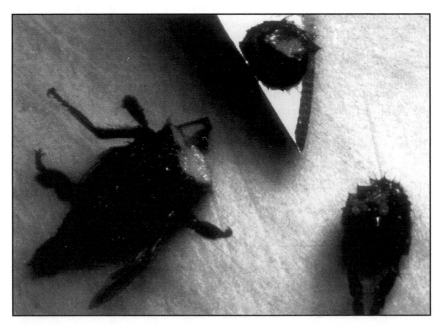

▲*Figure 6.3 Cutting a disc containing thoracic tracheae. The discs are subsequently clarified with KOH and examined under microscope for the presence of tracheal mites.*

alcohol. Stained mites can be easily seen in the tracheae under a dissecting microscope at 10-25 X.

The choice of technique for estimating mite populations depends on the objectives of the study and how the data will be used. Economics, such as the cost of sampling and data collection becomes a factor. The most precise method is the direct counting of all mite stages in the tracheae. This method requires proper laboratory facilities and is time consuming. The counts become more difficult as mite density increases. Sampling can be simplified if one is willing to accept categorical data. Tracheae can be scored from 0-5, respectively, depending on their membership in one of the following six descriptive categories: 0 mites, 1-8, 9-30, 31-80, "some" scarring, or "major" scarring[17] (Fig. 6.4). Although precision is sacrificed, this method allows for rapid examination of a large number of samples.

Alternative methods for diagnosis. Camazine[6] found that honey bee thoraces can be collected from honey bees which have been stored in alcohol or a freezer. Thoraces are broken apart in water using a household blender. After this blending process, the air-filled tracheae float to the top and can be collected for microscopic examination. This method is useful for examining tracheae for the presence or absence of mites, but it is not reliable for determining rates of infestation in a sample because many mites may be lost.

An extraction of frozen bee samples can be tested for the presence

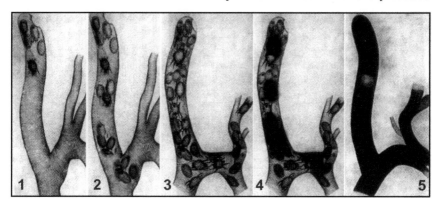

▲*Figure 6.4   Tracheae with different levels of infestations as scored from 1-5.*

of tracheal mites using a biochemical test known as enzyme-linked immunosorbent assay (ELISA). Antibodies produced by bees specifically for tracheal mites are used in the analysis[11,19,20]. ELISA can detect an infestation rate as low as 5% of the bees in a sample[11]. However, the test is expensive and requires special laboratory facilities.

Economic treatment thresholds. Lessons of recent decades have taught agriculturalists that pesticides are not the only answer for pest problems. Pesticides are important tools in pest control, but their abuse has led to environmental problems and chemical-resistant pests. Growers in all commodities are increasingly adopting an alternative approach to pest control called *integrated pest management* (IPM). Integrated pest management is defined as the use of compatible combinations of genetic, cultural, regulatory, physical, and chemical methods to manage pests in an economically and environmentally sound manner. This chapter is concerned with the IPM concept of economic treatment thresholds for miticides against tracheal mites. Other aspects of IPM are covered elsewhere, namely, cultural controls (Chapter 8) and the use of genetically-resistant bee stock (Chapter 9). Information about specific miticides is given in Chapter 7.

To use miticides in a manner consistent with IPM, one must: (1) detect the pest to be managed, (2) monitor the pest population, and (3) develop a treatment strategy based on economic treatment thresholds. Points 1 and 2 are covered above in the sections on sampling and diagnosis. Colony sampling to determine whether one should treat should be done in early spring or in fall.

IPM practitioners recognize that miticides are an important, if not the most important, mite management tool (Chapter 7). However, an IPM practitioner is concerned with reducing the frequency of miticide applications and reducing the overall amount used. This is done with economic treatment decision levels. Economic decision levels can be described by defining the following three concepts. First, the *economic injury level* (EIL) is the lowest pest level that will cause economic damage and justify the cost of control. The *economic threshold* (ET) is the infestation level at which control measures should be implemented to prevent an increasing pest population from reaching the EIL. The *equilibrium position* (EP) is the average pest level that develops over time unaffected by the temporary interventions of control measures.

The EIL, ET, and EP can vary according to the population dynamics of bees and mites, genotype of bees, time of the year, climate, and location. Rennie[21] and Morgenthaler[15] reported that the economic injury level (EIL) is 50% of the bees infested in a colony. However, this figure was found to be smaller in later studies from Europe and North America. Bailey[2], Furgala & others[9], and Eischen & others[8] found that honey production is reduced when over 25-30% of the bees in a colony are infested; winter survival decreases as the infestation increases. Therefore, these authors considered 25-30% infestation to be the EIL. Mite levels exceeding the EIL can be expected to cause increasing damage to bee colonies[16].

For tracheal mites, the economic threshold (ET) may be close, or even identical to published EILs. The ET was suggested to be 25-30% of bees infested in spring or fall based on a dissection of 50 bees per colony[2,8,10]. In the case of pooled apiary sampling, the ET was estimated to be 10% infestation[13].

Bailey[2] reported the equilibrium position (EP) to be below 10% in Europe. Many factors, such as environmental conditions, bee genotype, and bee health, may affect the EP.

These published threshold levels can help beekeepers make informed chemical treatment decisions. A beekeeper faced with, for example, a <10% infestation in autumn could justifiably delay or avoid a chemical treatment, while a neighboring beekeeper with 25% infestation would know to treat as soon as possible. An understanding of thresholds can allow the beekeeper to eliminate chemical applications that are arbitrary or based simply on the calendar. The goal of IPM-based treatment thresholds is to delay or minimize miticide treatments. Even a short delay in treatment may be beneficial if it allows another mite generation to reproduce without the enormous selection pressure for chemical resistance involved in even one miticide application. It is helpful to think of such a delay as conserving chemical-susceptible genes in a mite population (Chapter 17). Chemical resistance reduction is just one benefit of using economic thresholds. The practice also saves beekeepers money, minimizes risk of unwanted contaminants in honey, and minimizes risks to bees and beekeepers from materials that are inherently hazardous.

Summary. Accurate and efficient sampling techniques are required to maximize the probability of detecting tracheal mites and for monitoring their population growth. Taking large numbers of samples and large numbers of bees per sample, randomly, increases the probability of detecting mites at low densities and improves accuracy of the sampling program. The use of pooled bee samples from colonies in an apiary and the use of sequential sampling are adequate, fast and relatively inexpensive methods. The economic threshold (ET) is the mite level at which miticide applications are warranted in order to prevent mites from reaching an economic injury level. Published values for ET range from 10% to 25-30%.

Acknowledgments. I thank D. McRory and S. Corrigan for making helpful comments on this chapter. Thanks are also extended to the Canadian Adaptation Council, the Ontario Ministry of Agriculture, Food and Rural Affairs, and the Ontario Beekeepers' Association for financially supporting the IPM research program in Ontario, Canada.

References cited.

1. **Anonymous. 1992.** Protocol for the importation of queen bees from Hawaii, p. 129. Proceedings, Canadian Association of Professional Apiculturists, 5 July 1992.

2. **Bailey, L. 1961.** The nature of incidence of *Acarapis woodi* (Rennie) and the winter mortality of honey bee colonies. Bee World 42: 96-100.

3. **Betts, A.D. 1922.** The examination of bees for disease. Bee World 3: 298-299.

4. **Bradbury, F.C.S. 1924.** Some calculations on acarine disease. Bee World 5: 145-147.

5. **Calderone, N. W. & H. Shimanuki. 1992.** Evaluation of sampling methods for determining infestation rates of the tracheal mite (*Acarapis woodi* R.) in colonies of the honey bee (*Apis mellifera*): spatial, temporal, and spatial-temporal effects. Exp. Appl. Acarol. 15: 285-298.

6. **Camazine, S. 1985.** Tracheal flotation: a rapid method for the detection of honey bee acarine disease. Am. Bee J. 125: 104-105.

7. **Delfinado-Baker, M. 1984.** *Acarapis woodi* in the United States.

Am. Bee J. 124: 805-806.

8. Eischen, F.*A.*, D. Cardoso-Tamez, W.T. Wilson & *A.* Dietz. 1989. Honey production of honey bee colonies infested with *Acarapis woodi* (Rennie). Apidologie. 20: 1-8.

9. Furgala, B., S. Duff, S. Aboulfaraj, D. Ragsdale, & R. Hyser. 1989. Some effects of the honey bee tracheal mite (*Acarapis woodi* Rennie) on non-migratory, wintering honey bee (*Apis mellifera* L.) colonies in east central Minnesota. Am. Bee J. 129: 195-198.

10. Giavarini, I. & G. Giordani. 1966. Study of acarine disease of honey bee. Final report, pp. 1-22. Nat. Inst. Apic., Bologna, Italy.

11. Grant, G.*A.*, D.L. Nelson, P.E. Olsen, & W.*A.* Rice. 1993. The "ELISA" detection of tracheal mites in whole honey bee samples. Am. Bee J. 133: 652-655.

12. Killion, E.E. & L.*A.* Lindenfelser. 1988. Observations on the honey bee tracheal mite in Illinois, pp. 518-525 *In* G.R. Needham, R.E. Page Jr., M. Delfinado-Baker & C.E. Bowman [eds.], Africanized honey bees and bee mites. Halsted Press, New York.

13. McRory, D. & M.E. Nasr. 1996. 1996 recommendations for disease and pest control in Ontario, Canada. Advisory Leaflet. Ontario Min. Agric. Food, & Rural Affairs. Guelph, Ontario, Canada, 3 pp.

14. Ministry of Agriculture, Fisheries & Food. 1956. The examination of bees for acarine disease. Advisory Leaflet No. 362, Min. Agric. Fish. & Food, London.

15. Morgenthaler, O. 1931. An acarine disease experimental apiary in the Bernese Lake District and some results obtained there. Bee World 12: 810.

16. Otis, G.W. & C.D. Scott-Dupree. 1992. Effects of *Acarapis woodi* on overwintered colonies of honey bees (Hymenoptera: Apidae) in New York. J. Econ. Entomol. 85: 40-46.

17. Otis, G.W., J.B. Bath, D.L. Randall, & G.M. Grant. 1987. Studies on the honey bee tracheal mite (*Acarapis woodi*) (Acari: Tarsonemidae) during winter. Can. J. Zool. 66: 2122-2127.

18. Peng, Y.S. & M.E. Nasr. 1985. Detection of honeybee tracheal mites (*Acarapis woodi*) by simple staining techniques. J. Invertebr.

Pathol. 46: 325-331.

19. **Ragsdale, D.W. & B. Furgala. 1987.** A serological approach to the detection of *Acarapis woodi* parasitism in honey bees using an enzyme-linked immunosorbent assay. Apidologie 18: 1-10.

20. **Ragsdale, D.W. & K.M. Kjer. 1989.** Diagnosis of tracheal mite (*Acarapis woodi* Rennie) parasitism of honey bees using a monoclonal based enzyme-linked immunosorbent assay. Am. Bee J. 129: 550-553.

21. **Rennie, J. 1922.** Notes on acarine disease: XI. Bee World. 3: 237-239.

22. **Robinson, F.A., K.L. Thel, R.C. Littell, & S.B. Linda. 1986.** Sampling apiaries for honey bee tracheal mite (*Acarapis woodi* Rennie): effects of bee age and colony infestation. Am. Bee J. 126: 193-195.

23. **Tomasko, M., J. Finley, W. Harkness & E. Rajotte. 1993.** A sequential sampling scheme for detecting the presence of tracheal mite (*Acarapis woodi*) infestations in honey bee (*Apis mellifera* L.) colonies. Pennsylvania State Univ. Coll. Agric. Sci. Bull. 871, 38 pp.

CHEMICAL
CONTROL OF
TRACHEAL MITES

W.T. Wilson
D.L. Nelson
K.J. Clark

*T*he association between honey bees (*Apis mellifera* L.) and tracheal mites (*Acarapis woodi* Rennie) can be traced through apicultural literature to the Isle of Wight and the British mainland starting in 1904[53,73]. The mite apparently spread rapidly across Great Britain, and it was soon reported from many sites in Europe[71]. Wherever this mite has been found, it has caused serious honey bee losses.

The introduction of tracheal mites into North America in the 1980s led to serious economic losses by beekeepers in Canada, the United States, and Mexico[30,49,88]. Scientists and beekeepers were forced to look for chemical treatments that would kill this mite and protect honey bee colonies. The list of effective miticides and application methods has expanded rapidly in North America, mainly because chemical treatment has been the only practical way of saving parasitized colonies. If bees are not treated, many colonies die during winter.

Beekeepers are often quick to adopt new miticides for control of parasitic mites. This was demonstrated in 1987 when menthol usage became widespread and quickly went from 0 tons to nearly 100 tons per year in the USA and Canada[97]. However, difficulties arise when the needs of beekeepers outpace research findings and regulatory approval. Beekeepers should remember that applying unregistered chemicals is illegal and should not be part of their management program.

This chapter outlines the history of miticide use and development against tracheal mites and reviews current chemical controls.

Evolution of miticide testing for tracheal mite control.

Initial European studies. Many chemical compounds (both natural and synthetic) were tested on honey bees in an attempt to control the tracheal mite in the 1920s, but few were effective. One of the first reported compounds was smoldering sulphur (sulfur) fumes. Bailey[7] said that Rennie recommended burning sulphur-impregnated fuel (cardboard with saltpeter) in a smoker and puffing smoke in the hive entrance, but others said it didn't work[76]. The most widely-used early treatment, named after its first proponent, R.W. Frow, was the vapors from a mixture of petrol (gasoline), nitrobenzene, and safrol. Frow's first tests with the treatment were made in 1927[41,42]. Frow's mixture also killed brood and shortened the life of adult bees[7,8]. Vapors of methyl salicylate (wintergreen oil) were also used in England and parts of Europe for control of *A. woodi*[3,4,8].

Studies in India. Asian honey bees (*Apis cerana*) proved to be highly susceptible to the tracheal mite, thus prompting several chemical control studies. Atwal & Sharma[6] reported an annual loss of 25-40 percent of bee colonies in northern India while Shah[78] reported losses as high as 90 percent. Some colony infestations encompassed 80 percent of the bees[5]. For control, Atwal & Sharma[6] recommended methyl salicylate (wintergreen oil) during brood rearing and in summer. They also listed chlorobenzilate (Folbex®) and methanol as effective miticides. Sharma & others[79] report excellent results with formic acid.

Folbex VA® controls A. woodi. Folbex (chlorobenzilate) was effectively used as a fumigant for tracheal mite control in Europe in the 1950s, but was replaced later by an equally effective miticide called Folbex VA (bromopropylate). The miticidal fumes were generated by igniting a paper strip that had been treated with potassium nitrate (saltpeter) and bromopropylate. The smoldering strip was hung in the top of a standard-size colony with the hive entrance plugged for 30 minutes[7]. One to three treatments at weekly intervals killed a high percentage of adult mites without damaging adult bees or brood. The most attractive aspect of Folbex VA is its efficacy against both varroa mites (*Varroa jacobsoni*) and the tracheal mite. The product is not registered for use in North America.

Menthol and other compounds in Italy. Giavarini & Giordanim[46] were the first to identify menthol (peppermint oil) fumes as a miticide for killing tracheal mites. However, they did not develop an efficient application method. Vecchi & Giordani[82] studied the effects of menthol and other medicinal products on the mite in laboratory tests. They also tested several naturally derived compounds such as pine oil, terpineol, and eucalyptol, but none was as effective as menthol.

Although menthol is highly effective, beekeepers in Europe did not use it as a routine treatment. Extensive use of menthol did not take place until after 1985 when beekeepers in the USA and Canada started making spring and fall applications.

Recent tests in Europe. Many scientists and beekeepers in Europe view the tracheal mite as a minor problem. Consequently, few miticides have been tested in Europe since the 1960s. However, extensive testing has taken place over the past twenty years in Europe to develop chemicals to control varroa, and this has benefitted North American scientists in their search for new controls for *A. woodi*. Miticides that have received the most attention are fluvalinate, flumethrin, amitraz (smoke) and formic acid fumes, but only the latter two control *A. woodi*.

First tests in North America. The rapid spread of tracheal mites across Mexico in the early 1980s created a dire need for miticides[89,98]. Mexican scientists conducted field tests and reported that menthol fumes were not effective for tracheal mite control, but Folbex VA gave 83 percent and Acarol® (nitrobenzene & methyl salicylate) gave 100 percent control[49]. However, Acarol was blamed for causing bee mortality and was not widely used. Garza-Q. & others[44] reported control of *A. woodi* with formic acid fumes in Mexico and later confirmed its efficacy[45].

Recent miticide research in the United States.
Helping beekeepers overcome tracheal mites. In 1985, USA

Department of Agriculture (USDA) scientists established efficacy tests at a Mexican federal research station near Rio Bravo in northeastern Mexico. Two insecticides (acephate and dimethoate) at sublethal doses and a varroacide (coumaphos, called Perizin®) at heavier than recommended doses for varroa proved ineffective against *A. woodi*[23].

Menthol works well. In May 1986, colony tests demonstrated that adult bees became mite free when exposed to screen packets of menthol crystals that gave off fumes for three weeks during hot weather[23,39,91]. Further studies in Maryland, Nebraska and Texas confirmed menthol's efficacy[25,50,62,94]. Menthol pellets in a perforated plastic bag are currently sold under the trade name of Mite-A-Thol®. Wilson & others[92] demonstrated that the synthetic, natural and L-form of menthol controlled mites, but the D-isomer did not.

Amitraz has limited value. Between 1985 and 1987, Cromroy & others[26] conducted efficacy tests with several miticides including amitraz for control of *A. woodi* in Florida. During this time Eischen & others[34,35] studied mite control with amitraz and Apitol® in Mexico. Moffett & others[61] reported that aerosol amitraz gave 93 percent mite reduction while plastic strips (cattle collars) impregnated with amitraz only controlled 70 percent.

Miticur®, a white plastic strip impregnated with amitraz, was touted as an effective control for the tracheal mite by the manufacturer in 1992-93, but studies by USDA showed little or no value[87]. The manufacturer stopped selling Miticur in 1993.

Several other methods of applying amitraz have been evaluated. Liquid Mitac® or Ovasyn® evaporated from paper pads in the top of a colony or cardboard strips soaked in Mitac and vegetable oil proved to be ineffective[86,87]. However, smoke from a strip of filter paper impregnated with saltpeter and liquid amitraz, when burned in the bottom of a colony, gave nearly 100 percent control of *A. woodi*[87]. Recently, Dag & others[27] reported excellent control of *A. woodi* in Israel using amitraz smoke.

Although Bogdanov[12] found that amitraz in honey degrades completely in 2-4 weeks at warm temperatures, beekeepers should nevertheless be careful to avoid contaminating honey or other hive products with miticides.

Fluvalinate doesn't kill tracheal mites. Wilson[84] found that smoke from a paper strip containing fluvalinate did not kill tracheal mites. Also, exposure to a fluvalinate plastic strip (Apistan®) did not prevent the transfer of mites between bees or reproduction in *A. woodi*[69]. However, a low level of mite mortality occurred when adult mites were placed directly on an Apistan strip for several hours[70].

Feeding systemics. Perizin® and Apitol® have each given effective control of varroa in Europe[13,72] but against *A. woodi* they have been less successful. Cox & others[23] found little or no control of tracheal mites from feeding Perizin (coumaphos) in sugar syrup. (Since coumaphos in plastic functions as a contact varroacide, it is questionable whether Perizin was ever systemic.) Eischen & others[35] obtained reasonable mite control (<30 percent prevalence) in Mexico from feeding Apitol (cymiazole) in sugar syrup, whereas colonies fed Apitol in sugar syrup showed minimal mite control (32-79 percent reduction) in the USA[96].

Formic acid kills mites quickly. In the 1980s several studies in Europe determined that formic acid is an effective miticide against both tracheal mites and varroa[51]. Studies on formic acid control of tracheal mites in North America were initiated in the early 1990s. Wilson & others[95] demonstrated the efficacy of three weekly 40-ml treatments of 65 percent formic acid liquid on paper pads. Treatments were effective in temperate zones in spring or fall[87].

Clark[15] added large quantities (90-200 ml) of formic acid to newspaper pads in zip closure plastic bags with micropores or with "windows" cut in the bag, similar to the "Kramer plates"[40] used in Europe for prolonged fumigation. Using this technique, Baxter[9] killed 97-99 percent of the mites in autumn.

Feldlaufer & others[38] and a private inventor (Dan Davis) each developed a gel matrix to prolong the fumigation period in a hive and improve applicator safety. Recently, formic acid in a gel matrix was tested against *A. woodi* in Arkansas[9] and Mexico[32] with moderate success.

An unpredictable but occasionally serious problem with formic acid is the loss of queens and worker bees. Losses can be as high as 20 percent of queens[1] with a significant increase in worker bee kill for 24 hours after treatment[65]. A few beekeepers have reported emergency cells (suggesting queen loss) a day or two after formic acid application, but the reappearance of a laying queen a few days later[17]. Queen loss seems to occur more frequently with the use of higher concentration (85 percent) acid during hot weather and with older queens or under conditions where bees are not able to escape pockets of concentrated fumes. Westcott & Winston[83] concluded that applications of formic acid as directed on the Canadian product label did not increase colony mortality or reduce honey production, and the benefits of the treatment outweigh potential problems.

Miticidal properties of plant smoke. It is well known that tobacco smoke gives moderate control of varroa[74] and causes low-level mortality in tracheal mites[55]. In expanded studies, Eischen & Wilson[33] tested smoke from more than 50 species of plants for varroa knock-down and mortality. Earlier, Eischen[31] noted that the smoke from the creosote bush (*Larrea tridentata*) killed tracheal mites. Much work remains in testing plant substances for *A. woodi* control.

Extender patties and vegetable oils for mite control. Gary & Page[43] and Smith & others[80] showed in laboratory studies that vegetable oil protects young bees from *A. woodi* infestation. Wilson[85] suggested that introducing a vegetable oil: sugar: antibiotic "extender patty"[90] into a hive might prevent tracheal mites from identifying and entering young bees. Clark[18] found that tracheal mite levels in colonies treated with a canola oil and sugar patty in the brood nest decreased by 40 percent. Vegetable oil-soaked corrugated cardboard was less effective[16].

Liu[54] reported that Crisco® vegetable shortening reduced mite infestation levels, and Delaplane[28] demonstrated that extender patties without antibiotics were effective in controlling tracheal mites in overwintering colonies. Delaplane further showed that mite counts were lowest in hives with a combination of extender patty and menthol. Research by Liu & Nasr[57] supported the findings of Delaplane. Sammataro & others[75] showed that continuous treatment with oil extender patties reduced mite levels. Calderone & Shimanuki[14] tested four types of vegetable oil and found that all reduced tracheal mite levels.

Amrine & others[2] suggested that oil patties with wintergreen oil might control tracheal mites. To test this hypothesis, a field study was established in Kansas in the fall of 1996 by USDA scientists from Weslaco, Texas. Large colonies were given patties of oil and sugar containing wintergreen. After one month, mite control was poor (mite reduction <20 percent) and by spring more treated colonies had died than non-treated colonies[10].

Botanical oils. Beekeepers have an intense interest in aromatic or essential oils of botanical origin such as thymol, camphor, menthol, wintergreen, patchouli oil, and many others as miticides for parasitic mite control. Many people advocate using these natural oils in hives even though efficacy data may not exist and research findings may not support the claim of mite control. Some botanical oils have shown great promise where valid tests have been conducted. Vecchi & Giordani[82] demonstrated that menthol was the best material for killing tracheal mites, but they tested many other less effective natural compounds such as cade oil, eucalyptol, camphor oil, creosote, pine oil, terpineol, and others. Ellis[36] tested several naturally-occurring compounds as fumigants under laboratory conditions, and determined that citral was highly effective against tracheal mites. Unfortunately, citral fumigation of standard-sized colonies in spring resulted in only moderate mite reduction (67 percent) over a four week period[96].

Beekeepers should be aware that some botanical oils are toxic to both bees and humans. When used as a miticide, natural oils of plant origin must comply with EPA (Environmental Protection Agency) regulations.

Mite levels and when to treat colonies. Bailey[7] reported that colonies with 30 percent or more of the bees infested with tracheal mites had a higher likelihood of dying during winter. Beekeepers in the northern USA believe that a prevalence of 10-15 percent in August predicts heavy winter losses in the absence of proper treatment. Thus, effective mite control must take place in spring or fall. Delaplane[29] advocates spring treatments before major nectar flows begin.

Registration of miticidal compounds. Currently in the USA, menthol is the only material registered with the EPA and sold for use in honey bee colonies to control tracheal mites. A formic acid gel pack has been approved by EPA[59].

Future of miticide research and emerging problems. With the discovery of fluvalinate resistance in varroa mites in parts of Europe, Argentina, and the USA[37], there is renewed interest in screening chemicals for miticidal activity. Some of these new miticides may control *A. woodi*. A major problem is finding companies that are willing to invest money to register new miticides for bees because beekeeping represents a small market compared to other agricultural products. Testing will continue at university and federal laboratories in hopes of finding effective materials that are relatively inexpensive and safe to use.

Although scientists and queen breeders have selected genetic lines of bees that show some resistance to *A. woodi* (Chapter 9), much work needs to be done before honey bees are protected at a level where chemicals will no longer be needed. In the meantime, the search for new miticides continues.

Miticide research in Canada.

Early mite control in Canada. After tracheal mites were found in the USA, a certification program was agreed to by package producers and officials from Canada and the USA. This was to ensure the shipment of mite-free packages and queens. However, in 1987, three years after the start of certification, tracheal mites were found in a USA shipment to Manitoba and Saskatchewan. These bees were killed.

The first Canadian study on the tracheal mite was conducted at La Ronge in northern Saskatchewan in an area isolated by about 150 km from agriculture and other beekeeping. The project was initiated in 1986 by the Saskatchewan Beekeepers' Association[68] to study the impact, control, and biology of tracheal mites in infested package bee colonies. Infested packages from Florida and non-infested packages from California were maintained in separate apiaries. The study continued for two years[48]. In both years, the mite-free colonies produced significantly more brood than did the infested colonies. In later shipments from Florida, varroa mites were found and all bees were destroyed[47].

Scott-Dupree & Otis[77] evaluated four miticides in northern New York. Fall treatments of menthol, amitraz, Apistan®, and Apitol® were tested. Contrary to other studies, the chemicals did not reduce mite levels relative to control colonies.

Menthol proved effective. Mite control using menthol crystals was tried in 1986 and 1987. Although high mite mortality was achieved in a few hives during summer weather, treatment at cooler temperatures was not successful. Different formulations were tested: menthol-dipped cardboard, menthol foam-strips, and menthol paste[64]. All were attempts at increasing surface area by combining menthol with vegetable oil on a solid substrate[24,93]. Each menthol treatment reduced mite count to less than one percent by late August, whereas mite levels in the non-treated controls were 25 percent.

In mating nuclei, menthol amounts ranging from 0 to 30 grams were applied at the time of queen cell placement[22]. While about 90 percent of queens emerged and mated in non-treated nucs, menthol-treated nucs produced as low as 28 percent laying queens. Most of the failures occurred in the first week after installation, resulting from non-emergence or destruction of the cell by worker bees.

Macdonald & Clark[58] applied 50 g packets of menthol pellets on the top bars of the bottom chamber of colonies for two weeks in June. Menthol was reapplied from August to October. Mite infestations in non-treated colonies increased from 9 to 31 percent by August and to 50 percent in January. Infestation level of the treated bees decreased from 9 to <2 percent.

A novel method of feeding microencapsulated menthol was described by Kevan & Kevan[52]. Microencapsulated menthol fed in candy patties to workers was absorbed through the gut wall into the bee's blood where it apparently killed tracheal mites.

Formic acid fumigation. Formic acid tests have been carried out in several provinces. In Alberta, liquid formic acid and a German product (Milben-Platten®) were evaluated for tracheal mite control[65]. All formic acid treatments reduced mite levels to less than 6 percent. However, dead bee trap counts were 8 times greater for treated colonies than for controls.

In British Columbia, liquid 65 percent formic acid (30 ml per dose) on paper pads applied weekly for three weeks on the bottom board or the top bars resulted in >95 percent mite mortality[21].

Formic acid slow release. Incorporating liquid formic acid into a gel-strip improved beekeeper safety and reduced the number of applications from three to one. Compared to liquid formic acid, efficacy of gel formulations ranged from that equal to three applications of liquid formic acid[20] to only 65-80 percent as effective[65]. A gel prototype provided adequate evaporation for only five days after an application[11].

The Mite Wipe Kit®, a pad of absorbent material inside a thin plastic perforated envelope, is being marketed in Ontario for application of formic acid[63]. For hive use, Mite Wipes are placed in a plastic bucket along with enough 65 percent formic acid to cover the pads. After the pads are saturated, individual Mite Wipes are removed and placed on the top bars of a hive. Pads are replaced in 4-10 days until three applications have been made.

Clark[15] tested "zip" closure plastic bags with 25 sheets (8.5 x 11 inches) of newspaper for absorbing up to 200 ml of 65 percent acid. The plastic bags had either micro-perforations (Ziploc® vegetable bag) or 2 to 3 rectangular openings (each 0.3 x 10 inches) to prolong evaporation over 15 to 20 days. Bags were placed on the top bars or bottom boards of hives. Mite mortality was about 95 percent.

Narrow plastic reservoirs and other devices have been developed to treat varroa by evaporating liquid formic acid over many days. The amount of acid and period of exposure provided by the VTD (*Varroa Treatment Device®*), the Liebefeld applicator, or Nassenheider Verdunster would be expected to kill a high percentage of tracheal mites.

Formic acid and human exposure. Application of liquid formic acid presents several hazards to the applicator: (1) liquid contacting skin or eyes can cause severe burns, (2) vapors can cause eye irritation, and (3) inhaled vapors can cause throat and lung irritation or damage. The permissible exposure limit for formic acid in air is 5 parts per million (ppm) over an eight hour period[66,81]. The odor threshold has been determined to be 21 ppm, but can vary from 15-40 ppm.

In order to assess the effectiveness of procedures to avoid harmful effects to beekeepers, Clark[19] measured the formic acid concentration in air encountered around a hive being treated or subsequently inspected during field applications. Using label directions for applying liquid 65 percent formic acid to absorbent materials on the top bars of bee colonies, beekeepers were exposed to 1 ppm or less. The exposure of persons inspecting treated colonies was also determined at 8, 24, 48 hours and one week post-application. Although air drawn from within 1 cm (<½ inch) of the formic acid treatment paper gave readings of 12 ppm at 8 hours post application, air breathed by the person conducting a typical inspection of the colony only indicated about 1 ppm.

It was concluded that adherence to proposed safety precautions would result in applicator or inspector exposure well below the permissible limit in Canada.

Bayvarol® was ineffective. Otis[67] conducted a study in the Mexican state of Veracruz with liquid flumethrin (active ingredient in Bayvarol) fed in sugar syrup to infested colonies, and concluded that it was not an effective miticide for tracheal mites. Liu[56] tested Bayvarol in northern Alberta and found that, with two strips per colony, the tracheal mite levels gradually decreased. Colonies treated with two strips of Bayvarol had significantly fewer adult mites and eggs. Bayvarol is not registered for use in honey bee colonies in Canada or the USA.

Neem being studied. Neem is derived from the tree, *Azadirachta indica*. Liu[56] observed fewer adult mites and eggs in neem-treated colonies and suggested that neem (Margosan-O®) might affect mite reproduction. The testing of neem products for bee parasite and disease control continues at Simon Fraser University[60]. Currently, none of the neem-based pesticides is registered for use in beekeeping.

Miticides used by industry. Menthol in pellet form became legally available to beekeepers in Canada in July 1992. Use of menthol has decreased greatly since March 1994 when formic acid became available through the scheduling provision of the Canada Pest Control Products Act. Some beekeepers continue to use menthol mixed with vegetable oil and applied on sheets of cardboard[93]. This method seems to work better than menthol pellets at low temperatures.

Future of miticide research and emerging problems. Work is ongoing with formic acid to determine optimal application methods. Various groups have active programs to select and breed bees for greater resistance to tracheal or varroa mites. Many of the selected lines are being evaluated by beekeepers for honey production and pollination.

Summary. Since 1904, the tracheal mite, *Acarapis woodi*, has caused serious problems for beekeepers worldwide. Apicultural scientists in North America have been testing acaricides since the mid 1980s in an attempt to control this mite. Several chemicals have therapeutic value when treating honey bee colonies, but only two have been widely used in North America: fumes of formic acid and fumes from menthol crystals. In Europe, Folbex VA fumigation is effective in tracheal mite control, but the cost of four weekly treatments is prohibitive for commercial beekeepers in the USA and Canada. More recently, scientists have tested extender patties containing vegetable oil or shortening for supplemental mite control, while others have explored the acaricidal properties of plant smoke. More than 50 species of plants have been tested against *Varroa jacobsoni*, and a few have proven effective against *A. woodi*. This chapter reviews all relevant literature concerning the chemical control of the tracheal mite.

Disclaimer. Mention of a proprietary product does not constitute a recommendation by the USDA or Canadian Ministry of Agriculture, nor does it imply registration under USA or Canadian pesticide laws.

References cited.

1. **Adee, R. 1993.** personal communication.

2. **Amrine, J. W., T. A. Stasny & R. Skidmore. 1996.** New mite controls investigated. Am. Bee J. 136: 652-654.

3. **Angelloz-Nicoud, M. 1929.** Experiments in the treatment of acarine disease. Bee World 10: 12-14.

4. **Angelloz-Nicoud, M. E. 1930.** Treatment of acarine disease with methyl salicylate. Bee World 11: 26.

5. **Atwal, A. S. & G. S. Dhaliwal. 1969.** Robbing between *Apis indica* F. and *Apis mellifera* L. Am. Bee J. 109: 462-463.

6. **Atwal, A. S. & O. P. Sharma. 1970.** Acarine disease of adult honeybees: prevention and control. Indian Farming. 20: 39-40.

7. **Bailey, L. 1963.** Infectious diseases of the honey-bee. Land Books, London.

8. **Bailey, L. & E. Carlisle. 1956.** Tests with acaricides on *Acarapis woodi* (Rennie). Bee World 37: 85-94.

9. **Baxter, J.B. 1997.** personal communication.

10. **Baxter, J.B. 1997.** unpublished data.

11. **Befus-Nogel, J. & D. L. Nelson. 1995.** Formic acid gel-strip place-

ment in honey bee colonies and the effect on evaporation rates, pp. 9-10. *In* D.L. Nelson & W.A. Rice [eds.], Research Highlights 1994. Agriculture & Agri-Food Canada, Beaverlodge, Alberta, Canada.

12. **Bogdanov, S. 1988.** Determination of amitraz and its metabolites in honey by HPLC. Sektion Bienen, Forschungsanstalt für Milchwirtschaft No. 3, Liebefeld, Switzerland (Apicultural Abstracts 984/89, 40: 279).

13. **Brodsgaard, C. & J. Beetsma. 1994.** Discussion group on control methods. *In A.* Matheson (ed.), New perspectives on varroa. International Bee Research Association; Cardiff, UK.

14. **Calderone, N. W. & H. Shimanuki. 1995.** Evaluation of four seed-derived oils as controls for *Acarapis woodi* (Acari: Tarsonemidae) in colonies of the honey bee, *Apis mellifera* (Hymenoptera: Apidae). J. Econ. Entomol. 88: 805-809.

15. **Clark, K. J. 1996.** personal communication.

16. **Clark, K. J. 1997.** personal communication.

17. **Clark, K. J. 1998.** unpublished data.

18. **Clark, K. J. 1990.** 1990 field trials comparing vegetable oil and menthol as a control for tracheal mites. Am. Bee J. 130: 799.

19. **Clark, K.J. 1992.** Human exposure to formic acid from applications for the control of honey bee tracheal mite. In-house publication 1-4. B.C. Min. Agric. Fish. Food, Dawson Creek, British Columbia, Canada.

20. **Clark, K.J. 1992.** Applications of formic acid liquid or gel for the control of tracheal mites. In-house publication 1-9. B.C. Min. Agric. Fish. Food, Dawson Creek, British Columbia, Canada.

21. **Clark, K. & J. Gates. 1992.** Investigations of the use of formic acid for the control of tracheal mites in British Columbia. In house publication 1-11. B.C. Min. Agric. Fish. Food, Dawson Creek, British Columbia, Canada.

22. **Clark, K. J., D. L. Nelson & D. McKenna. 1989.** Effect of menthol on queen rearing. Am. Bee J. 129: 811.

23. **Cox, R. L., W. T. Wilson, D. L. Maki & A. Stoner. 1986.** Chemical control of the honey bee tracheal mite, *Acarapis woodi.* Am. Bee J.

126: 828.

24. Cox, R. L., J. O. Moffett & W. T. Wilson. 1989. Techniques for increasing the evaporation rate of menthol when treating honey bee colonies for control of tracheal mites. Am. Bee J. 129: 129-131.

25. Cox, R.L., J.O. Moffett, W.T. Wilson & M. Ellis. 1989. Effects of late spring and summer menthol treatment on colony strength, honey production and tracheal mite infestation levels. Am. Bee J. 129: 547-549.

26. Cromroy, H. L., L. C. Cutts, D. L. Harris, W. R. Carpenter, J. C. E. Nickerson & S. Yocom. 1990. Tracheal mite research in Florida. Am. Bee J. 130: 187.

27. Dag, A., Y. Slabezki, H. Efrat, Y. Kamer, B. A. Yakobson, R. Mozes-Koch & U. Gerson. 1997. Control of honey bee tracheal mite infestations with amitraz fumigation in Israel. Am. Bee J. 137: 599-602.

28. Delaplane, K.S. 1992. Controlling tracheal mites (Acari: Tarsonemidae) in colonies of honey bees (Hymenoptera: Apidae) with vegetable oil and menthol. J. Econ. Entomol. 85: 2118-2124.

29. Delaplane, K.S. 1996. Practical science—research helping bee keepers I. tracheal mites. Bee World 77: 71-81.

30. Delfinado-Baker, M. 1984. *Acarapis woodi* in the United States. Am. Bee J. 124: 805-806.

31. Eischen, F. A. 1997. Natural products, smoke and varroa. Am. Bee J. 137: 107.

32. Eischen, F. A. & J. S. Pettis. 1997. personal communication.

33. Eischen, F. A. & W. T. Wilson. 1997. The effect of natural products smoke on *Varroa jacobsoni*. Am. Bee J. 137: 222-223.

34. Eischen, F. A., J. S. Pettis & A. Dietz. 1986. Prevention of *Acarapis woodi* infestation in queen honey bees with amitraz. Am. Bee J. 126: 498-500.

35. Eischen, F. A., D. Cardoso-Tamez, A. Dietz & G. O. Ware. 1987. Apitol, a systemic acaricide for the control of *Acarapis woodi*: an apiary test. Am. Bee J. 127: 844.

36. Ellis, M. D. 1994. Toxic effects of monoterpenoids on the honey

bee, *Apis mellifera* L., and its tracheal mite parasite, *Acarapis woodi* (Rennie). Ph.D. dissertation, University of Nebraska, Lincoln.

37. **Elzen, P. J., F. A. Eischen, J. B. Baxter, J. Pettis, G. W. Elzen & W. T. Wilson. 1998.** Fluvalinate resistance in *Varroa jacobsoni* from several geographic locations. Am. Bee J. 138: 674-676.

38. **Feldlaufer, M. F., J. S. Pettis, J. P. Kochansky & H. Shimanuki. 1997.** A gel formulation of formic acid for the control of parasitic mites of honey bees. Am. Bee J. 137: 661-663.

39. **Ferguson, J. L. 1986.** Menthol crystals reduce tracheal mite populations. Am. Bee J. 126: 760.

40. **Fries, I. 1993.** *Varroa* in cold climates. *In A.* Matheson (ed.) Living with varroa. International Bee Research Association; Cardiff, UK.

41. **Frow, R. W. 1934.** The Frow treatment for acarine disease. Bee World 15: 29-31.

42. **Frow, R. W. 1940.** Treatment with the nitro-benzene formula for acarine disease. Bee World 21: 55-56.

43. **Gary, N. E. & R. E. Page Jr. 1987.** Phenotypic variation in susceptibility of honey bees, *Apis mellifera*, to infestation by tracheal mites, *Acarapis woodi*. Exp. Appl. Acarol. 3: 291-305.

44. **Garza-Q., C., J. H. Dustmann, W. T. Wilson & R. Rivera. 1990.** Control of the honey bee tracheal mite (*Acarapis woodi*) with formic acid in Mexico. Am. Bee J. 130: 801.

45. **Garza-Q., C. & J.-H. Dustmann. 1993.** The problem of acariosis in honey bees (*Apis mellifera* L.) in north-east Mexico; investigations into incidence, disease patterns and possible therapy. *Anim. Res. Dev.* 38: 7-31. Inst. Sci. Co-op., Germany.

46. **Giavarini, I. & G. Giordani. 1966.** Study of acarine disease of honey bee. Final report, pp. 1-22. Nat. Inst. Apic., Bologna, Italy.

47. **Gruszka, J. 1987.** Examination of sample methods to detect low level infections of the honey bee tracheal mite. Saskatchewan Beelines. 81: Sask. Dept. Agric., Prince Albert, Saskatchewan, Canada.

48. **Gruszka, J., D. Peer & A. Tremblay. 1990.** The impact of *Acarapis*

woodi on the development of package bee colonies. Saskatchewan Beelines. 89: Sask. Dept. Agric., Prince Albert, Saskatchewan, Canada.

49. **Guzman-Novoa, E. & A. Zozaya-Rubio. 1984.** The effects of chemotherapy on the level of infestation and production of honey in colonies of honey bees with acariosis. Am. Bee J. 124: 669-672.

50. **Herbert, E. W., H. Shimanuki & J. C. Matthenius. 1987.** The effect of two candidate compounds on *Acarapis woodi* in New Jersey. Am. Bee J. 127: 776-778.

51. **Hoppe, H., W. Ritter & E. W.-C. Stephen. 1989.** The control of parasitic bee mites: *Varroa jacobsoni*, *Acarapis woodi* and *Tropilaelaps clareae* with formic acid. Am. Bee J. 129: 739-742.

52. **Kevan, S. D. & P. G. Kevan. 1997.** Protecting bees from tracheal mites: a novel approach. Am. Bee J. 137: 149-150.

53. **Kjer, K. M., D. W. Ragsdale & B. Furgala. 1989.** A retrospective and prospective overview of the honey bee tracheal mite, *Acarapis woodi* R. Am. Bee J. 129: 25-28, 112-115.

54. **Liu, T. P. 1991.** Vegetable oil and tracheal mites—is there any pheromone connection, or is it a myth? Am. Bee J. 131: 303.

55. **Liu, T. P. 1991.** Tobacco smoke and tracheal mites. Am. Bee J. 131: 435.

56. **Liu, T. P. 1995.** Controlling tracheal mites in colonies of honey bees with neem (Margosan-O) and flumethrin (Bayvarol). Am. Bee J. 135: 562-566.

57. **Liu, T. P. & M. E. Nasr. 1993.** Preventive treatment of tracheal mite, *Acarapis woodi* (Rennie) with vegetable oil extender patties in the honey bee, *Apis mellifera* L. colonies. Am. Bee J. 133: 873-875.

58. **Macdonald, J. & K. J. Clark. 1990.** 1989 field trials of menthol as a control for tracheal mites. Am. Bee J. 130: 804.

59. **Mann Lake Supply Ltd. 1999.** press release.

60. **Melathopoulos. A. 1997.** personal communication.

61. **Moffett, J. O., W. T. Wilson, R. L. Cox & M. Ellis. 1988.** Four for-

mulations of amitraz reduced tracheal mite, *Acarapis woodi*, populations in honey bees. Am. Bee J. 128: 805-806.

62. **Moffett, J. O., R. L. Cox, M. Ellis, R. Rivera, W. T. Wilson, D. Cardoso-T. & J. Vargas-C. 1989.** Menthol reduces winter populations of tracheal mites, *Acarapis woodi*, in honey bees from Mexico and Nebraska. Southwest. Entomol. 14: 57-65.

63. **Nasr, M. E. 1995.** Development of a safe method for applying formic acid to control bee mites in honey bee colonies. Canadian Beekeeping 18: 164.

64. **Nelson, D., P. Sporns, P. Kristiansen, P. Mills & M. Li. 1993.** Effectiveness and residue levels of three methods of menthol application to honey bee colonies for the control of tracheal mites. Apidologie 24: 549-556.

65. **Nelson, D., P. Mills, P. Sporns, S. Ooraikul & D. Mole. 1994.** Formic acid application methods for the control of honey bee tracheal mites. BeeScience 3: 134-140.

66. **OSHA & NIOSH. 1978.** Occupational health guideline for formic acid. Occupational Safety and Health Administration (OSHA) and National Institute for Occupational Safety and Health (NIOSH), U.S. Depts. Labor and Health and Human Services. Washington D.C.

67. **Otis, G. 1987.** unpublished data.

68. **Peer, D., J. Gruszka, & *A.* Tremblay. 1987.** Preliminary observations on the development of *Acarapis woodi* on the development of package bee colonies. Saskatchewan Beelines. 81: 6-16. Sask. Dept. Agric., Prince Albert, Saskatchewan, Canada.

69. **Pettis, J. S., R. L. Cox & W. T. Wilson. 1988.** Efficacy of fluvalinate against the honey bee tracheal mite, *Acarapis woodi*, under laboratory conditions. Am. Bee J. 128: 806.

70. **Pettis, J. S., W. T. Wilson, H. Shimanuki & P. D. Teel. 1991.** Fluvalinate treatment of queen and worker honey bees (*Apis mellifera* L.) and effects on subsequent mortality, queen acceptance and supersedure. Apidologie 22: 1-7.

71. **Phillips, E. F. 1925.** The status of Isle of Wight disease in various countries. J. Econ. Entomol. 18: 391-395.

72. Rademacher, E. 1993. Apitol-Kombi—a new product for controlling *Varroa jacobsoni*, pp. 530-540. *In* L.J. Connor, T. Rinderer, A. Sylvester & S. Wongsiri [eds.], Asian apiculture. Wicwas Press, Cheshire, Connecticut, USA.

73. Rennie, J., P. B. White & E. J. Harvey. 1921. Isle of Wight disease in hive bees (1) The etiology of the disease. Trans. R. Soc. Edinburgh 52: 737-748.

74. Ruijter, A. de. 1982. Tobacco smoke can kill varroa mites. Bee World. 63: 138.

75. Sammataro, D., S. Cobey, B. H. Smith & G. R. Needham. 1994. Controlling tracheal mites (Acari: Tarsonemidae) in honey bees (Hymenoptera: Apidae) with vegetable oil. J. Econ. Entomol. 87: 910-916.

76. Sanctuary, C. T. 1924. A successful experiment in the eradication of acarine disease. Bee World 6: 91-92.

77. Scott-Dupree, C. D. & G. W. Otis. 1992. The efficacy of four miticides for the control of *Acarapis apis* (Rennie) in a fall treatment program. Apidologie 23: 97-106.

78. Shah, F. A. 1987. 20 years of acarine mite in India. Glean. Bee Cult. 115: 517.

79. Sharma, O. P., R. Garg & G. S. Dogra. 1983. Efficacy of formic acid against *Acarapis woodi* (Rennie). Indian Bee J. 45: 1-2.

80. Smith, A. W., R. E. Page Jr. & G. R. Needham. 1991. Vegetable oil disrupts the dispersal of tracheal mites, *Acarapis woodi* (Rennie), to young host bees. Am. Bee J. 131: 44-46.

81. Van Waters & Rogers, Ltd. 1990. Material safety data sheet for formic acid. CAS no. 64-18-6. 4 p.

82. Vecchi, M. A. & G. Giordani. 1968. Chemotherapy of acarine disease. I. laboratory tests. J. Invertebr. Pathol. 10: 390-416.

83. Westcott, L. C. & M. L. Winston. 1999. Sublethal effects of three acaricide treatments on honey bee (*Apis mellifera* L.) colony development and honey production. Can. Entomol. 131: 363-371.

84. Wilson, W. T. 1987. unpublished data.

85. Wilson, W. T. 1990. Tracheal mite control. Am. Bee J. 130: 186.

86. Wilson, W. T. & J. R. Baxter. 1993. unpublished data.

87. Wilson, W. T. & A. M. Collins. 1993. Formic acid or amitraz for spring or fall treatment of *Acarapis woodi*. Am. Bee J. 133: 871.

88. Wilson, W. T. & R. A. Nunamaker. 1982. The infestation of honey bees in Mexico with *Acarapis woodi*. Am. Bee J. 122: 503-505, 508.

89. Wilson, W. T. & R. A. Nunamaker. 1985. Further distribution of *Acarapis woodi* in Mexico. Am. Bee J. 125: 107-111.

90. Wilson, W. T., J. R. Elliott & J. J. Lackett. 1970. Antibiotic treatments that last longer. Am. Bee J. 110: 348, 351.

91. Wilson, W. T., J. O. Moffett, R. L. Cox, D. L. Maki, H. Richardson & R. Rivera. 1988. Menthol treatment for *Acarapis woodi* control in *Apis mellifera* and the resulting residues in honey, pp. 535-540. *In* G.R. Needham, R.E. Page Jr., M. Delfinado-Baker & C.E. Bowman [eds.], Africanized honey bees and bee mites. Halsted Press, New York.

92. Wilson, W. T., J. S. Pettis & A. M. Collins. 1989. Efficacy of different isomers of menthol against the honey bee tracheal mite. Am. Bee J. 129: 826.

93. Wilson, W. T., R. L. Cox & J. O. Moffett. 1990. Menthol-grease board: a new method of administering menthol to honey bee colonies. Am. Bee J. 130: 409-412.

94. Wilson, W. T., R. L. Cox, J. O. Moffett & M. Ellis. 1990. Improved survival of honey bee (*Apis mellifera* L.) colonies from long-term suppression of tracheal mites (*Acarapis woodi* Rennie) with menthol. BeeScience 1: 48-54.

95. Wilson, W. T., J. R. Baxter, A. M. Collins, R. L. Cox & D. Cardoso-T. 1993. Formic acid fumigation for control of tracheal mites in honey bee colonies. BeeScience 3: 26-32.

96. Wilson, W. T., M. Ellis & A. M. Collins. 1994. Citral fumigation and three methods of feeding apitol for tracheal mite control. Am. Bee J. 134: 839.

97. Wilson, W. T., J. S. Pettis, C. E. Henderson & R. A. Morse. 1997. Tracheal mites, pp. 253-277. *In* R.A. Morse & K. Flottum [eds.],

Honey bee pests, predators, and diseases, 3rd ed. A.I. Root Co., Medina Ohio, USA.

98. Zozaya-R., J. A., E. Tanus-S. & E. Guzman-N. 1982. Mexicans report on acarine mite survey. Speedy Bee 10: 16.

Chapter 8

CULTURAL AND NATURAL CONTROL OF TRACHEAL MITES

Frank A. Eischen

Historically, non-chemical control practices have been used extensively in Europe for the control of *Acarapis woodi*[21]. Partially this was due to the lack of safe and efficacious chemical control, but there was also reluctance by beekeepers to use toxic materials in their hives and jeopardize the image of honey as a natural product. Currently, interest in non-chemical control is sporadically rekindled, usually for similar reasons or as an attempt to hold down treatment costs. Because tracheal mite infestations tend to be relatively slow-growing and chronic, these mites are more amenable to cultural controls than are *Varroa jacobsoni*.

Cultural control.

Manipulative techniques. Several techniques have been described wherein young parasite-free bees are emerged in isolation or under conditions of reduced contact with older and potentially infested bees[14,20,21,27,36]. Historically, this approach gained considerable favor with

European beekeepers and is even credited with eradicating *A. woodi* in some locations[21]. Initially, this did not seem applicable to U.S. commercial beekeeping until it was realized that the basic principles were frequently employed when making colony splits. Typically, one to two nuclei are taken from the strongest colonies. This usually involves combining 2-3 frames of brood and adhering bees with a frame of honey and a feeder. These nuclei are then moved to a new location and managed separately from the parent colonies. By selecting strong colonies, beekeepers tend to avoid those that are heavily infested (this is not always true, but it is far better to use large colonies than weak ones showing signs of distress). By using brood frames with adhering nurse bees, the most heavily-parasitized bees are avoided and the new unit will probably include a substantial number of young noninfested bees. When nuclei are made up in the usual manner (ie., brood in all stages and a sealed queen cell), a one-week gap occurs during which no young bees (within 0-5 days of age) are available for migratory female mites. If only sealed brood is used then a 2½-week gap occurs. If splits are made during or after the spring nectar flow, it further limits the inclusion of infested foragers as infestations frequently drop precipitously after a honey flow[10]. Moving the nuclei to a new location eliminates drifting foragers from parent colonies.

Requeening. The importance of having young vigorous queens heading infested colonies was quickly recognized as an important factor in diminishing the impact of *A. woodi*[20,22,32]. The prolific egg laying by a young queen tends to reduce the average mite load by increasing the number of bees in relation to the number of young migratory female mites. Earlier observers called attention to this, albeit without empirical evidence. Eischen & others[10] found that in heavily-infested colonies in northeastern Mexico, colonies headed by young queens had significantly fewer mites than colonies with old queens. Using vigorous young queens is probably the single most effective cultural control available.

Rennie[31] considered queens to be a continuing source of infestation and this appears to be supported by Burgett & Kitprasert[6], although Pettis & others[29] found that many queens showed evidence of only previous infestations. Morgenthaler[26] found *A. woodi* in queens imported from France into Switzerland. Warnings about imported queens have been echoed many times[1]. Nevertheless, queens generally show a lower incidence of infestation than the colonies they head. Young queens are not as hairy as workers and this may lower their chances of becoming infested. Mites seeking a new host crawl to the tip of a body hair (called questing behavior), and if a potential new host is relatively hairless then it seems plausible that it will be less likely to pick up a mite. Changing queens also changes genetic stock, a time-honored technique for dealing with a honey bee problem.

Reducing stress. The concept of stress, though intuitively obvious, is inadequately defined for insects. In mammals, stress has been described primarily in physiological concepts, where an exterior agent or force causes a changed physiology and the animal attempts to reestablish homeostasis[35]. Probably analogous processes occur in honey bees[18], and perhaps are due to some of the same causes such as poor food, environmental toxicants, etc.[13]. Parasites like *A. woodi* no doubt stress honey bees as evidenced by poor wintering ability, reduced honey gathering and lowered reproductivity[9,12,15]. It is unclear whether multiple sources of stress act with a simple additive effect or act synergistically which means that more bees die than would from the individual factors acting separately. Mammalian physiology indicates synergistic effects. In any case, most infested colonies die during winter, a time of apparently increased stress due to both mites and the attendant problems caused by long periods of confinement.

Another case of compounded stress may exist in commercial migratory beekeeping. This notion is supported by observations made by Danka & others[7] who found that multiple hive moves adversely affected Africanized colonies. Eischen & others[12] estimated the economic threshold of *A. woodi* to be about 30% (percent of bees in the hive which are infested) for relatively stationary colonies used in northeastern Mexico for commercial honey production. Bach (personal communication) estimated the economic threshold for colonies rented for multiple pollination contracts in the Pacific Northwest to be only about 15%, half that of the stationary Mexican colonies.

Some disagreement in the scientific community continues over the amount of stress that *A. woodi* causes. Gary & Page[16] found little or no effect of mites on bee foraging or survivorship. Their observations followed individual bees, but only percentages of bees infested are reported. To evaluate their information the parasite load (number of parasites per bee) of individual bees is required. It is possible for the percentages of workers infested to be relatively high (about 50%), but the parasite number low (10 mites per bee). Individual bees can probably tolerate a few mites with little economic impact.

Beekeeping practices that reduce stress may either allow a colony to support higher infestation levels without exhibiting measurable decline in colony viability, or allow the colony to reduce its level of infestation by out-reproducing the mites, or both. Reducing the frequency of colony disturbance, maintaining foulbrood control[9], providing adequate winter stores[20], and any other practice that promotes vigor will probably help reduce the impact of *A. woodi* infestation.

Reducing mite dispersal from drift, absconding, robbing, and swarming. Drifting by workers and drones has long been recognized as an important source of infestation. Rennie[32] noted that one infested colony could infest many others by drifting drones and postulated that drone control was required to eradicate *A. woodi*. He also called for staggering colonies in an apiary to reduce inter-colony drift by workers. Dawicke & others[8] found that the percentage of drones parasitized was not different than workers, but that female migratory mites preferred drones. The spread of *A. woodi* by drones within an apiary has sufficient supporting evidence to indicate that it is important. The spread of mites by drones over long distances has not yet been thoroughly investigated, but Mossadegh[28] found that marked drones from infested colonies were found in noninfested colonies 800 meters distant. Worker drift within an apiary is well documented and probably causes substantial spread of this mite. Drift is pervasive in apiaries laid out in regular rows with little distinguishing differences among colony locations. Palletized colonies are likely to show high rates of drift (among the joined colonies) and perhaps few corrective options are available, although painting hive bodies different colors does help limit the problem.

Some evidence suggests that parasitism alters the host's behavior such that it increases the likelihood of the parasites finding another host[5]. As noted above, stress due to several causes including parasitism has been implicated in poor colony performance. Presumably parasitism debilitates individual workers, and their lowered performance causes colony degradation to the point that the society breaks down. Thoenes & Buchmann[37] recorded a case of workers drifting away from an infested colony over a period of several hours. If the drifting bees gain entry to healthy colonies, then this behavior increases the likelihood of mite dispersal and increases the mites' reproductive fitness, i.e. ability to produce offspring. Absconding is a related phenomenon that occurs with undetermined frequency, but appears with regularity in Africanized bees in Mexico and southern Texas. Absconding swarms sometimes move considerable distances and if infested may facilitate the spread of the parasites.

Robbing has been suggested as a means of mite dispersal, although information is largely anecdotal (but see Atwal & Dhahwal[2]). Mite transfer during tumultuous mass robbing has never been measured and it seems unlikely that such conditions are optimum for it. However, infested survivors of a robbed colony may drift into healthy colonies. Eliminating or segregating weak or infested colonies is probably worthwhile. Other practices such as reducing entrances and limiting colony inspection time during dearth periods can lower the risk of robbing-induced spread of mites. Progressive, or silent, robbing is a much quieter although pervasive activity and is difficult to prevent[33]. Mite transfer conditions during progressive robbing are more favorable than during mass robbing. One can discourage progressive robbing, and associated risks of mite spread, by maintaining uniformly strong colonies in an apiary and avoiding practices (such as open-barrel feeding) that encourage robbing. Unfortunately, the popular Italian bees are notably prone to robbing.

Royce & others[34] speculate that swarming functions to regulate tracheal mite populations in nature by two mechanisms. First, bees capable of departing with a swarm may have a lower rate of infestation than do bees remaining with the nest. Second, newly established swarms have no new workers for at least 21 days, during which time mite populations decline owing to the fact that mites reproduce most successfully on young bees (chapter 3). There may be a limit to this type of control, however. In Mexico, queen cell production and drone rearing decline dramatically when colony mite infestations reached about 50%[11].

Reducing mite dispersal due to migratory beekeeping practices. Long range trucking of infested colonies in the United States has probably spread *A. woodi* faster than any other factor. Nearly every state was found infested within three years of the parasite's discovery in 1984. Strong and predictable nectar flows create areas dense with honey bee colonies–colonies often owned by several outfits. Apiaries are set in close proximity to one another. Drifting and robbing are common and a well-known mechanism for spreading parasites. Migrating bee colonies are often placed in holding yards prior to trucking. Such dense populations of bees serve to spread mites, and reducing the time spent in these yards is helpful. During trucking, unscreened colonies frequently co-mingle under the net especially during daylight hours. Some beekeepers screen individual colonies, but this requires extra expense. Hosing down colonies with water before moving them in hot weather helps prevent overheating and extensive co-mingling. For many operations, keeping colonies strong and healthy is the only practical way to counteract the propensity of mechanized beekeeping for spreading mites.

In operations with a history of damaging mite levels, the combining of weak colonies with stronger ones should not be done as this invariably leads to spread of the parasite. Small colonies with high mite populations should be killed in the fall.

Natural effects and control.

Climatic effects. Jeffree[19] predicted that tracheal mites would flourish in only a limited portion of the United States—western Washington, California, and possibly in the mountains of Arizona, New Mexico, and Carolina. This prediction was based on rainfall and temperature ranges perceived to be the limits for *A. woodi*. Unfortunately, the prediction was wrong, but as with other failed hypotheses, some of the underlying principles have value. *A. woodi* breed in adult bees, and although winter may slow mite reproduction it is usually not stopped. Populations of mites typically reach their highest levels during late winter. Even though the mites prefer young bees, they can reproduce in older ones too. So during winter tracheal mite populations continue to rise. The close confinement of inside wintering colonies may be an advantage to transferring mites. Pettis & others[30] found that most tracheal mite transfers occur at night, perhaps because it is easier for the mites to transfer at this time or that this is when maximum contact occurs between older infested foragers and young bees which are the preferred hosts. Collectively, these findings may explain why tracheal mites seem to be a more serious problem in areas with harsh winters where bees must endure long periods of confinement.

Pathogens. Little is known about the biotic factors that affect *A. woodi*. However, Lavie[23] reported that the yeast *Acaromyces laviae* was capable of controlling tracheal mites when suspensions of it were sprayed on each comb of infested colonies. Martha Gilliam (United States Dept. Agriculture, Tucson, AZ; personal comm.), however has expressed reservations on the identity of the organism that Lavie worked with. My opinion is that there probably are microorganisms that adversely affect *A. woodi*. During a study in Mexico we observed mite levels in a heavily infested colony drop suddenly from 90% to nondetectable. Up to the time of this drop, the tracheae of infested bees contained a cottony-filamentous material. Other heavily infested colonies in the apiary did not have this material and continued to maintain high mite levels. The prevalence of this unidentified material is not high. We observed it in only a few of the many hundreds of colonies examined. Liu[24] reported finding virus-like particles in tracheal mites from Scotland that were not found in mites from California, USA. This raises the possibility that British bees are more resistant to *A. woodi* in part because of the presence of an endemic virus pathogen of mites. More recently, Grant & others[17] found no specific bacterial or fungal associations with tracheal mite-infested bees in Canada.

Parasite-host cycles. As a general rule of biology, high host populations frequently lead to unhealthy conditions for the host but favorable conditions for their parasites. An increase in parasite numbers can reduce the host population to lower numbers, and if conditions are right the cyclic process begins anew. As a result of this density-dependent relationship, parasites control or regulate host populations[25]. Bailey & Perry[4] suggested that the reason for the decline of tracheal mites in England was a density-dependent relationship between the number of managed colonies and tracheal mite populations. They noted that as colony density declined in England, so did the number of mites. They argued that as colony density fell, more nectar resources were available to the remaining colonies. This led to increased foraging and thus reduced the contact time between young, emerging noninfested bees and their older infested nestmates. This hypothesis is reasonable since reducing colony density is likely to increase average inter-colony distance making it more difficult for the parasite to move between colonies. The nectar component of the hypothesis must be incomplete if not incorrect, however, since Pettis & others[30] showed that most mite transfer to young bees occurs at night when most bees are in the nest, permitting maximal contact time. It also does not explain why some areas of the United States, such as the Lower Rio Grande Valley, have low mite populations even though they have a high density of managed colonies and poor nectar conditions. Further, Bailey's[3] prediction that areas of the United States with good nectar conditions would have low mite populations has generally proven incorrect. It should be said in defense of the Bailey hypothesis that commercial colonies in the USA may be more stressed than those in Britain, possibly allowing higher parasite populations to arise than would ordinarily develop.

Populations of *A. woodi* go through seasonal cycles. Frequently mite levels drop dramatically in spring and this has been attributed to a combination of increased nectar flows and brood production by bees. Intense foraging has been suggested as the cause for many heavily infested bees dying in the field, and we witnessed this several times in the mid 1980s in the presence of high mite populations in northeastern Mexico. In most areas in the USA, mite populations are highest during late fall and winter.

Future developments. If apiculture follows the path of other areas of commercial agriculture, it is likely that cultural controls coupled with strategically timed acaricide applications will play an increasing role. These two practices are tenets of the concept called *Integrated Pest Management* (IPM). This idea has proven useful in reducing the amount of pesticides needed and the number of yearly applications required in many cropping systems. Pest populations are carefully monitored and pesticides applied only when they exceed an empirically determined economic threshold. Monitoring *A. woodi* populations has not been practiced by most beekeepers in the past because it seems to be a formidable task. Actually, it's not. Various beekeeping shortcourses around the country provide training in mite diagnosis. Once the technique is mastered, all that is required is a judicious sampling scheme. Armed with actual mite counts, one can make intelligent decisions on whether cultural controls have been adequate or chemical intervention is warranted.

Summary. In many cases, populations of tracheal mites can be kept below damaging levels by employing cultural, non-chemical management techniques. Some of these methods exploit the fact that newly-emerged or relatively young bees have lower incidence of mite infestation than do older workers. Hive manipulations that increase the ratio of young bees, such as making splits and using prolific queens, can reduce overall colony mite levels. Good beekeeping management that reduces colony stress can help colonies withstand mites or else reduce the general level of infestation by increasing bee reproductive vigor. Practices that reduce robbing, drifting, and absconding can minimize local dispersement of mites to other colonies.

References cited.

1. Anonymous. 1980. Research and beekeeping. Bee World 61: 85-86.

2. Atwal, A.S. & G.S. Dhaliwal. 1969. Robbing between *Apis indica* F. and *Apis mellifera* L. Am. Bee J. 109: 462-463.

3. Bailey, L. 1985. *Acarapis woodi*: a modern appraisal. Bee World 66: 98-104.

4. Bailey, L. & J.N. Perry. 1982. The diminished incidence of *Acarapis woodi* (Rennie) (Acari: Tarsonemindae) in honey bees, *Apis mellifera* L. (Hymenoptera: Apidae) in Britain. Bull. Ent. Res. 72: 655-662.

5. Brodeur, J. & J.N. McNeil. 1989. Seasonal microhabitat selection by an endoparasitoid through adaptive modification of host behavior. Science 244: 226-228.

6. Burgett, M. & C. Kitprasert. 1992. Tracheal mite infestation of queen honey bees. J. Apic. Res. 31: 110-111.

7. Danka, R.G., T.E. Rinderer, A.M. Collins & R.L. Hellmich. 1987. Responses of Africanized honey bees (Hymenoptera: Apidae) to pollination-management stress. J. Econ. Entomol. 80: 621-624.

8. Dawicke, B.L., G.W. Otis, C. Scott-Dupree & M. Nasr. 1992. Host preference of the honeybee tracheal mite (*Acarapis woodi* (Rennie). Exp. Appl. Acarol. 15: 83-98.

9. Eischen, F.A. 1987. Overwintering performance of honey bee colonies heavily infested with *Acarapis woodi* (Rennie). Apidologie 18: 293-304.

10. Eischen, F.A., W.T. Wilson, D. Hurley, & D. Cardoso-Tamez.

1988. Cultural practices that reduce populations of *Acarapis woodi* (Rennie). Am. Bee J. 128: 209-211.

11. **Eischen, F.A., D. Cardoso-Tamez, A. Dietz & G.O. Ware. 1989.** Cymiazole, a systemic acaricide that controls *Acarapis woodi* (Rennie) infesting honey bees: II. an apiary test. Apidologie 20: 41-51.

12. **Eischen, F.A., D. Cardoso-Tamez, W.T. Wilson & A. Dietz. 1989.** Honey production of honey bee colonies infested with *Acarapis woodi* (Rennie). Apidologie. 20: 1-8.

13. **Erickson, E.H. 1990.** Stress and honey bees. Glean. Bee Cult. 130: 650-654.

14. **Fergusson, C.S.R. 1922.** The manipulative treatment of acarine disease. Bee World 4: 39-40.

15. **Furgala, B., S. Duff, S.A. Boulfaraj, D. Ragsdale, & R. Hyser. 1989.** Some effects of the honey bee tracheal mite (*Acarapis woodi* Rennie) on nonmigratory, wintering honey bee (*Apis mellifera* L.) colonies in east central Minnesota. Am. Bee J. 129: 195-197.

16. **Gary, N.E. & R.E. Page, Jr. 1989.** Tracheal mite (Acari: Tarsonemidae) infestation effects on foraging and survivorship of honey bees (Hymenoptera: Apidae). J. Econ. Entomol. 82: 734-739.

17. **Grant, G.A., D.L. Nelson, J. Befus-Nogel & J.D. Bissett. 1997.** Micro-organisms associated with tracheal mite-infested honey bees. J. Apic. Res. 36: 141-144.

18. **Harris, J.W. & J. Woodring. 1992.** Effects of stress, age, season, and source colony on levels of octopamine, dopamine and serotonin in the honey bee (*Apis mellifera* L.) brain. J. Insect Physiol. 38: 29-35.

19. **Jeffree, E.P. 1959.** The world distribution of acarine disease of honeybees and its probable dependence on meteorological factors. Bee World 40: 4-15.

20. **Jordan, R. 1963.** Was der Imker zurn Schutze seiner Völker vor Erkrankung an Milbe auf pflegliche Weise tun kann. Bienenvater 84: 35-43.

21. **Kaeser, W. 1952.** Bekämpfung der Milbenseuche auf biologischer

Grundlage. Deut. Bienenwirt 3: 21-25.

22. **Killick, C.R. 1923.** The control of acarine disease. Bee World 5: 93-94.

23. **Lavie, P. 1951.** Investigations on a mysterious micro-organism *Acaromyceslaviae* which appears to be a parasite of *Acarapis woodi*. Proceedings, 14th International Beekeeping Congress, Leamington Spa, England, paper 20.

24. **Liu, S. 1991.** Virus-like particles in the tracheal mite *Acarapis woodi* (Rennie). Apidologie. 22: 213-219.

25. **May, R.M. 1985.** Host-parasite associations: their population biology and population genetics, pp. 243-262. *In* D. Rollinson & R.M. Anderson [eds.], Ecology and genetics of host-parasite interactions. Linnean Society Symposium Series No. 11, Academic Press, New York.

26. **Morgenthaler, O. 1949.** Achtung vor ausländischen Königinnen. Schweiz Bienen Ztg. 72: 570.

27. **Morgenthaler, O. 1965.** Die natürlichen Widerstände gegen eine rasche Ausbreitung der Milbenseuche im Bienenvolk. Ved Pr. Vyzk. Ust. Vcelars. Dole. 4: 131-136 [Apicultural Abstracts 160/66].

28. **Mossadegh, M.S. 1993.** The biology of the tracheal mite *Acarapis woodi* (Acari: Tarsonemidae) and role of drone honey bees in inter colony spread of the mite in North Carolina [in Arabic]. Sci. J. Agric. 16: 2-3, 14-22 [Apicultural Abstracts 249/95].

29. **Pettis, J.S., A. Dietz & F.A. Eischen. 1989.** Incidence rates of *Acarapis woodi* (Rennie) in queen honey bees of various ages. Apidologie 20: 69-75.

30. **Pettis, J., W.T. Wilson, & F.A. Eischen. 1992.** Nocturnal dispersal by female *Acarapis woodi* in honey bee (*Apis mellifera*) colonies. Exp. Appl. Acarol. 15: 99-108.

31. **Rennie, J. 1921.** Notes on acarine disease II. Bee World 3: 5-7.

32. **Rennie, J. 1921.** Notes on acarine disease. III. Bee World 3: 35-36.

33. **Ribbands, R. 1955.** Community defense against robber bees. Am. Bee J. 95: 313 , 320.

34. Royce, L.*A.*, P.*A.* Rossignol & D.M. Burgett. **1989.** A suggested role of swarming in tracheal mite parasitism. Am. Bee J. 129: 821.

35. **Selye, H. 1950.** Stress and the general adaptation syndrome. British Med. J. 1: 1383-1392.

36. **Svoboda, J. 1947.** The mechanical eradication of acarine disease. Bee World 28: 41-43.

37. **Thoenes, S.C. & S.L Buchmann. 1992.** Colony abandonment by adult honey bees: a behavioural response to high tracheal mite infestation? J. Apic. Res. 31: 167-168.

RESISTANCE OF HONEY BEES TO TRACHEAL MITES

Chapter 9

Robert G. Danka

*I*t was suggested long ago that some genetic lines of honey bees resist infestation by tracheal mites. This possibility received little attention through many decades of this century, but the rise of mite associated problems in North America in the 1980s and 1990s prompted renewed interest in mite control techniques. Recent scientific inquiry has revealed much about genetic resistance to tracheal mites and beekeepers can use this knowledge to incorporate resistance into mite management strategies.

There are several important benefits of using resistant bees rather than chemicals to manage mites. A genetic resistance approach is less labor intensive and less expensive. After a queen of a resistant bee stock is installed in a colony, mite control is complete for at least as long as the queen lives, and a daughter queen may also provide useful level of resistance. When resistant bees are used, less acaricides are needed, and this reduces the exposure of bees and beekeepers to pesticides.

History. Anderson[2], writing about the outbreak of Isle of Wight disease in England that began at the turn of this century, noted that as early as 1911 some colonies of bees apparently were less susceptible than others to the problems that later were determined to be caused by tracheal mites. Anderson submitted a proposal in 1918 to test for resistance to the disease, but his application was denied; the beekeeping world perhaps lost an early chance to learn how bee stocks could be bred to resist hazards. Still, Anderson believed that genetic resistance would be the ultimate solution to the disease. He noted that the virulence of the disease subsided in an area through time, suggesting that surviving bees were resistant to the causative agent. He debated this issue with a Mr. Illingworth in the pages of *Bee World* in 1930 and 1931, and put forth ideas that we now know are correct.

Brother Adam at Buckfast Abbey in southwest England began breeding in 1916 from colonies that had survived the early tracheal mite problems. Colonies susceptible to mites probably were eliminated quickly from the breeding pool, given that an estimated 90% of colonies in England were killed. Adam[1] related that he first saw clear evidence of genetic control of mite susceptibility in 1922 and 1923 when two sister breeder queens of Italian origin produced daughter colonies that differed greatly in susceptibility to tracheal mites. His breeding of the Buckfast stock continued throughout the next seven decades with an emphasis on traits such as brood production, low swarming, etc., while the local intense pressure from mites was thought to have promoted mite resistance in the bees.

One beekeeping trial supported the contention of tracheal mite resistance in Buckfast bees. Calvert[5], in Ireland, reported that he was able to overcome severe mite infestations within 12 months by requeening his infested colonies with either pure-mated Buckfast queens or with Buckfast queens mated to his own susceptible stock.

Subsequent to the devastation wrought by the mites early in this century, tracheal mite problems declined in Europe and the mites are now considered to be only an infrequent problem[25]. This suggests that natural selection rendered European bees comparatively resistant to the parasite. However, it has not been established clearly that this is the case. Studies regarding possible differences in susceptibilities of mite-exposed European bees and non-exposed North American bees led Bailey[3,4] to conclude that British and American bees were equally susceptible. Yet it also has been argued that Bailey's data do in fact support the view that non-selected American bees were more susceptible than British bees[18]. There were no other investigations of possible resistance to tracheal mites in European bees, and seeking out and using resistant stock does not appear to have been a priority for European beekeepers. An apparent lack of need for active tracheal mite control is further circumstantial evidence that the susceptibility of European bees generally declined through years of exposure to tracheal mites.

Definitions. The term *resistant* is used to mean that it is unlikely that many bees in the described colony or population will become infested when exposed to tracheal mites. Colonies or populations in which few bees become infested are less likely to suffer damage or be killed by mites than are others which become highly infested[26]. Resistant bees are not *immune* to mite infestation. Rather, in the presence of mites, resistant colonies tend to have infestations that remain relatively low while *susceptible* colonies will tend to become infested to the point of being severely damaged or killed. It must be stressed that these infestation patterns are probabilities, not certainties, and resistant bees on occasion may be damaged by mite infestation. The term tolerance is less applicable than the term resistance because there are no data showing that colonies can perform well when infested with tracheal mites at levels known to cause problems (that is, when more than 15-25% of worker bees are infested in the autumn). Honey bees apparently are simply not able to tolerate high mite infestations.

Terminology suggested by the American Society of Parasitologists allows clear communication about the relationship of bees with their mite parasites. The percentage of mite-infested worker bees in a sample (or of infested colonies in a group) is called the *prevalence*. The number of mites per individual infested bee is the mite *intensity*, while the average number of mites per bee overall in a sample is the mite *abundance*. *Fecundity* refers to the number of offspring produced per female.

Scientific evidence of resistance. Soon after tracheal mites were found to cause severe beekeeping problems in North America, research in the United States and Canada turned to finding solutions to the mite problem. Several intensive searches for genetic resistance were among the research efforts. It did not take long for scientific inquiry to document that different lines of bees do indeed differ in susceptibility to the mites.

Gary & Page[14] showed that different lines of bees having lesser and greater susceptibility to the mites can be selected from a common population. A key to their research was to develop a comparative testing protocol whereby different bee lines are simultaneously exposed to a uniform source of mite-infested bees. Page & Gary[27] furthermore showed that the differences in response to mites had a genetic basis. These findings together demonstrated that bee selection and breeding might provide a solution to beekeeping problems caused by tracheal mites.

Studies using comparative tests in Canada found significant variation in resistance to tracheal mites among bees from commercial sources[6], and also within a closed population of bees originating from queens produced in California[29].

The longstanding reputation of Buckfast bees being resistant to tracheal mites garnered research attention, and this stock has been the richest source of material for study. Buckfast bees maintained commercially in the United States were tested first. Colonies maintained low mite prevalences when compared with another commercial U.S. stock during a 7-month test[21]. Variance in the responses of Buckfast colonies suggested that the stock was not uniformly resistant.

Queens of Old World Buckfast stock were imported in 1990 from Great Britain to the United States and Canada for testing. In the United States, Buckfast bees went through a standard Department of Agriculture (USDA) quarantine procedure and then were put immediately into a field test conducted in four commercial beekeeping operations. In comparisons with three other stocks, Buckfast bees had low mite prevalences during the 1-year test and had other desirable traits such as good honey production and survivability[12].

In Canada, work at the University of Guelph found that Buckfast both from England and the United States had lower mite prevalences and abundances than a standard Canadian stock[19]. Colonies within all stocks varied in response to the mite, suggesting that selection could further enhance resistance. Hybrids of British Buckfast and Canadian stocks generally had the superior resistance of the Buckfast parent. These tests were conducted using both a short-term assay of test bees placed into infested colonies (similar to Page & Gary[27]), and a field test in standard colonies for seven months. An important finding was that the two test methods gave comparable results, meaning that the short-term test is valid for evaluating the resistance of a stock. Further research also showed a congruence of results from field tests and short assays[9]. In sum, a variety of independent scientific tests verified earlier reports from beekeepers that Buckfast bees are resistant to tracheal mites.

Carniolan bees were imported from Yugoslavia by the USDA in 1989 and were found to resist tracheal mite infestation under commercial beekeeping conditions[12,17]. When hybridized with British Buckfast bees, the F_1 colonies resisted mite infestation as well as, but not better than, the parent stocks, which were about equal in resistance[16]. The Yugoslavian bees were released by the Agricultural Research Service of the USDA as ARS-Y-C-1 Honey Bee Stock and have been available to the U.S. beekeeping industry since 1993.

Another importation of potentially mite resistant stock was made by Morse and comprised queens donated by beekeepers in Great Britain[22]. Worker bees from these British queens were found not to be strongly resistant to tracheal mites when compared to bees of other lines[13,15]. The imported British stock was distributed to some North American beekeepers for cooperative testing, but was largely abandoned for beekeeping use.

The attempts of several individual beekeepers in the United States to develop resistant stock have been publicized. Taber[30,31] outlined a method whereby a queen producer could select among potential breeder queens for mite resistance. He later offered mite resistant queens for sale. Hines, a southern Arizona beekeeper, teamed with USDA scientists in a resistance improvement program. No acaricides were used in Hines' entire operation of 600-700 colonies. New queens were raised from colonies that had low mite prevalences and mated to drones from other surviving colonies; these queens were then used in colonies made up to replace those that had died. Within four years, colony mortality apparently due to tracheal mites decreased from 33% to about 3% in the operation[20]. Webster selected for mite resistance for several years by propagating from colonies that were thriving among others damaged or killed by parasitism in his Vermont apiaries[32]. In a field test, two of Webster's lines and Buckfast bees had relatively low mite prevalence[13]. Bees of a cross between Morse's British stock and some of Webster's selected lines generally had intermediate mite prevalences.

A common experience is that the impact of tracheal mites, as gauged by colony mortality, first increases but then decreases during the first few years that mites are present in an area. Around Baton Rouge,

Louisiana, for example, mites were first detected in 1989 and colony mortality of 30-50% was common in the winters of 1989-90 and 1990-91. Losses decreased dramatically thereafter, and colony deaths attributed to tracheal mite parasitism are now rare. Wilson & others[33] reported that a similar trend occurred in Mexico. After tracheal mites spread throughout the country in the 1980s, sampling in 1992-1995 revealed that mites continued to be found in about half of the colonies, but mite prevalences in worker bees were markedly lower than they were in the mid 1980s. The authors concluded that "surviving colonies now appear less susceptible to" tracheal mites. They also noted that the trend of lower infestations during the period was coincident with increased Africanization of bees in Mexico; Africanized bees are known to be somewhat resistant to tracheal mites[8].

Details of resistance. After resistance was documented scientifically, questions arose regarding what mechanisms regulate resistance and how the characteristic of resistance is inherited when bees are hybridized. Answers to both of these questions are potentially important in enabling bee breeders to select resistant bees more effectively and efficiently. Work to address these issues has been carried out mostly using bees derived from Buckfast stock in comparative tests against stocks known to be susceptible.

Mechanism. Resistant bees significantly reduce the number of tracheal mites that are able to enter and become established in the tracheae[9,19]. A direct mechanism by which infestation is suppressed is by autogrooming; young resistant stock bees apparently are more effective at cleaning migrating mites off themselves[10]. Autogrooming can occur as part of a "grooming dance" which occurs more frequently when mite infestation is high[28]. Susceptible bees are able to autogroom to some extent, and the frequency of this trait probably can be increased in a random population by selection. It does not appear that differences in cuticle chemistry, the presence of the hairs surrounding the prothoracic spiracles, or grooming among nestmates are major determinants of resistance[11]. Resistant bees cause little or no reduction in fecundity of the mites which infest them[9,19].

Inheritance. The beekeeper Calvert[5] successfully reduced tracheal mite problems by requeening with Buckfast bees, and wrote that "the resistance characteristic is inherited and holds good in a first cross" (of Buckfast queens mated to susceptible drones). Recent studies have confirmed this assertion about the inheritance of resistance. In crosses of British Buckfast or commercially available U.S. Buckfast bees with a susceptible Canadian stock, hybrids had intermediate mite prevalences both in short bioassays and in a field test[19]. Cobey & Smith[7] reported that Buckfast-Carniolan reciprocal crosses were intermediate in prevalences, although the data are difficult to interpret because of the very low infestations in all test colonies. Three recent tests[11] confirmed and expanded our understanding of inheritance. In the first test, resistance was improved when resistant stock drones were mated to five commercial U.S. stocks including Italian, Carniolan and Caucasian types. Resistance therefore is transferable in a variety of crosses. Each of the commercial stocks was intermediate in susceptibility between known resistant and susceptible stocks. In the second test, resistance was improved when resistant bees were crossed to highly susceptible bees, regardless of whether the resistant parent was represented by queens or by drones. Thus queen breeders using only natural matings can impart resistance by two approaches: by propagating queens from a resistant source and mating those daughter queens to drones of any source; or by mating queens of any stock in an area "flooded" with resistant stock drones produced by either resistant queens or daughters of resistant queens. In the third test, the heritability of the trait of resistance was estimated to be high; traits with high heritability are easily selected for within a breeding population.

ARS-Y-C-1 bees also pass resistance to tracheal mites to their offspring. This was found when these bees were crossed to another Carniolan stock that was less resistant[17]. Hybrids were as resistant as the ARS-Y-C-1 parents.

Resistant stocks in North American beekeeping. The most successful system for improving tracheal mite resistance in commercial bee stocks has been a joint program of the Ontario Bee Breeders' Association and the provincial government. Progeny of potential breeder queens are screened for relative resistance using a short bioassay and participating queen producers use the test results to select their breeder queens[24]. From 1992 to 1997, the number of participating beekeepers rose from five to 28, and the number of breeder colonies evaluated annually increased concurrently. After initially screening 28 colonies in 1992, about 350 colonies were tested during the peak of selection in 1994 and 1995 and about 165 colonies now are evaluated annually to maintain selection pressure in the breeding stock. Mite resistance was improved quickly by selection. Overall mite abundance in stock tested by the program decreased from 13 to 1.5 mites per bee from 1992 to 1997. A comparison of progeny of selected and non-selected stock showed 72% of selected stock colonies versus 19% of non-selected colonies had mite abundances below the mean for the entire group after just two generations of selection[23] (Fig. 9.1). This testing and selection system stands as a model by which other local, regional or national groups could design stock improvement programs.

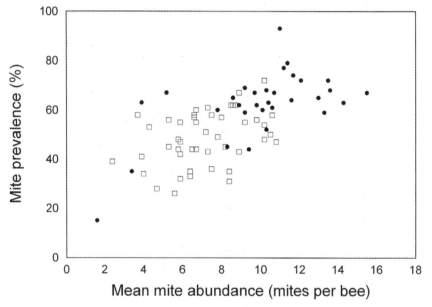

▲*Figure 9.1 Progress in selection for tracheal mite resistance as exemplified by data from Ontario, Canada[23]. Compared are progeny of the second generation of stock selected for tracheal mite resistance (□, representing 46 colonies) and progeny of non-selected stock (•, representing 31 colonies). Colonies were tested using a colony level bioassay similar to that described in the text and shown in Fig. 9.2. Tracheal mites were significantly less abundant and prevalent in the progeny of selected resistant stock. Approximately 72% of resistant stock colonies (versus 19% of non-selected colonies) had less than the average abundance of all colonies in the test (8.3 mites per bee).*

Although there seems to have been a slackening of efforts to breed tracheal mite resistant bees in the United States in recent years, bee-keepers interested in keeping resistant bees have several stocks available from which to choose. Various stocks of domestic and foreign origin have been advertised in industry publications within the past five years as being mite resistant.

Recommendations for stock selection. A queen breeder can make the best improvement in mite resistance by making careful comparisons of potential breeding sources. There are two common approaches to making such comparisons. Each involves exposing bees from the various sources to uniform conditions so that they are challenged equally by mites. As exemplified by the program in Ontario, Canada[24], newly emerged worker bees are obtained from potential breeder queens, marked to identify their colony sources, and placed in a mite-infested colony. After about a week the marked bees are retrieved and their mite infestations are measured (Fig. 9.2). Breeder queens are selected based on their progeny having low mite prevalences and abundances. In another approach, a large group of mite infested bees can be divided into packages and used to start colonies which are then each given a potential breeder queen. Mite infestations are monitored through time to look for differences among the potential breeder colonies. Taber[30] described how he used this system in a commercial program.

A third option is to let natural selection enhance mite resistant bees. In areas where tracheal mites are known to cause problems, the simple approach of not treating with acaricides, accepting natural rates of colony loss from parasitism, and then propagating only from the best colonies has been shown to improve mite resistance in the population of selected colonies (for example, see Loper & others[20]).

In all these approaches, the best results are obtained when queens are raised from the best breeding colonies and mated to drones also of resistant colonies, either by instrumental insemination, by conducting matings in isolated areas, or by maintaining large populations of select-stock drones in mating areas. However, the high heritability of the trait of resistance suggests that acceptable progress could be achieved using queens outcrossed to non-selected drone sources.

Summary. These are times of both extraordinary challenges and opportunities in North American beekeeping. Beekeepers who are willing to broaden their management repertoire will be best able to cope with the challenges. It is clear that tracheal mite resistant stocks of bees exist and can be useful to mitigate problems. Several different resistant stocks are available, and bee breeders can use these to incorporate resistance into breeding lines as new stocks are being developed. Alternatively, breeders can select within existing stocks for improved resistance. A willingness for bee breeders to create new and improved bee stocks and for beekeepers to experiment with and adopt new stocks is essential for the continued vitality of the craft of beekeeping.

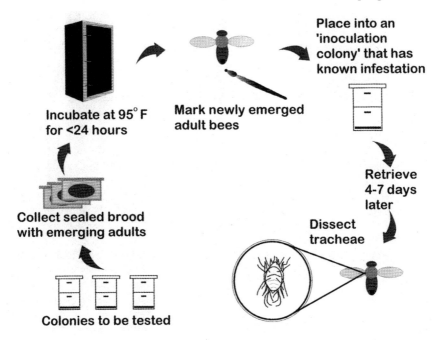

Place into an 'inoculation colony' that has known infestation

Incubate at 95°F for <24 hours

Mark newly emerged adult bees

Retrieve 4-7 days later

Collect sealed brood with emerging adults

Dissect tracheae

Colonies to be tested

▲*Figure 9.2 Schematic diagram of a procedure that can be used to determine the relative susceptibility of colonies to infestation by tracheal mites. Brood combs with emerging bees are brushed free of adult bees and then placed in cages or screen bags to isolate bees of each test colony. The caged combs are held in an incubator or in a colony, and 30-60 worker bees that emerge within 12-24 hours are marked with plastic tags or enamel paint to differentiate colony sources. The young marked bees are placed into an inoculation colony in which the mite prevalence of worker bees ideally is 30-70%. After retrieval, marked bees are dissected to determine mite prevalences or mite abundances for the bees from each test colony source.*

Acknowledgments. I thank Keith Delaplane, Medhat Nasr, Dale Pollet and José Villa for comments on a draft of this chapter. Medhat Nasr kindly permitted use of the data in Fig. 9.1.

References cited.

1   Adam, Bro. 1968. "Isle of Wight" or acarine disease: its historical and practical aspects. Bee World 49: 6-18.

2. Anderson, J. 1930. "Isle of Wight disease" in bees—I. Bee World 11: 37-42, 50-53.

3. Bailey, L. 1965. The effect of *Acarapis woodi* on honeybees from North America. J. Apic. Res. 5: 105-108.

4. Bailey, L. 1967. The incidence of *Acarapis woodi* in North American strains of honeybee in Britain. J. Apic. Res. 6: 99-103.

5. Calvert, F.M.W. 1957. Acarine disease. Four years' experience with resistant strain of bees. Scot. Beekeeper 33: 39-41.

6. Clark, K.J., E. Huxter, N.J. Gates & T.I. Szabo. 1990. Screening breeder honey bee stock for resistance to tracheal mites. Am. Bee J. 130: 800.

7. Cobey, S. & B.H. Smith. 1994. Analysis of tracheal mite infestation levels of Buckfast and Carniolan honey bees and their reciprocal hybrids. Am. Bee J. 134: 829-830.

8. Danka, R.G. & J.D. Villa. 1996a. Comparative susceptibility of Africanized honey bees from south Texas to infestation by *Acarapis woodi*. Southwest Entomol. 21: 451-456.

9. Danka, R.G. & J.D. Villa. 1996b. Influence of resistant honey bee hosts on the life history of the parasite *Acarapis woodi*. Exp. Appl. Acarol. 20: 313-322.

10. Danka, R.G. & J.D. Villa. 1998. Evidence of autogrooming as a mechanism of honey bee resistance to tracheal mites. J. Apic. Res. 37: 39-46.

11. Danka, R.G. & J.D. Villa. Unpublished data.

12. Danka, R.G., J.D. Villa, T.E. Rinderer & G.T. Delatte. 1995. Field test of resistance to *Acarapis woodi* (Acari: Tarsonemidae) infestation and of colony production by four stocks of honey bees (Hymenoptera: Apidae). J. Econ. Entomol. 88: 584-591.

13. Frazier, M.T., J. Finley, B. McPheron, W. Harkness & G. Stiles. 1995. Evaluating honey bee lines for tracheal mite resistance in the Northeastern United States. Am. Bee J. 135: 635-638.

14. Gary, N.E. & R.E. Page Jr. 1987. Phenotypic variation in susceptibility of honey bees, *Apis mellifera*, to infestation by tracheal mites, *Acarapis woodi*. Exp. Appl. Acarol. 3: 291-305.

15. Gary, N.E., R.E. Page Jr., R.A. Morse, C.E. Henderson, M.E. Nasr & K. Lorenzen. 1990. Comparative resistance of honey bees (*Apis mellifera* L.) from Great Britain and United States to infestation by tracheal mites (*Acarapis woodi*). Am. Bee J. 130: 667-669.

16. Guzman, L.I. de; T.E. Rinderer & L.D. Beaman. 1996. Attractiveness to infestation by tracheal mites, *Acarapis woodi* (Rennie) in three stocks of honey bees and two of their hybrids. BeeScience (in press).

17. Guzman, L.I. de; T.E. Rinderer & G.T. Delatte. 1998. Comparative resistance of four honey bee (Hymenoptera: Apidae) stocks to infestation by *Acarapis woodi* (Acari: Tarsonemidae). J. Econ. Entomol. 91: 1078-1083.

18. Kjer, K.M., D.W. Ragsdale & B. Furgala. 1989. A retrospective and prospective overview of the honey bee tracheal mite, *Acarapis woodi* R. Am. Bee J. 129: 25-28, 112-115.

19. Lin, H., G.W. Otis & C. Scott-Dupree. 1996. Comparative resistance in Buckfast and Canadian stocks of honey bees (*Apis mellifera* L.) to infestation by honey bee tracheal mites (*Acarapis woodi* (Rennie). Exp. Appl. Acarol. 20: 87-101.

20. Loper, G.M., G.D. Waller, D. Steffens & R.M. Roselle. 1992. Selection and controlled natural mating: A solution to the honey bee tracheal mite problem. Am. Bee J. 132: 603-606.

21. Milne, C.P., G.W. Otis, F.A. Eischen & J.M. Dormaier. 1991. A comparison of tracheal mite resistance in two commercially available stocks of honey bees. Am. Bee J. 131: 713-718.

22. **Morse, R.A. 1990.** Importation of British queen honey bees into the United States. Am. Bee J. 130: 106-107, 116-120.

23. **Nasr, M.E. 1995.** Tracheal mite resistance technology transfer, annual report. Ontario Beekeepers' Association, Department of Environmental Biology, University of Guelph, Guelph, Ontario, Canada, 29 pp.

24. **Nasr, M.E. & D. McRory. 1998.** Integrated parasitic mite management in honey bees: from laboratory tests to field implementation. Am. Bee J. 138: 298.

25. **Otis, G.W. 1990.** Results of a survey on the economic impact of tracheal mites. Am. Bee J. 130: 28-31.

26. **Otis, G.W. & C.D. Scott-Dupree. 1992.** Effects of *Acarapis woodi* on overwintered colonies of honey bees (Hymenoptera: Apidae) in New York. J. Econ. Entomol. 85: 40-46.

27. **Page, R.E. Jr. & N.E. Gary. 1990.** Genotypic variation in susceptibility of honey bees (*Apis mellifera*) to infestation by tracheal mites (*Acarapis woodi*). Exp. Appl. Acarol. 8: 275-283.

28. **Pettis, J.S. & T. Pankiw. 1998.** Grooming behavior by *Apis mellifera* L. in the presence of *Acarapis woodi* (Rennie) (Acari: Tarsonemidae). Apidologie 29: 241-253.

29. **Szabo, T.I., L.P. Lefkovitch & K.J. Clark. 1991.** Comparative resistance of honey bees from a closed population to infestation by tracheal mites. Am. Bee J. 131: 643-645.

30. **Taber, S. 1989.** Our breeding program for resistance to the tracheal mite. Am. Bee J. 129: 593, 595.

31. **Taber, S. 1990.** Breeding acarine resistant bees—second generation. Am. Bee J. 130: 115-116.

32. **Webster, K. 1991.** Honey bee breeding in the Northeast—starting again. Am. Bee J. 131: 20-24.

33. **Wilson, W.T., J.R. Baxter, W.L. Rubink, C. Garza-Q & A.M. Collins. 1995.** Parasitic mite population changes during Africanization of managed honey bee colonies in Mexico. Am. Bee J. 135: 833.

Chapter 10

BIOLOGY AND LIFE HISTORY OF VARROA MITES

Stephen J. Martin

The ectoparasitic mite *Varroa jacobsoni* Oud. belongs to a small group of three highly specialized blood-feeding mite species which are closely associated with the Asian cavity-nesting honey bees *Apis cerana* and *A. koschevnikovi*. The Asian bush-nesting honey bees *A. florea* and *A. andreniformis* are hosts to the closely related *Euvarroa* spp., while *A. dorsata* and *A. laboriosa* are hosts to the *Tropilaelaps* mites (Table 10.1). All of these mites reproduce within the sealed honey bee brood. *V. jacobsoni* cannot survive on any non-*Apis* species, for example wasps or bumble bees. When man moved the western honey bee *A. mellifera* colonies into the Asian region, *V. jacobsoni* was able to cross over to the *A. mellifera* bee which was ill-adapted to cope with this new 'exotic' parasite. However, this did not occur immediately as *A. mellifera* and *A. cerana* colonies were kept together for 50-100 years in Japan and China[34] before any *A. mellifera* colony deaths were reported. A similar situation has been reported in Papua, New Guinea and Indonesia[1] and an explanation is currently

Natural honey bee-brood mite relationships

Mite species[1]		Bee species	Nesting habitat
Varroa jacobsoni V. underwoodi V. rindereri		Apis cerana A. cerana A. koschevnikovi	Cavity
Euvarroa sinhai E. wongsirii		A. florea A. andreniformis	Bush
Tropilaelaps clareae T. koenigerum		A. dorsata A. laboriosa	Cliff/tree

1 Not drawn to scale

▲ *Table 10.1 Associations of mites which reproduce in the brood of honey bees* (Apis *spp.). (Adapted from Martin[32])*

being investigated.

The first records of *A. mellifera* colonies collapsing due to *V. jacobsoni* occurred in the 1960s and since then it has spread rapidly around the world, reflecting the world-wide trade in honey bees. It is absent only from Australia[36].

The female *V. jacobsoni* mite, known commonly as varroa, is a large (length 1.1 mm; width 1.6 mm) reddish brown, crab shaped mite (Fig. 10.1a). In relation to the size of its host the female mite represents one of the largest ectoparasites known. The spherical shaped soft bodied, greenish-white male (Fig. 10.1b) is much smaller (length 0.8 mm; width 0.7 mm) and seldom seen, living entirely within the sealed honey bee brood cell.

The mite's life history falls into two distinct phases (Fig. 10.2):
(1) The phoretic (carrying) phase, during which the adult female mite lives on the adult bee, and
(2) The reproductive phase, during which the mite reproduces within the sealed honey bee brood cell.

Phoretic phase. When the bees emerge from their cells they release the

▲*Figure 10.1a Scanning electron microscope photograph of the adult female* Varroa jacobsoni.

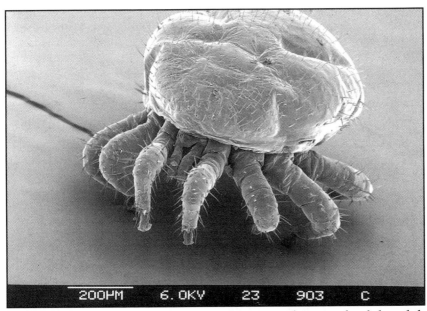

▲*Figure 10.1b Scanning electron microscope photograph of the adult male* Varroa jacobsoni.

mites into the hostile hive environment. The male mite and any immature females soon perish. However, the adult female mite is very well
adapted for life on the adult bees. The flattened crab-like body shape,
which is unusual in mites, enables the mites to fit neatly in between the
segments of the bee's abdomen. Claws which can grasp the hairs of the
bee at the end of each leg[40], and stiff ventral setae (hairs), which mesh
with the bee's hairs, allow the mites to remain firmly attached to their
host. The mite's cuticle (skin) is heavily sclerotized (thickened), which
helps reduce water loss. It has a chemical pattern similar to that of the
bee's cuticle, which may help camouflage the mite within the bee
hive[38]. Mites are normally found tucked between the 3rd and 4th
abdominal sclerites (segmental plates) predominantly on the left hand
side[11]. Once established in this position the mites are difficult to
remove even by the social grooming of *A. cerana* bees, a behavior generally lacking in *A. mellifera*[18]. This position also allows the mites to
pierce the thin intersegmental membrane which joins the bee's segments together and so feed undisturbed on the blood of the bee, using
their modified stylet-shaped mouthparts (Fig. 10.1c).

These adaptations allow the mite to survive the long time (55-134
days) between drone rearing periods in *A. cerana*[41]. Hence the varroa
mite was already well suited for surviving the long winter broodless
periods of its new host *A. mellifera* in temperate regions. Mites in the

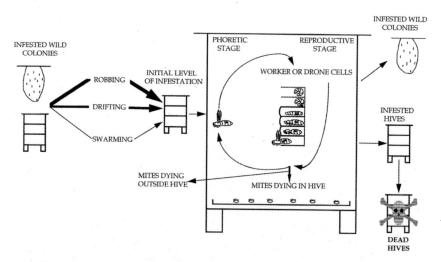

▲*Figure 10.2 Life cycle of the* Varroa jacobsoni *and mode of dispersal
in apiaries.*

laboratory have been observed to live for up to 80-100 days[44] while reproducing, but their life expectancy under natural conditions has been estimated at an average of 27 days when *A. mellifera* brood is present[12]. It must exceed 5-6 months during the winter broodless period.

The duration of the phoretic period is dependent on the mite's chances of being taken to a suitable cell by its host, which depends on the number of brood cells in relation to the number of adult bees[6]. Therefore, more brood cells and fewer bees increase the chance that a mite is carried close enough to a suitable cell to invade, thus shortening the phoretic period. When brood is present, phoretic periods of between 4.5 to 11 days have been recorded, while an average period of 4 to 6 days can be predicted by using the above concept in a model[35].

Mites artificially transferred from one cell to another, without passing any time on the adult bee, are still able to reproduce[44] although at a reduced rate when compared with mites that have spent some time on an adult bee[3]. However, under natural conditions mites need only a short time on the adult bee, less than one day, for their subsequent reproductive ability to be unimpaired[8]. The minimum necessary phoret-

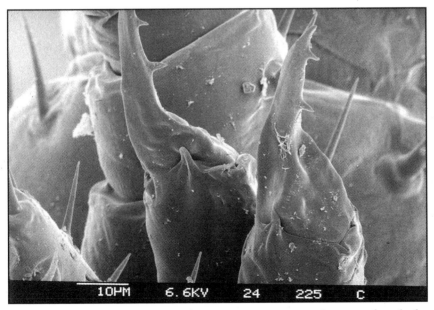

▲*Figure 10.1c Scanning electron microscope photograph of the* Varroa jacobsoni *mite along with the modified mouthparts for feeding in the female.*

ic period is probably linked to maturation of the sperm within the female (see **Mating**, below).

Dispersal. Only the adult female mites disperse between colonies, aided by the behavior of the adult bees. The mites can live only a limited time (2-3 days) if they become accidentally detached from the bee[21]. This period can be extended to 5-10 days when high humidity is present. However, despite this dependence on the host the mites are able to disperse very effectively. Nearly all *A. cerana* colonies are infested[41] and the same applies regionally to *A. mellifera* colonies, once the mite becomes established within an area. The mites are able to disperse between bee colonies by utilizing three different bee behaviors: robbing, drifting and swarming.

Robbing. Infested colonies weakened by the activities of the mite are prone to robbing by other stronger colonies. Sakofski[46] showed that 35% of the mites can be transferred into the robbing colony via the robber bees picking up mites or infested robbed bees which desert their hive and return with the robber bees.

Drifting. Bees have long been known to drift from hive to hive, especially the drones which may visit many hives during their lifetime and would appear to be excellent dispersal agents for the mite. However, Greatti & others[20], have shown that mite invasion rates into *A. mellifera* colonies were similar irrespective of whether drones were excluded or not, suggesting that in at least *A. mellifera* it is the worker bees which play the major role in mite dispersal. It has been suggested[43] that the mites may disorientate the bees, thus aiding their dispersal by drifting but this attractive idea needs to be substantiated.

Swarming. Although of minor importance in managed *A. mellifera* colonies swarming is possibly the main method of mite dispersal in natural *A. cerana* colonies. When any infested colony swarms, both halves of the colony will contain a proportion of the mite population.

Dispersal rates appear to be linked to a combination of mite buildup and changes in bee behavior, with peak dispersal occurring in September and October in northern temperate regions. This corresponds with the peak in mite numbers and the peak in robbing activity due to the lack of nectar flow. Since at this time there is little brood production, the majority of mites will be on the adult bees resulting in up to 100 mites being transferred daily[20].

Reproductive phase. Varroa's entire reproductive cycle consists of four developmental stages: egg, protonymph, deutonymph, and adult. Mating is completed within the sealed honey bee brood cells. So the behavior and physiology of the mites exhibit a high degree of adaptation to changes that occur in their host during this time[14]. Many of these adaptations have been revealed by a variety of studies. They have recently been linked together by continuous observations, using transparent cells, of the mite's reproductive activity[13].

Most of the reproductive biology of the mite has been determined from observations using *A. mellifera* since only limited data from *A. cerana*[10] exist. However, these limited data and the large body of data from *A. mellifera* studies suggest that at present the reproductive biology, with certain exceptions, is similar in both the new and natural hosts.

Cell invasion. Mite invasion of either a worker or drone cell starts when the bee larva completely covers the cell bottom and continues until the cell is sealed. In *A. mellifera* this period lasts for 40-50 hours (drone brood) or 15-20 hours (worker brood)[5,23]. During this time the rate of invasion is fairly constant. Video observations have revealed that when a mite is carried by a bee close to a suitable cell, the mite moves directly from the bee down the side of the cell and immerses itself in the brood food under the larva[7]. The stimulus informing the mite which cell is suitable for invasion may be a volatile chemical, since changes in the cell volume alter the attractive period of that cell[9].

Mites have a strong preference (6 to 12 times) for drone brood over worker brood, although 60% of this preference is probably due to larger size of drone larvae[35]. The mites also show a preference for younger (nurse) bees over older (foraging) bees, which enhances their chances of coming into contact with suitable brood cells to invade[24].

Once the mite enters the brood food under the larva it becomes immobilized. While immersed in this liquid environment it erects its peretrimes (aquatic breathing tubes) which aid respiration[17].

Oviposition (egg laying). After the cell is capped by the adult bee, the larva consumes the remaining brood food within the first five hours and so releases the mites. This explains the observations of Infantidis[23] and Martin[28,29] that within six hours after cell capping 100% (in worker cells) or 90% (in drone cells) of the mites are released from the brood food. The mite remains on the larva, feeding regularly as the larva spins its cocoon and thus avoids becoming entombed between the cell wall and cocoon[16]. During this early stage the mite repeatedly probes the anal zone of the bee and defecates at random on the cell wall[14].

Mites artificially introduced into cells which have been sealed longer than 24 hours fail to reproduce, suggesting that the timing of the first feeding is crucial if the mite is to reproduce[48]. High humidity levels (80%+) also cause the mites not to reproduce[25]. Often 'infertile' mites remain in the anal region for the entire larval development period and establish atypical feeding and defecation sites[34].

As soon as the mite starts to feed, her first egg starts to develop. This is completed in around 30 hours and is followed by the equally rapid development of the embryo. The first egg hatches to an eight-legged protonymph around 60 hours after cell sealing. In *A. cerana* drone brood, the first egg in laid around 68-70 hours after cell sealing; hence the mites' development runs around 8-10 hours behind that found in *A. mellifera*[10].

Because the entire mite reproductive cycle must be completed within the limited period imposed by the development of the bee, *V. jacobsoni* has greatly compressed its early developmental stages, omitting the normal 6-legged larval stage[48]. Also, proteins ingested by the mite from the bee's blood can be detected unaltered in the mite's egg[50], which again may help speed up development. This direct use of unaltered host proteins is known to occur in only a few other parasitic arthropods and indicates a high degree of parasitic adaptation with its host.

The first egg, which is unfertilized, develops into a male and is laid in the top part of the cell near the entrance. The protonymph hatches some 30 hours later if it is facing the cell wall and therefore successfully emerges from the eggshell, otherwise it will perish. This position protects the egg from disturbance during the moulting of the bee from the larva to a pupa, since disturbed eggs often fail to hatch. All subsequent eggs, are fertilized, develop into females and are laid in the base of the cell near the bee fecal area at approximately 25-30 hour intervals after the first (male) egg is laid[14,22,29].

The developing eggs swell the body of the foundress mite, and since the developmental periods of individual eggs overlap, the foundress remains in a swollen state until egg laying ceases.

Feeding and fecal sites. After bee pupation the mother mite attempts to increase the free space around the newly established feeding site, usually located on the 5th ventral abdominal segment, by pushing aside the bee's third pair of legs. An area for voiding feces is established on the cell wall near to the feeding site. The fecal site is used by the mother mite and her offspring to rest between feeding bouts and as a rendezvous site for mating. The mother mite's feeding activity at the site enables the protonymphs to feed easily. They die if the mother mite is absent, indicating that *V. jacobsoni* shows some parental care and therefore basic sociality[14].

Development of the progeny. The developmental time of the mite's offspring has been the world-wide focus of much research over the past decade since it is an important factor when determining the speed at which infestations can develop. An error in the assumed order in which the sexes are laid, corrected by Rehm and Ritter[42], resulted in an overestimation of developmental times. More recent studies in the field[28,29] and laboratory[14] have shown that the development of the mites occurs at a similar rate in drone or worker cells and in different races of *A. mellifera*. Figure 10.3 illustrates the daily development of each mite in *A. mellifera* brood cells. The mite has yet to adapt to its new host since it could greatly increase its reproductive efficiency by decreasing, by two, the number of eggs laid in *A. mellifera* worker brood and even increasing, by one, the number of eggs laid in *A. mellifera* drone cells.

Egg mortality and the speed of mite development are very sensitive to changes in temperature[39]. The optimal temperature for the mite is similar to that for the bee, 36°C.

During the last moult the deutonymph sheds an exuvium (skin). It provides a useful aid for determining the number of adult offspring produced in that cell, since the pale, newly moulted adult female mites soon darken and become indistinguishable from their mother.

Mating. Mating in *V. jacobsoni* is between brother and sister (inbreeding) and occurs within the protected environment of the sealed cell. During the final moult the male's mouth-parts change from spear shaped feeding structures to hollow tubes (Fig. 10.1d). These allow the male to transfer packets of sperm (spermatozoa) to the openings at the

DRONE

WORKER

Figure 10.3 Daily development of Varroa jacobsoni offspring in both Apis mellifera worker and drone brood. The survivorship of each offspring at bee emergence is given. (after Martin[32]).

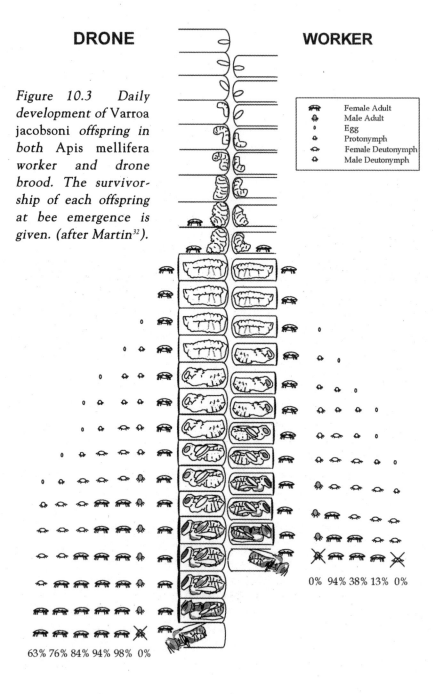

	Female Adult
	Male Adult
	Egg
	Protonymph
	Female Deutonymph
	Male Deutonymph

0% 94% 38% 13% 0%

63% 76% 84% 94% 98% 0%

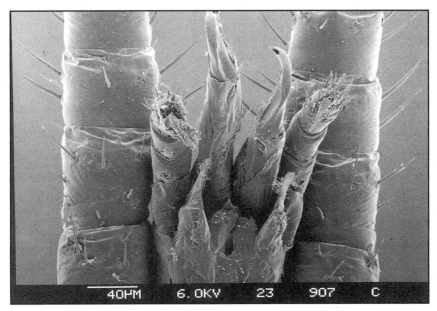

▲*Figure 10.1d Scanning electron microscope photograph of the male* Varroa jacobsoni *mouth parts modified for sperm transfer.*

base of the third pair of legs on the female. Despite this dramatic change in the mouth-parts the male is able to feed, due to the feeding site having been kept open by the mother mite and her daughters[15].

Due to the differences between male and female development times, the male matures immediately prior to the first female (Fig. 10.3) and mates with her and all subsequent female offspring as soon as they have completed their final moult. Mating occurs at the fecal area to which the mites return after each feeding bout. Multiple matings are required if the female's spermatheca is to be filled[15]. Soon after mating is completed the sperm transport system in the female degenerates[2] thereby preventing any future mating. If females are not mated soon after moulting, e.g. due to the premature death of the male, they are unable to produce any viable offspring and are therefore non-reproductive, or infertile[34]. Newly fertilized females cannot lay fertilized eggs immediately since the final stages of spermatogenesis occur in the female reproductive system, taking 4-13 days depending on the maturity of the female[2]. Inbreeding and the very stable environment within the cell may account for the very low level of genetic variability observed between mite populations[24]. Matings by different males in multiply invaded cells will reduce the level of inbreeding. However, in *A. cerana* this will occur infrequently since a multiple infestation is more likely to kill the drone pupa and with it the mites[41].

Mortality. Although the sealed cell within the bee hive provides a protected and very stable environment (the brood nest temperature varies by ± 0.5 C°), it contains many hazards for the mites. In *A. mellifera* a small number (1-3%) of the mother mites become entombed between the cell wall and the cocoon, so fail to escape from the brood food, with a further 1-5% dying during reproduction[26,28,29]. In contrast, mite offspring suffer much higher rates (4-100%) of mortality, depending on the sex and time when they are laid (Fig. 3). Although the pattern of offspring mortality is similar, the levels are much lower in drone cells than worker cells. However, in *A. cerana* drone cells the levels of offspring mortality are greatly reduced[10]. The development time of *A. mellifera* worker bees (12 days) is shorter than the drones which means there is insufficient time for the fifth offspring (fourth female) to mature before the bee emerges, so these offspring always die. There is also barely enough time for the fourth offspring, which matures at the same time as the bee. During the emergence of infested worker brood in *A. mellifera* there is an associated natural mite fall to the hive bottom predominantly consisting of pale mites. Almost half of these mites are still alive and probably fail to get established on the bees immediately after emergence[33].

Multiply-invaded cells. If an *A. cerana* drone cell is invaded by more than one mite, there is a greatly increased chance that those mites will kill their host. This results in the death of the bee pupa and therefore all the mites within the cell since they cannot remove the thick drone capping[41]. This is a critical difference between *A. mellifera* and *A. cerana*[4] since in *A. mellifera* many mother mites can invade a single cell and reproduce successfully without killing the host bee. When *A. mellifera* cells are invaded by more than one mite, competition between offspring at the feeding site increases the offspring mortality, especially of the younger stages[30]. Also the mother mites in heavily infested cells show a decrease in the number of eggs laid per mite[27,49].

Fertility and population growth. When mites are artificially transferred from cell to cell, they can produce a maximum of 30 eggs[44]. This figure is supported by studies[2] which reveal that V. *jacobsoni* ovaries contain around 25 eggs. Each mite can alter the number of eggs it lays depending on the type of cell it invades[31]. In *A. mellifera* brood cells, it normally lays five eggs in worker cells and six in drone cells. More eggs are laid in drone than worker cells because, although egg laying ceases when the pupa are of a similar physiological age, the longer developmental period of the drone brood means that this point is reached some 30 hours later than in the worker brood.

In temperate Europe where most of the mite research has been conducted, a normally reproducing mite whose offspring suffer no mortality can produce 2-3 mated females in *A. mellifera* worker cells or 5 in drone cells. However, after offspring mortality and infertile mites are taken into account, the average number of new viable female offspring produced per mite after invading a brood cell falls to around 1 (worker) and 2-2.2 (drone) in *A. mellifera*. Subsequent mortality of the new female mites before they invade cells to reproduce will reduce these figures even more. In *A. cerana* drone brood the combination of lower offspring mortality and very high (90-100%) levels of fertile mothers, results in 4.5-4.6 daughters being produced per mite after 9 days[10].

This means that for the mite population to increase in *A. mellifera* colonies, each mother mite must invade a cell and reproduce more than once during its lifetime. Artificial transfers of mites from cell to cell have shown that mites can reproduce up to seven times[37,44] with an average of 3.6 cell entries per mite. Field trials put this figure between 1-1.5[47], although past experiments have always suffered from large losses of mites due to the experimental techniques. Recent field work has suggested that the mean number of reproductive cycles is around 1.7-2[19] or 2-3[33].

These figures combine to allow a mite population to increase 12 fold in a colony which has brood present 128 days yearly or 800 fold where brood is present continuously through one year[35]. This means a mite population can recover to previous levels within a year even after a highly effective (90%) treatment has been administered.

Summary. The life history of *Varroa jacobsoni* consists of a phoretic phase and a reproductive phase. During the phoretic phase the adult female mite is attached between the segments of the bee's abdomen. Mites disperse among hives by the robbing, drifting and swarming behavior of the bees. The mite begins its reproductive phase by leaving the adult bee and entering a bee brood cell. Approximately 60 hours after the invading mite begins to feed, her first egg, a male, is laid. All subsequent eggs develop at 25 to 30 hour intervals to become females. Mating between the offspring occurs within the brood cell. When the parasitized bee emerges, the male and any immature mites die. The average number of mature female offspring produced is about one in a worker cell and 2.2 in a drone cell, when mite mortality and infertility are taken into account.

References cited.
1. Anderson, D. L. & Sukarsih. 1996. Changed *Varroa jacobsoni* reproduction in *Apis mellifera* colonies in Java. Apidologie 27: 461-466.

2. Akimov, I. A., A. V. Yastrebtsov & V. T. Gorgol. 1988. Functional and morphological specialisation of *Varroa jacobsoni* for parasitism, pp. 475-497. *In* G. R. Needham, R. E. Page, M. Delfinado-Baker, C. E. Bowman [eds], Africanized honey bees and bee mites. Halsted Press, New York.

3. Beetsma, J. & K. Zonneveld. 1992. Observations on the initiation and stimulation of oviposition of the *Varroa* mite. Exp. Appl. Acarol. 16: 303-312.

4. Boecking, O. & W. Ritter. 1994. Current status of behavioural tolerance of the honey bee *Apis mellifera* to the mite *Varroa jacobsoni*. Am. Bee J. 134: 689-694.

5. Boot, W. J., J. N. M. Calis & J. Beetsma 1992. Differential periods of *Varroa* mite invasion into worker and drone cells of honey bees. Exp. Appl. Acarol. 16: 295-301.

6. Boot, W. J., D. J. A. Sisselaar, J. N. M. Calis & J. Beetsma. 1994. Factors affecting invasion of *Varroa jacobsoni* (Acari: Varroidae) into honeybee, *Apis mellifera* (Hymenoptera: Apidae), brood cells. Bull. Entomol. Res. 84: 3-10.

7. Boot, W. J., J. Beetsma & J. N. M. Calis. 1994. Behaviour of *Varroa* mites invading honey bee brood cell. Exp. Appl. Acarol. 18: 371-379.

8. Boot, W. J., J. N. M. Calis & J. Beetsma. 1995. Does time spent on adult bees affect reproductive success of *Varroa* mites ? Entomol. Exp. Appl. 75: 1-7.

9. Boot, W. J., R. G. Driessen, J. N. M. Calis & J. Beetsma. 1995. Further observations on the correlation between attractiveness of honey bee brood cells to *Varroa jacobsoni* and the distance from larva to cell rim. Entomol. Exp. Appl. 76: 223-232.

10. Boot, W. J., N. Q. Tan, P. C. Dien, L. V. Huan, N. V. Dung, L. T. Long & J. Beetsma. 1997. Reproductive success of *Varroa jacobsoni* in brood of its original host, *Apis cerana*, in comparison to that of its new host, *A. mellifera* (Hymenoptera: Apidae). Bull. Entomol. Res. 87: 119-126.

11. Bowen-Walker, P. L., S. J. Martin & A. Gunn. 1997. Preferential distribution of the parasitic mite, *Varroa jacobsoni* Oud. on overwintering honeybee (*Apis mellifera* L.) workers and changes in the level of parasitism. Parasitology 114: 151-157.

12. Calatayud, F. & M. J. Verdu. 1995. Life expectancy of the mite *Varroa jacobsoni* Oud. (Mesostigmata: Varroidae) in colonies of the honey bee *Apis mellifera* L. during brood rearing periods. Invest. Agr.: Prod. Sanid. Anim. 10:153-161. (in Spanish)

13. Donzé, G. 1995. Behavioural attributes of the parasitic mite *Varroa jacobsoni* during its reproductive phase in the brood of the honey bee *Apis mellifera*. PhD thesis. Université de Neuchâtel, Switzerland.

14. Donzé, G., & P. M. Guerin. 1994. Behavioural attributes and parental care of *Varroa* mites parasitizing honeybee brood. Behav. Ecol. Sociobiol. 34: 305-319.

15. Donzé, G., M. Herrmann, B. Bachofen & P. M. Guerin. 1996. Effect of mating frequency and brood cell infestation rate on the reproductive success of the honeybee parasite *Varroa jacobsoni*. Ecol. Entomol. 21: 17-26.

16. Donzé, G. & P. M. Guerin. 1997. Time-activity budgets and space structuring by the different life stages of *Varroa jacobsoni* in capped brood of the honey bee *Apis mellifera*. J. Ins. Behav. 10: 371-393.

17. Evans, G. O. 1992. Principles of Acarology. C.A.B. International, 563 pp.

18. Fries, I., W. Huazhen, S. Wei & C. S. Jin. 1996. Grooming behaviour and damaged mites (*Varroa jacobsoni*) in *Apis cerana cerana* and *Apis mellifera ligustica*. Apidologie 27: 3-11.

19. Fries, I. & P. Rosenkranz. 1996. Number of reproductive cycles of *Varroa jacobsoni* in honey-bee (*Apis mellifera*) colonies. Exp. Appl. Acarol. 20: 103-112.

20. Greatti, M., N. Milani, & F. Nazzi. 1992. Reinfestation of an acaricide-treated apiary by *Varroa jacobsoni* Oud. Exp. Appl. Acarol. 16: 279-286.

21. Guzman, De. L. I., T. E. Rinderer & L. D. Beaman. 1993. Survival of *Varroa jacobsoni* Oud. (Acari: Varroidae) away from its living host *Apis mellifera* L. Exp. Appl. Acarol. 17: 283-290.

22. Ifantidis, M. D. 1983. Ontogenesis of the mite *Varroa jacobsoni* in worker and drone brood cells. J. Apic. Res. 22: 200-206.

23. Ifantidis, M. D. 1988. Some aspects of the process of *Varroa jacobsoni* mite entrance into honey bee (*Apis mellifera*) brood cells. Apidologie 19: 387-396.

24. Kraus, B., & G. Hunt. 1995. Differentiation of *Varroa jacobsoni* Oud. populations by random amplification of polymorphic DNA (RAPD). Apidologie 26: 283-290.

25. Kraus, B. & H. H. W. Velthuis. 1997. High humidity in the honey bee (*Apis mellifera* L.) brood nest limits reproduction of the parasitic mite *Varroa jacobsoni* Oud. Naturwissenschaften 84: 217-218.

26. Kustermann, T. 1990. Untersuchungen zur Populationsstruktur der Milbe *Varroa jacobsoni* Oud. in Zellen schlupfender Arbeiterinnenbrut von *Apis mellifera* L. Diplomarbeit; Universitat Hohenheim, Stuttgart-Hohenheim, Germany; 70 pp.

27. Marcangeli, J. & M. Eguaras. 1997. [Reduced reproductive potential in *Varroa jacobsoni* (Acari: Varroidae) caused by multiple infestation of drone brood cells of *Apis mellifera* (Hymenoptera: Apidae).] Rev. Soc. Entomol. Argent. 56: 137-140 (in Spanish).

28. Martin, S. J. 1994. Ontogenesis of the mite *Varroa jacobsoni* Oud. in worker brood of the honeybee *Apis mellifera* L. under natural conditions. Exp. Appl. Acarol. 18: 87-100.

29. **Martin, S. J. 1995.** Ontogenesis of the mite *Varroa jacobsoni* Oud. in drone brood of the honeybee *Apis mellifera* L. under natural conditions. Exp. & Appl. Acarol. 19: 199-210.

30. **Martin, S. J. 1995.** Reproduction of *Varroa jacobsoni* in cells of *Apis mellifera* containing one or more mother mites and the distribution of these cells. J. Apic. Res. 34: 187-196.

31. **Martin, S. J. & C. Cook. 1996.** Effect of host brood type on the number of offspring laid by the honeybee parasite *Varroa jacobsoni*. Exp. & Appl. Acarol. 20: 387-390.

32. **Martin, S. J. 1997.** Life and death of *Varroa*, pp 3-10. *In* P. Munn & R. Jones [eds.], Varroa! Fight the mite. Int. Bee Res. Assoc., Cardiff.

33. **Martin, S. J. & D. Kemp. 1997.** Average number of reproductive cycles performed by the parasitic mite *Varroa jacobsoni* in *Apis mellifera* colonies. J. Apic. Res. 36: 113-123.

34. **Martin, S. J., K. Holland, & M. Murray. 1997.** Non-reproduction in the honeybee mite *Varroa jacobsoni*. Exp. Appl. Acarol. 21: 539-549.

35. **Martin, S. J. 1998.** A population model for the ectoparasitic mite *Varroa jacobsoni* in honey bee (*A. mellifera*) colonies. Ecological Modeling 109: 267-281.

36. **Matheson, A. 1995.** World bee health update. Bee World 76: 31-39.

37. **Mikityuk, V. V. 1979.** Reproductive ability of *Varroa* females. Pchelovodstvo 9:21 (In Russian).

38. **Nation, J. L., M. T. Sanford & K. Milne. 1992.** Cuticular hydrocarbons from *Varroa jacobsoni*. Exp. Appl. Acarol. 16: 331-344.

39. **Piletskaya, I. V. 1988.** [Features of *Varroa jacobsoni* mite development in bee and drone brood]. Vestn. Zool. 2: 40-43 (In Russian).

40. **Ramirez W. B. & J. G. Malavasi. 1991.** Conformation of the ambulacrum of *Varroa jacobsoni* Oud. (Mesostigmata: Varroidae): a grasping structure. Int. J. Acarol. 17: 169-173.

41. **Rath, W. 1991.** Investigations on the parasitic mites *Varroa jacobsoni* Oud. and *Tropilaelaps clareae* Delfinado & Baker and their hosts *Apis cerana* Fabr., *Apis dorsata* Fabr. and *Apis mellifera* L.,

PhD Thesis, Mathematisch-Naturwissen- schaftlichen Fakultät der Rheinischen Friedrich Wilhelms Universität Bonn.

42. **Rehm, S. M. & W. Ritter. 1989.** Sequence of the sexes in the off-spring of *Varroa jacobsoni* and the resulting consequences for the calculation of the developmental period. Apidologie 20: 339-343.

43. **Ruano, V. M., F. M. Fernandez & A. C. Ochoa. 1991.** [Varroasis alters bees' sense of direction]. Vida Apicola 48: 55-57.

44. **Ruijter, A. 1987.** Reproduction of *Varroa jacobsoni* during successive brood cycles of the honeybee. Apidologie 18: 321-326.

45. **Ruttner, F. 1988.** Biogeography and taxonomy of the honey bee. Springer-Verlag Berlin Heidelberg 284 pp.

46. **Sakofski, F. 1989.** Transfer of *Varroa jacobsoni* by robbing. *In* Cavalloro, R [ed] Present status of varroatosis in Europe and progress in the *Varroa* mite control: Proceedings of a meeting of the EC expert's group, Udine, Italy, 28-30 November 1988, CEC, Luxembourg; pp 177-181.

47. **Schulz, A. E. 1984.** [Reproduction and population dynamics of the parasitic mite *Varroa jacobsoni* Oud. and its dependence on the brood cycle of its host *Apis mellifera* L.]. Apidologie 15: 401-420. (In German).

48. **Steiner, A., F. Dittmann, P. Rosenkranz & W. Engels. 1994.** The first gonocycle of the parasitic mite (*Varroa jacobsoni*) in relation to preimaginal development of its host, the honey bee (*Apis mellifera carnica*). Invertebr. *Repro. Develop.* 25: 175-183.

49. **Steiner, A., P. A. Diehl & M. Vlimant. 1995.** Vitellogenesis in *Varroa jacobsoni*, a parasite of honeybees. Exp. Appl. Acarol. 19: 411-422.

50. **Tewarson, T. & W. Engels. 1982.** Undigested uptake of non-host proteins by *Varroa jacobsoni*. J. Apic. Res. 21: 222-225.

Chapter 11

INTRODUCTION, SPREAD AND ECONOMIC IMPACT OF VARROA MITES IN NORTH AMERICA

M.T. Sanford

*I*ntroduction. The most significant event affecting 20th century apiculture has been human-assisted spread of the parasitic bee mite, *Varroa jacobsoni*. The Varroa mite transferred from its original host, *Apis cerana*, to the Western honey bee, *Apis mellifera*, in the 1950s and 1960s. This was a direct result of human colony movement between Asia and Europe. The mite quickly spread westward into Europe and was transferred from there to North Africa. It was also introduced from Japan into Paraguay, establishing a foothold in the Americas. It was first detected in North America in 1987 and since then spread to most regions except for isolated areas, such as the prairie provinces of Canada.

Because it is newly introduced to the European western honey bee (*Apis mellifera*), varroa does not have a "mature" relationship with this host. Thus, for most of North America, this means that almost all varroa-infested honey bee colonies eventually die, unless the beekeeper intervenes to reduce mite populations. This host-parasite relationship, however, does not appear to be the same everywhere. Although honey bees in North America appear to be extremely vulnerable to the mite, those in Brazil and Mexico, descendents of the African honey bee (*Apis mellifera scutellata*), appear to be less affected[35].

So far, eradication of varroa is not an option anywhere it has been introduced. Unfortunately, chemically treating for parasites hidden within the confines of one of nature's most complex insect societies, is no easy task. Worldwide it is estimated that beekeepers had experimented with over 140 different treatments with little success until adopting those based on the synthetic pyrethroids, fluvalinate and flumethrine. Both of these are highly effective and are today's most widely used varroacides. In spite of the effectiveness of treatment using this class of chemicals, the search for others continues as resistance is thought to be the result of routine use of only one class of substances. After a decade of synthetic pyrethroid use, resistance has in fact appeared in Italy, France and the United States (Chapter 17).

The worldwide introduction and spread of varroa has been well documented[8]. The purpose of this paper is to chronicle the mite's invasion of North America subsequent to its first detection. The history of the mite's treatment and varroa's economic effect on beekeeping in the region is also discussed.

Introduction of Varroa into the United States. With its history of successful invasion of three continents, it was only a matter of time until *Varroa jacobsoni* would be introduced to North America. It was no surprise, but still a shock, therefore, when the mite was finally discovered in Wisconsin, September 25, 1987. This find was officially confirmed by the Beltsville Bee Laboratory on September 29 the same year. The apiary consisting of twenty-one colonies of bees was subsequently destroyed. The source of the bees was determined to be packages from Florida. By October 20, nineteen of Florida's sixty-seven counties had positive finds[23].

Exactly how varroa was introduced into Florida remains an enigma. Although first found in 1987, the mite was probably introduced at least two to three years earlier. Many investigators believe it may take several years for an introduced population to reach detectable levels. Pinpointing the source of the mite is not just an academic exercise. There is information that various varroa subspecies might exist, some more virulent than others[12] (and see Chapters 1 and 18). One of the mechanisms thought to make mites less virulent is the variability that exists in reproductive rates on honey bees. At least two genetically distinct populations with different reproductive abilities have been reported[1].

Varroa First Found in Florida. Subsequent to the first find in Wisconsin, varroa was quickly discovered in a number of central Florida counties. The rapidity with which the mite was detected in the state was astounding, considering that Florida regulators had been collecting tracheal mite samples in earnest for several years without a single varroa mite being reported.

Events surrounding first detection in the state are found in official notices of the Apiary Bureau, Florida Department of Agriculture and Consumer Services:

September 28, 1987—Florida is notified that varroa apparently has been found in Wisconsin and that a connection with Florida is suspected.

September 29, 1987—*Varroa* is confirmed in Wisconsin by the United States Department of Agriculture. All Florida bee inspectors begin surveying for the mite.

September 30, 1987—A single bee colony near Oakland, Florida is found to be infested with varroa.

October 1, 1987—A meeting is held in Winter Garden, Florida to train bee inspectors and others in identifying and detecting the mite.

October 2, 1987—*Varroa* is found in a 14-colony beeyard south southeast of the first find in Orange County.

October 5, 1987—USDA APHIS (Animal and Plant Health Inspection Service) personnel and state inspectors find varroa in three beeyards in Lake County.

October 6, 1987—A field office for USDA APHIS and state inspectors is set up in Minneola, Florida.

October 7, 1987—Six survey teams are inspecting in the central part of the state. Mites are found in Lee, Brevard and Indian River counties.

October 9, 1987—The Honey Bee Technical Council of the Florida Department of Agriculture and Consumer Services convenes to discuss possible actions. The following measures are taken:
1. Quarantine movement of all bees in the state.
2. Prohibit moving honey supers from beeyard to honey house.
3. Provide for emergency movement of bees, if certified mite free.
4. Permit bees to enter the state and quarantining them in the unloading yard, unless found mite free.
5. Seek emergency authorization to use amitraz.

October 16, 1987—*Varroa* is found in thirteen central Florida counties, involving 1,740 colonies.

October 20, 1987—The Animal and Plant Health Inspection Service (USDA APHIS) approved a Section 18 crisis exemption to use plywood strips soaked with fluvalinate (Mavrik® or Spur®) as a survey tool for certification to move colonies. The Florida Department of Agriculture and Cooperative Extension Service establish several venues for beekeeper training around the state[24] USDA-APHIS also commissions a video on *Varroa* mite detection, completed in October 1988 by the Florida Cooperative Extension Service[25].

Surveys of beekeeping operations in Florida continued to discover mites on a regular basis. By February 6, 1988, twenty-nine counties contained 9,279 infested colonies.

Although the mite is universally present and routinely treated in Florida, the state has yet to deregulate varroa. This is to help comply with what is known as the "Eastern States' Agreement." This accord by a number of northeastern states ensures continued orderly movement of honey bees out of Florida for vital early spring pollination.

Varroa found in other states. The spread of varroa throughout the U.S.A. does not appear to have been orderly. As early as December 1987, eleven states had been found infested. On April 6, 1988, the USDA quarantined those (FL, IL, ME, MI, MS, NB, NY, OH, PA, SD, WI), plus two more (SC and WA)[2]. No varroa were found in California as late as March 1989[3] and Iowa was not reported infested until March

29 the following year[6]. In Kentucky it was detected as late as 1991[45]. A map of the eventual spread has been published[46]. Hawaii has yet to report the mite's presence. Over time, varroa continues to become a part of the beekeeping landscape everywhere in continental U.S.A.

Varroa introduced elsewhere in North America. Both Canada and Mexico closed their borders quickly following confirmation of varroa in the U.S.A. in 1987. Like similar measures in other infested countries in Europe, however, these actions probably delayed, but failed to keep the mite from becoming established. The first Canadian find was in New Brunswick, close to the Maine border in 1990[4]. By 1995, general finds were reported from a few operations in Alberta, Manitoba, Nova Scotia and Saskatchewan[46]. Pockets of varroa continue to show up in Canada. *Varroa* was recently discovered on Vancouver Island[44]. To date it has not yet been found on Prince Edward Island[19] and in portions of the Canadian prairie provinces, Alberta, Manitoba and Saskatchewan[13].

A reason for the lack of spread on the Canadian prairies is the relatively little movement for pollination that exists in these areas. Nevertheless, there continue to be regulations about bee movement in those areas and for Prince Edward Island, the only Canadian province still varroa free. Imports into these regions are confined to bees from New Zealand, Australia and Hawaii.

It took somewhat longer for varroa to be first detected in Mexico than in Canada. That occurred in 1992 near Veracruz[22]. Most of that country is now infested. Like elsewhere on the Continent, spread has not been uniform. *Varroa* was reported as far south as Yucatán in 1998[9]. As in other parts of tropical America inhabited by Africanized honey bees (*Apis mellifera* scutellata), the mite does not appear to be as virulent as in more temperate regions populated by European bees[5].

Initial Varroa treatment in Florida: Use of fluvalinate. On December 30, 1987, a Section 18 special exemption to use plywood strips soaked with fluvalinate (Mavrik® or Spur®) as treatment for varroa mites was approved. At that time, the treatment could only be used under compliance agreement with the Florida Department of Agriculture and Consumer Services. In 1998, the Training Division of the Department of Agriculture and the Florida Cooperative Extension Service conducted workshops around the state to train beekeepers in both formulating the treatment and following the specific regulations.

Permission to use wooden strips was rescinded on March 21, 1988. At that time, Apistan® plastic strips impregnated with the active ingredient fluvalinate entered the market place. This product still had to be used under a compliance agreement, however. A Section three general-use label, however, was subsequently issued for Apistan®[27].

At first, a once-a-year treatment with Apistan® was recommended in Florida. However, because of the warm climate with brood present all year long, Florida beekeepers have moved to a twice a year treatment schedule. There still remains no adequate economic threshold level that is generally accepted throughout the state, although the inspection service recommends treatment when standard ether rolls exceed 20 mites. Recommended thresholds have been established, however, in nearby Georgia and South Carolina[7].

Other treatments. An alternative treatment to Apistan®, Miticur®, a formulation of the active ingredient amitraz, received section three labeling in 1993[28]. The product was also effective in controlling the honey bee tracheal mite (*Acarapis woodi*). Thus, it would have provided a much-needed treatment that could be rotated with fluvalinate to delay the build up of pesticide resistance in mite populations.

Unfortunately, Miticur's® release was plagued with problems. Some honey bees in central Florida were alleged to have been damaged by the product. After legal action was taken by beekeepers, the manufacturer, Hoechst-Roussel Agri- Vet, settled out of court. Thus distribution of Miticur® was discontinued in late 1993, leaving the beekeeping industry with only one registered treatment[29]. There continues to be limited interest by some manufacturers in amitraz. That chemical is formulated on plastic strips for use in Europe under the trade name Apivar®.

In early 1999, partly because of resistance to fluvalinate, the coumaphos-based product (Bayer Bee Strip) was approved by the Environmental Protection Agency under a Section 18 exemption. Once approved for a Section 3 general use label, the product has been called CheckMite+®[42].

Formic acid, a so-called "soft" control is also an alternative control possibility. Canada already has registered the material and it is employed in Mexico as well. The use of other soft chemicals including oxalic acid and essential oils are also being explored both by researchers and beekeepers[36].

Varroa resistance to fluvalinate. First reports of possible resistance to fluvalinate in North America began to trickle in by July 1997; most had a Florida connection. Resistance was confirmed in Florida the next year, along with moderate levels detected in Arkansas, Montana, California and Wyoming[10].

Those in Florida, finding that fluvalinate was no longer effective, were left with no legal alternative until the approval of Bayer Bee Strips® in January 1999 under a Section 18 exemption. Universal resistance has yet to be proclaimed, however, and fluvalinate continues to be effective in many areas of the state and nation. As a consequence of this, however, the Florida Apiary Inspection Service published the following in February 1998:

As a result of recent discoveries of varroa mites that are resistant to Apistan® treatments, we will no longer require proof of treatment for certification. Current requirements are: an average of two mites or less on a post-treatment survey of five percent of the colonies in a yard (with a minimum of 10 hives per yard where applicable) using the standard ether roll of approximately 200 bees.

Past research has indicated a doubling of varroa mites every six weeks under Florida conditions, therefore listed below are levels that will provide equitable certification in cases where we are unable to survey immediately after treatment.
1. A tolerance of four mites in a six weeks post-treatment.
2. A tolerance of eight mites in a 12 weeks post-treatment.

Again, these regulations are in response to growers on the Eastern seaboard, who want orderly movement of bees out of Florida for early spring pollination activities.

Detecting resistance is difficult because it is a moving target with many shades of gray[41]. At the present time, at least one field test has been designed to screen colonies for resistance to the most often used chemical, fluvalinate[18].

Regulations about Varroa. Individual regulations promulgated by states to control varroa spread were found to impede bee movement early on to the detriment of commercial pollination. USDA-APHIS at the behest of growers, therefore, convened a meeting of beekeeping industry officials to establish a national quarantine that would have provided for orderly movement of bees for pollination. A process called "negotiated rule making" was initiated. Out of this process a proposed varroa movement rule was published in the *National Register* on March 16, 1988. However, it was abruptly withdrawn by APHIS April 13[26.] This action again left each state to develop its own regulations.

As noted elsewhere, however, states along the eastern seaboard continued to allow bee movement based on the Eastern States Agreement. Again, other North American regulations involved the closing of both the Mexican and Canadian borders to honey bees from the U.S.A. Some movement restrictions continue to this day in un-infested areas of Canada. These measures may have delayed the eventual introduction of varroa, but have not prevented it in most areas.

Varroa seems to have been independently introduced to Mexico as the U.S. border has been closed since detection in the U.S.A. Reports that it is not as virulent in some areas may indicate a South American source was involved.

Economic impact of Varroa. There is little question that introduction of varroa has been economically devastating to the U.S.A. beekeeping industry in several ways. Unfortunately, exact figures are not available and several other factors have also exacerbated the situation. These include previous introduction of the honey bee tracheal mite and several years of reduced prices because of extensive honey importation from China and Argentina. These economic conditions resulted in fewer resources at beekeepers' disposal to both manage and/or treat infested colonies.

In Florida, introduction of the tracheal mite and then varroa killed much of the extant package bee and queen industry. Package bees were routinely used to replace colonies killed during harsh winters in the north. In some cases, beekeepers in Canada and the midwest even purposefully killed colonies because they would be less expensive to replace than to feed during winter. Florida had a large share of this market prior to mite introduction and border closure.

To this date, the Canadian border remains closed and this will probably be the case until after the turn of the millennium[38]. In any case, reopening it will not ensure a return to conditions present when it was closed. Many Canadians have taken up queen rearing and also are importing queens from Australia and New Zealand.

The advent of varroa has changed beekeeping in other fundamental ways, besides the traditional queen and package bee trade. It killed off the bee colonies of many hobby beekeepers. The era of let-alone beekeeping vanished. Managed colonies remain extremely vulnerable to mites[11], as do feral or wild (unmanaged) honey bees[16].

Growers and home gardeners have noticed a shortage of honey bees in their plots[17]. For beekeepers and others interested in the honey bee's welfare, this represents an "educable" moment. At long last these insects are able to get the respect sought for so long as pollination providers for the nation's crops and gardens[32]. Anecdotal reports indicate that pollination fees have increased due to this perception, at least for some beekeepers. The continued importance of the honey bee as a pollinator of many crops is reflected in the continuance of the Eastern States' Agreement between Florida and several northeastern states for over a decade. At the same time, many western beekeepers have become more involved in this activity[37].

Varroa has caused beekeeper production costs to rise, often with no concomitant increase in honey prices. Chemical treatments are expensive and varroa parasitization may exacerbate other less virulent problems[15]. In addition, there is increased labor cost attached to treating, as well as removing honey supers while treatment is progressing. Longterm use of chemicals in colonies and the inevitable buildup of that material in colonies may also be responsible for as-yet-unknown effects. Sublethal doses of fluvalinate, for example, have been suspected of affecting colonies[39]. Drones appear to be particularly at risk[21].

Resistance to fluvalinate and perhaps other chemicals means a stint on the infamous pesticide treadmill[41]. Beekeepers must now resort to more and more treatments or materials, or see their investment be irreparably damaged by this parasite. Part and parcel of this is the ever-present risk that the beekeeper's main product, honey, could have its reputation sullied. Accidental or purposeful contamination of the sweet many consumers have come to rely on as the most "natural" of agricultural products would potentially be a disaster of major proportions for the honey market. Other products such as beeswax also appear to be at risk[33].

Because of varroa, beekeepers may have to rethink the independence they enjoyed previously in solving their own problems. The parasite affects the whole system, which includes both managed and feral colonies[46]. As such, treatment regimes might have to be mandated over large areas because of the likelihood of re-infestation[30].

Beyond chemicals, other solutions rest on finding or importing varroa-tolerant bees[20], selecting for hygienic behavior[43] or breeding for tolerance[14] (Chapter 15). Mechanical control measures can also help keep varroa populations at bay. These include drone brood trapping[31] and especially designed varroa trapping bottom boards[40]. Controlling mite populations by integrated pest management (IPM) using a combination of measures (chemical, cultural, and genetic) is probably the best strategy to pursue[31].

In spite of the havoc it has wrought in North America, *Varroa* also appears to be responsible for some interesting reversals of fortune in beekeeping. The entrenched mite population may be largely responsible for halting the eastward overland migration of the Africanized honey bee (*Apis mellifera scutellata*) from Texas. As a consequence, large portions of southeastern North America, originally thought vulnerable, have yet to be populated by this over defensive insect[34].

Finally, varroa, because of its severe effects on colony survival, may have helped create a "better" breed of beekeeper. The mite's presence demands even the most casual apiculturist proactively manage the honey bee colony if it is to reach it fullest potential.

Summary. Without doubt, introduction of the parasitic mite *Varroa jacobsoni* has been catastrophic for North American beekeeping. *Varroa* mites were detected in Florida in 1987. The history of the spread and economic impact of this mite are cataloged here along with efforts by beekeepers to treat their colonies for this organism. The varroa mite is now an integral part of beekeeping on this continent. Its control will continually challenge the apicultural community.

References cited.

1. **Anderson, D. L. & S. Fuchs. 1998.** Two genetically distinct populations of *Varroa jacobsoni* with contrasting reproductive abilities on *Apis mellifera*. J. Apic. Res. 37: 69-78.

2. **Anonymous. 1987.** More states find *Varroa*: No decision yet on national action. Am. Bee J. 127: 817.

3. **Anonymous. 1988.** Miscellaneous news reports cited in text. Am. Bee J. 128: 157.

4. **Anonymous. 1989.** *Varroa* mites found in New Brunswick: only the second official find in Canada. Am. Bee.J. 129: 765.

5. **Cauich, D. C. & C. L. Medina. 1998.** Infestación del Ácaro *Varroa Jacobsoni* Oud. En Colonias de Abejas *Apis mellifera* L en Yucatán, México. Memorias VI Congresso Ibero-Americano de Apicultura, Mérida, Yucatán, México.

6. **Cox, B. 1989.** Varroa discovered in Iowa. Am. Bee J. 129: 293.

7. **Delaplane, K. & M. Hood. 1997.** Effects of delayed acaracide treatment in honey bee colonies parasitized by *Varroa jacobsoni* and a late-season treatment threshold for the southeastern USA. J. Apic. Res. 36: 125-132.

8. **Dietz, A. & H. R. Hermann. 1988.** Biology, detection and control *Varroa jacobsoni*: A parasitic mite on honey bees. Commerce Georgia, USA: Lei-Act Publishers, 81 pp.

9. **Echazarreta, C. M., J. J. Quezada-Euan, L. A. Medina & C. Pasteur. 1998.** La Apicultura en la Peninsula de Yucatán. Memorias VI Congresso Ibero-Americano de Apicultura, Mérida, Yucatán, México.

10. **Elzen, P. J., F. A. Eischen, J. B. Baxter, J. Pettis, G. W. Elzen & W. T. Wilson. 1998.** Fluvalinate resistance in *Varroa jacobsoni* from several geographic locations. Am. Bee J. 138: 674-676.

11. **Finley, J., S. Camazine & M. Frazier. 1996.** The epidemic of honey bee colony losses dDuring the 1995-1996 Season. Am. Bee J. 136: 805-808.

12. **Guzman, L. I. de, T. Rinderer & J Stelzer. 1997.** DNA Evidence of the origin of *Varroa jacobsoni* Oudemans in the Americas. Biochem. Gen. 35: 327-335.

13. **Gruszka, J., Saskatechewan Provincial Apiarist, personal communication, April, 1999.**

14. **Harbo, J. R. & R. A. Hoopingarner. 1997.** Honey Bees (Hymenoptera: Apidae) in the United States That Express Resistance to *Varroa jacobsoni* (Mesostigmata: Varroidae) J. Econ.

Entomol. 90: 893-898.

15. **Hunt, G. 1998.** The war against *Varroa*: How are we doing? Am. Bee J. 138: 372-374.

16. **Loper, G. M. 1995.** A documented loss of feral bees due to mite infestations in S. Arizona. Am. Bee J. 135: 823-824.

17. **Martz, E. 1998.** Where have all the bees gone?, Penn State Agriculture, Pennsylvania State University College of Agriculture, Winter/Spring <http://aginfo.psu.edu/PSA/ws98/bees.html>

18. **Pettis, J., H. Shimanuki & M. Feldlaufer. 1998.** Detecting fluvalinate-resistant *Varroa* mites. Am. Bee J. 138: 535-537.

19. **Prouse, Chris Prince Edward Island Apiarist, personal communication, April 1999.**

20. **Rinderer, T. E., V. Nuznetsov, R. Danka & G. Delatte. 1997.** An importation of potentially *Varroa*-resistant honey bees from far eastern Russia. Am. Bee J. 137: 787-790.

21. **Rinderer, T E., L. de Guzman, V. Lancaster, G. Delatte, & J Stelzer. 1999,** *Varroa* in the mating yard: I. The effects of *Varroa jacobsoni* and Apistan® on drone honey bees. Am. Bee J. 139: 134-139.

22. **Rodriquez, S. R., J. M. Moro & G. C. Otero. 1992.** *Varroa* Found in Mexico. Am. Bee J. 132: 728-729.

23. **Sanford, M. T. 1987.** APIS: Apicultural Information and Issues, University of Florida, October <http://www.ifas.ufl.edu/~mts/apishtm/apis87/apoct87.htm#1>.

24. **Sanford, M. T. 1988a.** APIS: Apicultural Information and Issues, University of Florida, January <http://www.ifas.ufl.edu/~mts/apishtm/apis88/apjan88.htm#1>.

25. **Sanford, M. T. 1988b.** APIS: Apicultural Information and Issues, University of Florida, November <http://www.ifas.ufl.edu/~mts/apishtm/apis88/apnov88.htm#1>.

26. **Sanford, M. T. 1988c.** APIS: Apicultural Information and Issues, University of Florida, May <http://www.ifas.ufl.edu/~mts/apishtm/apis88/apmay88.htm#1>.

27. **Sanford, M. T. 1990.** APIS: Apicultural Information and Issues,

University of Florida, November
<http://www.ifas.ufl.edu/~mts/apishtm/apis90/apnov90.htm#1>

28. **Sanford,M. T. 1993.** APIS: Apicultural Information and Issues, University of Florida, January
<http://www.ifas.ufl.edu/~mts/apishtm/apis93/apjan93.htm#1>.

29. **Sanford, M T. 1993.** APIS: Apicultural Information and Issues, University of Florida, October
<http://www.ifas.ufl.edu/~mts/apishtm/apis93/apoct93.htm#1>.

30. **Sanford, M. T. 1993.** APIS: Apicultural Information and Issues, University of Florida, March
<http://www.ifas.ufl.edu/~mts/apishtm/apis93/apmar93.htm#1>.

31. **Sanford, M. T. 1996.** APIS: Apicultural Information and Issues, University of Florida, October
<http://www.ifas.ufl.edu/~mts/apishtm/apis96/apoct96.htm#3>.

32. **Sanford, M. T. 1996.** APIS: Apicultural Information and Issues, University of Florida, May
<http://www.ifas.ufl.edu/~mts/apishtm/apis96/apmar96.htm#1>.

33. **Sanford, M. T. 1996.** APIS: Apicultural Information and Issues, University of Florida, August
<http://www.ifas.ufl.edu/~mts/apishtm/apis96/apaug96.htm#1>.

34. **Sanford, M. T. 1996.** ABF in Portland—Has the Federation Come Full Circle? The Speedy Bee. 25: Nos. 3-4, March, April, 1996.
<http://www.ifas.ufl.edu/~mts/apishtm/papers/portland.htm#13>.

35. **Sanford, M. T. 1997.** APIS: Apicultural Information and Issues, University of Florida, May
<http://www.ifas.ufl.edu/~mts/apishtm/apis97/apmay97.htm#2>.

36. **Sanford, M. T. 1997.** APIS: Apicultural Information and Issues, University of Florida, November
http://www.ifas.ufl.edu/~mts/apishtm/apis97/apnov97.htm#4

37. **Sanford, M. T. 1998.** APIS: Apicultural Information and Issues, University of Florida, June
<http://www.ifas.ufl.edu/~mts/apishtm/apis98/apjun98.htm#6>.

38. **Sanford, M. T. 1998.** Canadian Honey Council and Association of Professional Apiculturists Meet in Joint Symposium with Québec

Honey Producers'Federation, Bee Biz No. 8:pp. 3-6, July.
<http://www.ifas.ufl.edu/~mts/apishtm/papers/CANADA.HTM#7>.

39. **Sanford, M. T. 1998.** APIS: Apicultural Information and Issues, University of Florida, February
<http://www.ifas.ufl.edu/~mts/apishtm/apis98/apfeb98.htm#4>.

40. **Sanford, M. T. 1998.** APIS: Apicultural Information and Issues, University of Florida, December
http://www.ifas.ufl.edu/~mts/apishtm/apis98/apdec98.htm#6

41. **Sanford, M. T. 1999.** APIS: Apicultural Information and Issues, University of Florida, February
<http://www.ifas.ufl.edu/~mts/apishtm/apis99/apfeb99.htm>.

42. **Sanford,T., K. Flottum & B. Arthur. 1999.** Bayer Bee Strip. The newest weapon in beekeeping's arsenal against *Varroa* also controls the small hive beetle. Bee Culture. 127: 32-35.

43. **Spivak, M. & G. Reuter. 1998.** Honey Bee Hygienic Behavior. Am. Bee J. 138: 283-286.

44. **van Westendorp, P. 1997.** Bee Scene: BC Honey Producers Association Newsletter, June.

45. **Webster, T. Kentucky State University, personal communication, October 1998.**

46. **Wenner, A. & W. W. Bushing. 1996.** *Varroa* mite spread in the United States. Bee Culture 124: 341-343.

DETECTION AND MEASUREMENT OF VARROA MITE POPULATIONS

Chapter 12

Thomas C. Webster

*I*ntroduction. Detection and measurement of varroa populations in the honey bee hive are critical to careful beekeeping. The evaluation of hives and package bees prior to shipment or transportation is now a significant aspect of commercial beekeeping in many parts of the world. Countries and regions of the world which remain free of mites rely on periodic hive evaluations. The effectiveness of acaricides (Chapter 13), the value of mite resistance in bees (Chapter 15), the appropriate time for acaricide application (Chapter 16), and the appearance of mites with acaricide resistance (Chapter 17) can be determined only by monitoring varroa populations.

Two factors make varroa detection difficult. First, a low infestation is easy to overlook. For example an infestation on only 50 bees out of 50,000 is nearly impossible to detect by some methods. However that same hive could easily be a source of mites for other colonies, through drifting and robbing behavior in the vicinity (Chapter 10), or through shipment of package bees and divided hives.

To illustrate this first problem consider a hive in which only one out of 1000 adult bees carry mites. This is defined as having a prevalence of 0.1% (see terminology defined in Chapter 9), not counting mites in the brood. A sample of 200 bees taken randomly from the population of 50,000 would have only an 18.1 % chance of including a mite-infested bee. Other examples are shown in Table 12.1. A larger sample of bees improves the likelihood of finding mites. However, the prevalence must approach 2% for the sample to be nearly certain of including mites. In general, the probability of including an infested bee in a random sample of bees is given by:

$$P = 1 - (1 - r)^s$$

where r is the proportion of adult bees infested, and s is the number of bees in the sample.

The second difficulty is that varroa divides its life cycle between the adult bees and the brood. This partitioning of the mite population varies according to the ratio of adult bees to brood cells, which changes with season and colony condition. The pale, immature mites in the brood cells are difficult to observe without magnification. This problem is especially important during the height of the brood rearing season when an estimated 70 - 80% of the mites in a hive are in the capped brood cells[41]. Furthermore, varroa shows a decided preference for drone brood over worker brood, and the drone brood is also dependent on season, colony populaton and other factors.

The concerns of beekeepers and others who must monitor bee hives can be reduced to the issues of time, cost, sensitivity, accuracy, and time of year when the test may be performed. Time and cost of detection methods are especially critical to commercial beekeepers. The sensitivity and accuracy of a method are important concerns for research projects, and for regions which are threatened by varroa, but not yet invaded. The methods which are most accurate are generally most sensitive, i.e. most able to demonstrate the existence of a very few mites in a well populated hive. The time of year is critical because some tests require the existence of brood, or drone brood. Other tests can be done at any time, even when bad weather prohibits the opening of the hive. Each test is evaluated here according to the five practical criteria listed above. No single test is best by all criteria.

The methods for varroa detection which follow are listed according to which portion of the honey bee colony is examined. The mean number of mites per immature or adult bee is the "abundance" (Chapter 9)

Table 12.1 *Probability (as percent) of including a mite-infested bee in a random sample of worker bees from one hive, according to the prevalence of mite-infested bees in that hive.*

Prevalence of of infested bees in the hive	Number of bees in sample			
	100	200	300	400
0.1 %	9.5	18.1	25.9	33.0
0.5 %	39.4	63.3	77.8	86.5
1.0 %	63.4	86.6	95.1	98.2
2.0 %	86.7	98.2	99.8	99.9+
5.0 %	99.4	99.9+	99.9+	99.9+

for that subpopulation (worker brood, drone brood or adult bees) of the colony. Martin[35] developed calculations to estimate the number of mites in the entire colony, based on the number of mites in one such sample and the time of year. These calculations would be changed for regions of the world in which the seasons differ from those of the United Kingdom.

Varroa on adult bees.
The "ether roll". This is a simple and commonly used test in North America[49]. Several hundred worker bees are brushed into a large, wide-mouth, transparent glass or plastic jar. The jar should be at least one liter (one quart), and not filled more than one tenth of its volume with bees. The bees are then sprayed for one or two seconds with an aerosol can of ether, of the type commonly sold in automobile supply stores. The bees die quickly and the mites fall from the bees. The beekeeper then caps the jar, shakes it vigorously for a short time, and carefully examines the inner surface for mites. The name of this test is somewhat misleading, because various liquids can be used in place of ether. Furthermore, a vigorous shake will dislodge more mites than a "roll" of the bees in the jar. Isopropyl or ethyl alcohol, soapy water, vegetable

oil, or gasoline may be used in place of ether[10,11,46,50]. One should beware of the explosive nature of many organic liquids, which must not be used near a lighted bee smoker. Ether is also a potent general anesthetic, hazardous inside closed vehicles and rooms.

The test may be improved if the bees are agitated in a larger amount of liquid, and then poured over a wire screen which retains the bees and lets mites pass through. The liquid is then examined for mites[2,48,50].

To estimate the number of adult bees in the sample, either the weight or the volume may be used. Both are good estimators. The part of the hive from which bees are sampled is significant. Bees from the brood nest may have twice the infestation rate of those from the honey frames[6].

All versions of this test are quick, inexpensive, and can be done whenever weather allows the hive to be opened. Package bees and swarms can also be tested in this way. The main disadvantage of this test is its poor sensitivity and accuracy due to the use of a small sample of bees, as discussed above. At very low infestation rates, an ether roll sample would need to include at least 1000 bees to detect the presence of the mites[8]. In addition, some of the mites in a sample often do not appear on the jar's inner surface. A sample containing only one or two mites may appear to be free of mites[17,46]. This problem is made worse if too many bees are placed in the jar.

Mitefall with acaricidal smoke or vapor. Several substances will cause a rapid fall of mites from the adult bees. One is tobacco, (20g or ¾ of an ounce for two hives) mixed with smoker fuel in a bee smoker. A large sheet of white paper is placed under the bees, usually across the bottom board when the bees are in a hive. The smoke is puffed through the cluster of bees. The white paper is then examined for varroa within several minutes, because some mites will revive and crawl away[37,49]. Care must be taken in using a limited amount of tobacco to avoid killing the bees[16.]

Other acaricidal smokes or vapors are used in a similar manner[27]. Smoke containing fluvalinate or amitraz has been found to be more effective than tobacco[49]. Formic acid, when allowed to evaporate inside the hive, allows a more sensitive test than tobacco, the ether roll test, or the examination of 75 drone pupae[18] (see following sections). The time and expense of these tests depend on the duration of the treatment and the acaricide used.

Heating caged bees. A cage of several hundred bees is placed over a white surface and heated in an oven or incubator for 10 to 15 minutes at 46-47°C (115-117°F)[9]. This method is not widely used because it is inconvenient. Its accuracy and sensitivity would depend on the sample size, as for the other adult bee tests.

Varroa in the brood nest.

Varroa in capped drone brood. This test depends on the marked preference of the female mites for drone brood over worker brood, by a factor of six to twelve[24] (Chapter 10). Drone brood is most attractive to the mites when the colony contains less of it[26]. Drone pupae are removed from their cells and examined for mites. A honey capping scratcher[42] or forceps are useful for this task. The dark-colored adult mites are easily seen when crawling quickly over pale bee pupae. Often the pale, immature varroa may be seen on the pupae or in the cells. Direct sunlight and a magnifying glass are helpful, especially in observing immature mites.

Mite-infested cells are not evenly or randomly distributed among the drone cells in a colony. They are most often along the periphery of the brood nest[21], and concentrated in certain cells more than one would expect from a random disribution.[14,25] This is due to fluctuations in infestation rates[34]. It complicates attempts to quantify the hive infestation by sampling drone brood.

This test is not very time consuming if incorporated into routine hive inspections, and the expense is nil. However, it was necessary to examine 75 drone pupae per hive for the test to be much more sensitive than the ether roll[18]. The chief problem lies in the need for capped drone brood. Clearly this test is useful only in spring and summer and it depends somewhat on recent weather, colony population and other factors which influence drone rearing.

Varroa in capped worker brood. In early spring and from late summer through fall, little drone brood is present in the hive. Worker brood may be examined instead, although this will be a less sensitive test because fewer mites inhabit a given number of cells compared to drone brood. Infested worker brood cells tend to be clumped rather than evenly distributed among the other capped cells[21,25]

The removal and examination of many pupae is tedious. In order to minimize the number of pupae examined for each colony, Floris[22] presented a method by which one may make a decision according to the number of mites discovered, given a certain number of pupae.

Varroa on bees emerging from brood cells. This test relies on the relative abundance of the mites on bees which are emerging from their brood cells[46]. Mites continue to reproduce within a capped brood cell until the bee emerges from its cell as a young adult. Shortly after their host has emerged, the mature female mites disperse to other bees. Consequently, the number of mites infesting a bee peaks at the time the bee emerges.

Sampling is done by removing a frame containing nearly mature capped brood, free of adult bees, and placing it inside a white plastic bag for at least one day. The bees which emerge are then examined for mites by the ether roll test, and the inside of the bag is also inspected for mites. The brood frame may then be returned to the bag and the sampling may continue over subsequent days as long as more bees emerge. The frame may be kept at room temperature (25°C or 77°F), although the use of an incubator would enhance survival of the brood and the number of bees which emerge. Vegetable oil makes a convenient and effective substitute for ether, especially when testing newly emerged bees which cannot fly[44].

The emerging bee test may be too time-consuming for a commercial beekeeper, especially if the frame must be returned to the hive afterward. The cost is almost nothing and it is much more sensitive than the ether roll. The need for mature brood limits the test to established colonies during brood rearing season.

This test should be much more sensitive if used with drone brood. Frames containing only drone cells may be produced using drone brood foundation, which is available from some beekeeping supply companies. The increased sensitivity of the emerging bee test with drone brood could justify the extra time required. Removal of mite-infested drone brood would also support the beekeeper's control program (Chapter 14). By removing capped drone brood on a regular basis, the beekeeper could incorporate both survey and control in a single procedure.

Varroa feces in brood cells. Mature female varroa defecate in the brood cell just before they leave the cell with their host bees. Consequently, this can be used as a measure of varroa in the brood nest. The fecal material is white guanine, easily seen on the upper wall of the vacated brood cell[19,20].

Apparently, the fecal material is not removed quickly by bees, although the amount of time it remains on the comb has not been reported. The accuracy and sensitivity of this technique depend on how long the material remains visible. Its sensitivity has not been compared to that of other methods of detecting varroa. Presumably this test is useful only during the season bees rear brood. If these observations are incorporated into routine hive inspections, the beekeeper's expended time is minimal.

Varroa on adult bees and in the brood. A method for sampling mites which are living on the adult bees and the brood of the entire honey bee colony is accomplished by counting mites caught on a sticky board which has been placed on the hive bottom board. Sticky boards may be constructed from plastic sheets or heavy, white paper cut to fit across the entire bottom board. Glossy "freezer paper", such as that used to wrap meat and other foods, is much better than paper which will absorb water and deteriorate. Laminated white paper is ideal. The paper is then covered with a liberal layer of sticky material that will retain fallen varroa. "Sticky-stuff"[®6] or a mix of one part vegetable shortening to one part petroleum jelly[1] are effective. Vegetable oil alone has been recommended,[49] but I have found it less effective in retaining mites. Wire screen or plastic webbing is placed over the sticky board so that the bees are able to walk over it. The best design is a thin wooden frame that suspends wire screen (3 openings / cm., or 8 / inch) just above the sticky board. Sticky boards designed to standard bottom board dimensions are sold by several beekeeping supply companies.

Often the sticky board can simply be inserted and removed through the hive entrance. The expense is modest if the boards are constructed by the beekeeper rather than purchased. The board should be examined every two weeks, or more often, when warm weather allows the bees to forage. A populous hive will quickly generate a large amount of debris. Collection and sieving the debris for mites has been recommended[37], but direct examination of the board is easier.

The time required for this test is considerable if many, perhaps thousands, of mites must be counted. To save time, the beekeeper may wish to count a fraction of the sticky board. However, it is important to divide the sticky board into subunits which will collectively give an unbiased estimate. Mitefall will not be evenly distributed across the sticky board. Most mites will accumulate below the spaces between frames. If the colony is small, it will cluster in one part of the hive and mitefall will be mainly underneath that cluster. A system for choosing subsamples of the sticky board, for a minimally biased estimate of overall mitefall, is described by Calderone[5].

This method is more sensitive and accurate than any other if the boards are used over a sufficient time period. If the sticky boards can be inserted and removed without opening the hive, the method is useful at any time of year. I have found that monthly exchange and examination of the boards through winter in Kentucky reliably indicates the presence of varroa.

Mitefall without acaricide. A large fraction of the varroa in a hive eventually fall from the bees to the hive's bottom board. Presumably, many of these mites simply die from senescence. Mites which have not matured by the time their host bee emerges from its cell will also die. Possibly, some mites are killed by the bees before they fall from the cluster, as a part of grooming behavior.

Routine checks with sticky boards through spring and summer can be good indicators of varroa populations. This method was evaluated for 15 hives by comparing total mitefall without acaricide over 18, 46 and 65 days to the total number of mites found at the end of this time period using Apistan®. The correlation was good after 46 days and excellent after 65 days[4].

A more accurate estimate of a hive's mite population can be calculated from mitefall and the dates of the initiation of worker brood rearing, the end of worker brood rearing, and the initiation of drone brood rearing[38]. Brood rearing is an important factor because many of the mites fall from bees, especially worker bees, as they emerge from brood cells. A higher proportion of pale, incompletely sclerotized adult mites fall from emerging workers, compared to emerging drones. This is because many mites are unable to complete their development within the shorter worker developmental time[33] (and see Chapter 10).

Mitefall with acaricide. This test is the best estimate of the mite population in an entire bee colony, including the brood, if the acaricide treatment lasts long enough for the parasitized bee brood to mature and emerge as adult bees. Plastic strips containing 10% fluvalinate (Apistan®) and a sticky board are installed at the same time. After at least one week, the sticky board is removed and examined for mites.

This is by far the most time-consuming and expensive of the tests discussed here. If the colonies are due for acaricide treatment anyway, there is little additional cost. The value of the test lies in its great sensitivity and accuracy. However, some beekeepers may wish to sacrifice sensitivity in favor of time by examining the sticky boards only a short time after the strips have been placed. If the board is examined after 4 hours, the test is only slightly more sensitive than the ether roll[27]. After 6 days, the test is much more sensitive than the ether roll[17]. After four weeks, nearly all the mites in the hive are exposed to the fluvalinate, and fall to the board[46].

Formic acid may be used in place of Apistan, although it is less effective. Over 120 hours it causes fewer mites to fall from the bees than a 24-hour treatment with fluvalinate strips[18]. The test is versatile, as it can be done whenever weather allows the beekeeper to open the hive.

Even this method is not entirely accurate, however. Mite reproduction will occur in the brood nest during the time period of the treatment. Some mites will die away from the hive. Bees with mites will drift to and from other hives, and die outside of the hive. Resistance to the acaracide used (Chapter 17) will certainly reduce the accuracy of the test. In Finland, ants were found to remove varroa from paper inserts inside bee hives, but sticky material on the paper prevented this "sabotage"[29].

Detecting new infestations in a region previously free of varroa. Hawaii, parts of Canada and some other countries are still apparently free of varroa. A high priority in these regions should be the detection of incipient infestations as early as possible. Fries & others[23] followed the development of newly infested hives at an isolated apiary in Finland. Sticky boards, adult workers, worker brood, and drone brood were examined periodically as the infestations increased over 16 months. The sticky boards gave more sensitive and accurate measures of mite levels than the other methods.

Similarly, the source of a new infestation, and subsequent mite dispersal patterns within an apiary, are most readily determined by sticky board techniques. The "ether roll" is the least useful for this purpose because of its low sensitivity[46].

Sampling colonies within an apiary. Commercial beekeepers and apiary inspectors are often faced with the problem of estimating infestations in apiaries containing many hives. Generally, there is time to sample only a few of the hives. An intra-apiary sampling scheme is needed to select a subset of hives which would give the best indication of overall apiary infestation. This would assist the estimation of treatment thresholds for the entire apiary.

Some apiary inspectors in the United States prefer to choose the hives at both ends when they are arranged in a row, with the idea that these two hives tend to have the highest infestations. This seems to be based on the fact that bees drift preferentially to the end hives, especially in large, windswept apiaries. Jay[28] quantified this drift before parasitic mites invaded North America. However, Jay's observations do not imply that mite infestations will follow the same patterns. Webster and Cho[47] showed that the end hives could tend to have the lowest infestation rates in a linear apiary, if mites do not affect drift behavior. The effects of mites on bee drift behavior are critical to the spread of mites by drift, and to the development of an intra-apiary sampling protocol.

The future. Progress in several areas of varroa research suggest that improved sampling methods may soon be available. Alternative miticides, including botanical compounds which are relatively safe to the beekeeper and the bees (Chapter 13), may be registered for beekeeping applications. These could be used in methods similar to those for the acaricides described above.

Recent research on varroa host-seeking behavior has been promising. Honey bee brood pheromones are attractive as kairomones to varroa. The mites can recognize bee brood and distinguish between drone and worker larvae by esters of straight-chain fatty acids[15,32,39,40,43,44,45]. Cell size[36] and the distance from the larva to the cell rim[3] are other important cues. *Varroa* are attracted to clove oil, and are more likely to infest brood cells built on beeswax containing clove oil[30]. The movement of the mite is influenced also by electrical charges[7] and temperature[31]. These could be factors in the development of a trap which could placed in a hive and removed later for examination.

Summary. Methods for the detection and measurement of varroa in honey bee colonies are confronted with two sampling problems. These are the difficulties posed by the large bee population of a typical colony and by the partitioning of mites between the capped brood and the adult population. Both problems complicate the methods and limit the sensitivity and accuracy of sampling methods.

Methods are described here according to which portions of the bee colony are to be assessed: the adult bee population, the drone brood, the worker brood, or the entire colony. The methods are also evaluated according to five criteria: time, cost, sensitivity, accuracy, and colony condition or time of year in which the test may be done. Beekeepers, apiary inspectors and researchers should choose a method according to which criteria meet their needs. Those wishing to intercept a new infestation in a region previously free of mites should choose a sticky board technique because of its great sensitivity. Intra-apiary sampling schemes have not been well studied. An objective method for choosing and sampling a subset of hives would be valuable for monitoring large apiaries. New sampling methods may be developed through the use of alternative miticides, or an improved understanding of the host-seeking behavior of the mite.

Acknowledgments. I thank Seppo Korpela for kindly providing results and translation. Keith Delaplane made many helpful comments. This review was supported by USDA CSREES Evans-Allen grants KYX -10-93-20P and KYX-10-99-30P to the author.

References cited.
1. **Anonymous. 1996.** How to make sticky boards. The Speedy Bee. September 1996.

2. **Bach, J. C., M. W. Klaus & G. Haubrich. 1988.** *Varroa* mite survey and treatment procedures in Washington State. Am. Bee J. 128: 682-685.

3. **Boot, W. J., R. G. Driessen, J. N. M. Calis & J. Beetsma. 1995.** Further observations on the correlation between attractiveness of honey bee brood cells to *Varroa jacobsoni* and the distance from larva to cell rim. Entomol. Exper. et Acta. 76: 223-232.

4. **Calatayud, F. & M. J. Verdu. 1993.** Hive debris counts in honeybee colonies: a method to estimate the size of small populations and

rate of growth of the mite *Varroa jacobsoni* Oud. (Mesostigmata: Varroidae). Exp. Appl. Acarol. 17: 889-894.

5. **Calderone, N. 1998.** Sub-sampling algorithms for estimating varroa counts on sticky-boards. Am. Bee J. 138: 291-292.

6. **Calderone, N. W. & R. M. Turcotte. 1998.** Development of sampling methods for estimating levels of *Varroa jacobsoni* (Acari:Varroidae) infestation in colonies of *Apis mellifera* (Hymenoptera: Apidae). J. Econ. Entomol. 91: 851-863.

7. **Colin, M. E., D. Richard, V. Fourcassie & L. P. Belzunces. 1992.** Attraction of *Varroa jacobsoni*, parasite of *Apis mellifera* by electrical charges. J. Insect Physiol. 38: 111-117.

8. **Collison, C. H., H. R. Fulton, M. Tomasko & J. Steinhauer. 1991.** Equating ether-roll sampling results with total number of varroa mites, *Varroa jacobsoni*, present. Am. Bee J. 131: 773-774.

9. **Crane, E. 1978.** The varroa mite. Bee World. 59: 164-167.

10. **DeJong, D. 1979.** Field identification of *Varroa jacobsoni*, a parasitic mite of honey bees. Glean. Bee Cult. 107: 639-640, 644.

11. **DeJong, D., D. De Andrea Roma & L. S. Gonsoalves. 1982.** A comparative analysis of shaking solutions for the detection of *Varroa jacobsoni* on adult honey bees. Apidologie. 13: 297-303.

12. **Delaplane, K. S. & W. M. Hood. 1997.** Effects of delayed acaricide treatment in honey bee colonies parasitized by *Varroa jacobsoni* and a late-season treatment threshold for the southeastern USA. J. Apic. Res. 36: 125-132.

13. **Delaplane, K. S. & W. M. Hood. 1999.** Economic threshold for *Varroa jacobsoni* Oud. in the southeastern USA. Apidologie. 30: 383-395.

14. **Donze, G., M. Herrmann, B. Bachofen & P. Guerin. 1996.** Effect of mating frequency and brood cell infestation rate on the reproductive success of the honeybee parasite *Varroa jacobsoni*. Ecol. Entomol. 21: 17-26.

15. **Donze, G. S. Schnyder-Candrian, S. Bogdanov, P.-A. Diehl, P.M. Guerin, V. Kilchenman & F. Monachon. 1998.** Aliphatic alcohols and aldehydes of the honey bee cocoon induce arrestment behavior

in *Varroa jacobsoni* (Acari: Mesostigmata), an ectoparasite of *Apis mellifera*. Arch. Insect Biochem. Physiol. 37: 129-145.

16. **Eischen, F. 1999.** Personal communication.

17. **Ellis, M., R. Nelson & C. Simonds. 1988.** A comparison of the flu-valinate and ether roll methods of sampling for *Varroa* mites in honey bee colonies. Am. Bee J. 128: 262-263.

18. **Ellis, M. D. & F. P. Baxendale. 1992.** Comparison of formic acid sampling with other methods used to detect *Varroa* mites. Am. Bee J. 132: 807-808.

19. **Erickson, E. H. 1996.** Fecal accumulations deposited by varroa can be used as a simple field diagnostic for infestations of this honey *bee parasite*. Am. Bee J. *136: 63-64.*

20. **Erickson, E. H., A. C. Cohen and B. E. Cameron. 1994.** Mite exc-reta: a new diagnostic for varroasis. Bee Science 3: 76-78.

21. **Floris, I. 1991.** Dispersion indices and sampling plans for the hon-eybee (*Apis mellifera* ligustica Spin.) mite *Varroa jacobsoni* Oud. Apicoltura 7: 161-170.

22. **Floris, I. 1997.** A sequential sampling technique for female adult mites of *Varroa jacobsoni* in the sealed worker brood of *Apis mellifera* ligustica Spin. Apidologie 28: 63-70.

23. **Fries, I., A Aarhus, H. Hansen & S. Korpela. 1991.** Comparison of diagnostic methods for detection of low infestation levels of *Varroa jacobsoni* in honey-bee (*Apis mellifera*) colonies. Exper. Appl. Acarol. 10: 279-287.

24. **Fries, I., S. Camazine & J. Sneyd. 1994.** Population dynamics of *Varroa jacobsoni*: A model and a review. Bee World. 75: 5-28.

25. **Fuchs, S. 1988.** The distribution of *Varroa jacobsoni* on honey bee brood combs and within brood cells as consequence of fluctuation [sic] infestation rates, pp. 73-76 R. Cavalloro [ed], European research on varroatosis control: Proceedings of a meeting of the EC expert's group. Bad Homburg, 15-17 October. 1986.

26. **Fuchs, S. 1990.** Preference for drone cells by *Varroa jacobsoni* Oud. in colonies of *Apis mellifera carnica*. Apidologie. 21: 193-199.

27. Herbert, E. W., Jr., P. C. Witherell, W. *A*. Bruce & H. Shimanuki. **1989.** Evaluation of six methods of detecting *Varroa* mites in bee hives, including the experimental use of acaricidal smokes containing fluvalinate or Amitraz. Am. Bee J. 129: 605-606,608.

28. Jay, S. C. **1966.** Drifting of honeybees in commercial apiaries. II. Effect of various factors when hives are arranged in rows. J. Apic. Res. 5: 103-112.

29. Korpela, S. **1997.** Mehiläisen loispunkkien integroitu torjunta. [Integrated control of honey bee parasitic mites.] Mehiläinen 14: 48-52.

30. Kraus, B., N. Koeniger & S. Fuchs. **1994.** Screening of substances for their effect on *Varroa jacobsoni*: attractiveness, repellancy, toxicity and masking effects of ethereal oils. J. Apic. Res. 33: 34-43.

31. Le Conte, Y. & G. Arnold. **1988.** Etude du thermopreferendum de *Varroa jacobsoni* Oud. (Study of thermal preference by *Varroa jacobsoni* Oud.) Apidologie. 19: 155-164.

32. Le Conte, Y., G. Arnold, J. Troiller, C. Masson, B. Chappe & G. Ourisson. **1989.** Attraction of the parasitic mite *Varroa* to the drone larvae of honey bees by simple aliphatic esters. Science. 245: 638-639.

33. Lobb, N. & S. Martin. **1997.** Mortality of *Varroa jacobsoni* Oudemans during or soon after the emergence of worker and drone honeybees *Apis mellifera* L. Apidologie. 28: 367-374.

34. Martin, S. J. **1995.** Reproduction of *Varroa jacobsoni* in cells of *Apis mellifera* containing one or more mother mites and the distribution of these cells. J. Apic. Res. 34: 187-196.

35. Martin, S. **1998.** *Varroa jacobsoni*: monitoring and forecasting mite populations within honey bee colonies in Britain. Ministry of Agriculture, Fisheries and Food and Central Science Laboratory, Sand Hutton, York, United Kingdom.

36. Message, D. & L. S. Gonçalves. **1995.** Effect of the size of worker brood cells of Africanized honey bees on infestation and reproduction of the ectoparasitic mite *Varroa jacobsoni* Oud. Apidologie. 26: 381-386.

37. Mobus, B. & C. de Bruyn. **1993.** The new varroa handbook.

Northern Bee Books, Mytholmroyd, UK.

38. **Omholdt, S. W. & K. Crailsheim. 1991.** The possible prediction of the degree of infestation of honeybee colonies (*Apis mellifera*) by *Varroa jacobsoni* by means of its natural death-rate: a dynamic model approach. Norwegian J. Agric. Sciences. 5: 393-400.

39. **Rickli, M., P. M. Guerin & P. A. Diehl. 1992.** Palmitic acid released from honeybee worker larvae attracts the parasitic mite *Varroa jacobsoni* on a servosphere. Naturwissenschaften. 79: 320-322.

40. **Rickli, M., P. A. Diehl & P. M. Guerin. 1994.** Cuticle alkanes of honeybee larvae mediate arrestment of bee parasite *Varroa jacobsoni*. J. Chem. Ecol. 20: 2437-2453.

41. **Schulz, A. E. 1984.** Reproduktion und Populationsentwicklung der parasitischen Milbe *Varroa jacobsoni* Oud. in Abhängigkeit vom Brutzyklus ihres Wirtes *Apis mellifera* L. [Reproduction and population dynamics of the parasitic mite *Varroa jacobsoni* Oud. and its dependence on the brood cycle of its host *Apis mellifera* L.] Apidologie 15: 401-420.

42. **Szabo, T. I. 1989.** The capping scratcher: A tool for detection and control of *Varroa jacobsoni*. Am. Bee J. 129: 402-403.

43. **Trouiller, J., G. Arnold, Y. Le Conte, C. Masson & B. Chappe. 1991.** Temporal pheromonal and kairomonal secretion in the brood of honeybees. Naturwissenschaften. 78:368-370.

44. **Trouiller, J., G. Arnold, B. Chappe, Y. LeConte, C. Masson. 1992.** Semiochemical basis of infestation of honey bee brood by *Varroa jacobsoni*. J. Chem. Ecol. 18: 2041-2053.

45. **Trouiller, J., G. Arnold, B. Chappe, Y. Le Conte, A. Billion & C. Masson. 1994.** The kairomonal esters attractive to the *Varroa jacobsoni* mite in the queen brood. Apidologie 25: 314-321.

46. **Webster, T. C. & D. J. Callaway. 1992.** The use of emerging bees for detecting low infestations of *Varroa jacobsoni* in honey bee colonies. Bee Science. 2: 125-129.

47. **Webster, T. C. & E. C. Cho. 1998.** Effects of drifting bees on *Varroa* distribution within an apiary. Am. Bee J. 138: 300.

48. **Witherell, P. C. & E. W. Hebert, Jr. 1988.** Evaluation of several

possible treatments to control *Varroa* mite *Varroa jacobsoni* (Oud.) on honey bees in packages. Am. Bee J. 128: 441.

49. **Witherell, P. C. & W. A. Bruce. 1990.** *Varroa* mite detection in beehives: evaluation of sampling methods using tobacco smoke, fluvalinate smoke, Amitraz smoke and ether-roll. Am. Bee J. 130: 127-129.

50. **USDA, ARS, BBII, Beneficial Insects Laboratory. 1987.** *Varroa jacobsoni* - Detection techniques. Am. Bee J. 127: 755-757.

Chapter 13

CHEMICAL CONTROL OF VARROA MITES

Marion Ellis

*T*he need for chemical control. *Varroa* management is an essential aspect of successful beekeeping. Unlike most parasites that coexist with their host, varroa eventually destroy honey bee colonies of European descent unless the beekeeper intervenes. Currently, chemical control is the most effective varroa management tool available to beekeepers. Without effective chemical control tools, beekeeping would be neither profitable nor enjoyable in many areas of the world.

Genetic, biological, and biotechnical control measures can reduce the growth rate of varroa in a colony (Chapters 14 and 15). These measures are generally used to reduce the frequency of chemical treatment rather than as a substitute for chemical control. Chemical control tools are essential in protecting honey bees from varroa injury. Without them, the profitability of beekeeping would be decimated and crops that rely on honey bee pollination would suffer disastrous yield losses. It is critical that beekeepers recognize their current reliance on chemical tools and that they utilize them in a sustainable manner. The cost of developing and registering new pesticides in the U.S.A. is approximately $35-50 million[25]. The beekeeping market, 2,570,000 colonies in the U.S.A.[45], is not large enough to induce manufacturers to generate a variety of control tools if currently registered products fail. In addition, varroa is a difficult organism to control with chemicals. Both varroa and honey bees belong to the phylum Arthropoda, and they share many systems and structures (Chapter 1). Most pest control situations do not involve such closely related organisms.

Classification of chemical control tools. Chemical control tool classification can be based on a variety of criteria depending on the needs and interest of the classifier. For example: target organ (liver, kidney, nervous system), use (pesticide, solvent, food additive), source (synthetic, animal, plant), physical state (gas, dust, liquid), poisoning potential or toxicity (dose lethal to 50% of a population). In this review, four ways of examining poisons are examined: (1) method of application, (2) mode of action, (3) poisoning potential, and (4) safety to user. Application methods refer to how the material is delivered. The mode of action designates the target site within the mite that is affected by the poison. The poisoning potential is a measure of the toxicity of the chemical to the target organism and to non-target organisms (such as bees). Safety to user indicates the poisoning potential for humans. Classification based on biochemical mode of action is the most informative.

Method of application. Application may be by fumigation, feeding to the bees, or direct contact. Fumigation includes materials dispersed on paper and burned in the colony, atomized products that are applied as aerosols, and volatile substances that evaporate when placed in the colony. Some fumigants kill mites on both adult bees and in brood cells. Other materials do not affect mites in brood cells.

Application by feeding includes all medications that are administered in sugar syrup. They kill mites on adult bees, but do not affect mites located in sealed brood cells. The toxic compounds accumulate in the bees' blood and mites are poisoned when they feed on bees that have fed on medicated syrup. The material is distributed among all adult members of the colony by food exchange or *trophallaxis*. Mites that emerge with brood may also be killed if the toxin has extended residual activity.

Toxins requiring direct contact are frequently applied in miticide-impregnated plastic strips that are suspended between frames in the brood nest. They are ineffective if they are placed outside the cluster and bees do not contact them. Proper placement can be a problem in the fall if treatments are applied on warm days. When the temperature drops, the cluster may form away from the strips. Proper placement is easier in the spring as the cluster position is more distinct due to the presence of brood and a smaller bee population. Contact strips that have extended residual activity (three weeks or longer) are especially effective in controlling varroa. They kill mites as they emerge from brood cells and effectively expose the entire mite population of a colony to the toxicant. If left in colonies beyond the recommended treatment period, they exert a strong selection pressure for mite resistance to the miticide in the strip (Chapter 17).

Dusts and materials that are sprayed directly onto the bees also work by contact. Sprays are labor intensive to apply, since combs of bees must be removed and sprayed individually. Direct spraying is most frequently used with relatively safe substances such as lactic acid. Dusts are sprinkled on the bees and distributed by bee movement and grooming behavior. They may contain miticides or inert powders such as talcum powder or powdered sugar that induce mites to drop from the bees to a sticky trap placed below the colony.

Modes of action. An understanding of miticide pharmacology can help beekeepers manage their selection of chemical control tools. As more control options become available, miticide selection will be an important aspect of resistance management. If a mite population is not effectively reduced by a compound, another compound with a similar mode of action would not be a good choice for subsequent treatments. Most toxins interfere with specific metabolic processes. Brown[4] indicated a rough grouping of insecticides by their mode of action (Table 13.1). The same groupings can be applied to miticides. In addition to toxins, some compounds serve as *synergists* which act by increasing the toxicity of another compound. The mode of action of some compounds, such as various essential oils, remains unknown[26].

Toxicity. A poison is any agent capable of producing a deleterious response in a biological system, seriously injuring functions or produc-

Table 13.1 Classification of insecticides on the basis of their mode of action[48].

Groups	Subgroups	Examples
Physical poisons	——	Heavy mineral oil, inert dust
Protoplasmic poisons	——	Heavy metals, e.g. Hg acids
Metabolic Inhibitors	Respiratory poisons	HCN, CO, H_2S, rotenone, dinitrophenols
	Inhibitors of mixed-function oxidase	Pyrethrin synergists
	Inhibitors of carbohydrate metabolism	Sodium fluoroacetate
	Inhibitors of amine metabolism	Chlordimeform
	Insect hormones	Juvenile hormone analogues
	Inhibitors of chitin synthesis	Diflubenzuron
Neuroactive agents (non metabolic)	Anticholinesterases	Organophosphorus compounds, carbamates
	Effects on ion permeability	DDT analogues, pyrethroids
	Agents for nerve receptors	Nicotine analogues, cyclodiene compounds, BHC
Hormone mimics		Methoprene
Stomach Poisons		*Bacillus thuringiensis* toxin

ing death. For example: two aspirins will cure a headache, but 200 will kill you. A pesticide bioassay is an experiment to estimate the probability that a pest population will respond in the desired manner. If the desired outcome is death, the results are reported as the LD$_{50}$, LC$_{50}$, or LT$_{50}$ (lethal dose, lethal concentration, or lethal exposure time, respectively, to 50 percent of a population). Variation is a characteristic of almost all biological systems, and toxicologists always report their results in terms of a population of organisms.

Pesticide bioassays measure a *quantal* (all or none) response. For example, the test organism dies or lives, molts or does not molt. To conduct a pesticide bioassay, one must apply a range of concentrations of a test compound to a population of test subjects. A good bioassay will have six or more replications of ten subjects for each concentration[40]. Assays of one randomly selected dose of a candidate compound provide little information about the potential value of that compound, but they are commonly reported in popular beekeeping literature and in some scientific literature. Experimental laboratory techniques for making serial concentrations and conducting exposures are described by Busvine[5], Shephard[43], Chen and Moss[8], Gage[20], Phalen[35], and Nelson[33].

The results of pesticide bioassays are interpreted by using *probit analysis*[16]. Probit analysis provides an estimate of the expected response of a test organism population to various concentrations of the candidate compound. It also establishes a confidence interval around the estimated values. Results of pesticide bioassays are frequently reported by providing the slope of the dose-response regression and the LD$_{50}$ of test organisms. Both measures are usually accompanied by confidence intervals around the estimated values.

In the case of a parasite, the response of the pest and its host must be determined separately. When both values are known, the relative toxicities can be compared. If the dose-response regressions are parallel, the relative toxicity will have a fixed value for all concentrations. If the regression lines are not parallel, the relative toxicities may only be compared at a specific response level (such as LD$_{50}$ or LD$_{90}$).

Safety to user. The major factors that influence user safety are the toxicity of the chemical, the route of administration, and the frequency of exposure. The effect(s) may be acute or chronic. Acute toxicity results from short-term exposure that occurs in less than 24 hours. *Chronic* toxicity results from repeated exposure for long periods of time.

Toxicity ratings charts are available for oral, dermal, and inhalation exposure. Table 13.2 provides a toxicity rating chart for acute oral and dermal exposure[48]. While acute effects are immediately apparent, chronic exposure can have equally damaging results if the toxin accumulates in tissues or organs. Pesticide labels indicate protective measures applicators should take to protect themselves. As stated previously, toxicology is a science of doses, and most pesticides will injure humans if the exposure is great enough.

Chemicals used for control. As early as the 16th century, Paracelsus (1493-1541) observed that toxicology is a science of doses. The right dose often separates a poison from a remedy. The potential value of a chemical treatment cannot be fairly evaluated by applying a randomly

Table 13.2 Pesticide toxicity classes[4].				
Routes of Absorption				
Toxicity Rating	Commonly Used Term	LD_{50} Single Oral Dose Rats mg/kg	LD_{50} Single Dermal Dose Rabbits mg/kg	Probable Lethal Oral Dose For Man
1	Extremely toxic	1 mg or less	20 mg or less	A taste, a grain
2	Highly toxic	1-50 mg	20-200 mg	A pinch-1 tsp.
3	Moderately toxic	50-500 mg	200-1,000 mg	1 tsp.-2 tbsp.
4	Slightly toxic	500-5,000 mg	1,000-2,000 mg	1 oz.-1 pint
5	Practically non toxic	5,000-15,000 mg	2,000-20,000 mg	1 pint-1 quart
6	Relatively harmless	> 15,000 mg	> 20,000 mg	> 1 quart

selected dose to a colony. A methodical approach that examines the effect of the chemical at a range of concentrations is needed to fairly evaluate its potential value. To obtain reliable results, studies should be replicated, test subjects should be randomly assigned to treatment groups, and untreated controls should be included in the test. Scientific publications require peer review to assure that the scientific method was followed and that the results obtained are reliable. Beekeepers should seek research-based information about chemical treatments. Likewise, they should be wary of anecdotal advice and recommendations that have not been published in a scientific journal and subjected to scrutiny. In the information age, where ideas circulate the globe at incredible speed, it is especially important that beekeepers carefully scrutinize their sources of information. It is also important that beekeepers understand the legal status of any chemical treatments that they consider using.

Most chemical controls for varroa are based on chemicals that have been previously developed as pesticides to control mite pests of crops and livestock. For use as varroacides, they are used at concentrations that are lethal to varroa but harmless to bees. Other treatments use commonly available or naturally occurring compounds that exhibit some varroacidal activity. To date, no new chemical has been developed primarily for the purpose of controlling varroa in honey bee colonies.

Fluvalinate. Fluvalinate is a synthetic pyrethroid chemical that was first developed for use on ornamental plants. Lubinevski and others[28] observed activity against varroa at concentrations that had no observable effect on bees. It is currently packaged by Wellmark Inc. for beekeepers in a miticide impregnated strip, Apistan®. Three strip concentrations are available. Ten percent strips are used to treat colonies, 2.5% strips are used to treat package bees, and 1% strips are used to treat caged queen bees and their attendants. The target site for fluvalinate is the axonal transmission of nerve impulses. Package bee and queen strips should be left in place for 3-4 days (usually accomplished when they are in transit). For treating colonies, one strip should be applied for every five frames of bees and brood. They should be suspended in the brood nest for 6-8 weeks. When properly applied they are 98-100% effective on susceptible mite populations. Care should be taken to avoid exposing the strips to sunlight as they are rapidly degraded by ultraviolet light. Apistan strips can be used at any time except when bees are storing surplus honey for harvest.

Fluvalinate is a contact toxin. It is essential that strips are located in contact with the bee cluster. Improper placement can result in poor control. It is distributed in the hive by bee to bee contact. Fluvalinate is a lipophilic molecule. If residues are detected in hive products, they are more likely to be found in beeswax than in honey.

In 1995, resistance to fluvalinate was reported in Italy[27]. In 1998, fluvalinate resistance was found in Florida[11]. Apistan remains an effective miticide for most varroa populations, but recent studies[12] indicate that resistance to fluvalinate is spreading and beekeepers should monitor their colonies for resistance (Chapter 17). Pettis and his colleagues[34] have developed a resistance monitoring protocol that can be used to determine if Apistan will be effective before applying treatment. The protocol calls for assaying two groups of adult bees in separate pint jars using sections of 2.5% and 10% fluvalinate strips stapled to note cards. The assay requires no specialized equipment, and it can be performed by beekeepers. Elzen and her colleagues[14] have developed a laboratory bioassay using a discriminating dose of 2.4 microliters of technical grade fluvalinate to coat 20 ml scintillation vials. Ten adult mites are transferred from brood cells to the vials along with one bee pupa as a food source. The vials are held in darkness at 26°C for 24 hours and then evaluated for mite mortality. Eighty to 90% of the mites should die in fluvalinate-susceptible populations. A lower response indicates that a varroa population has developed resistance to fluvalinate.

Flumethrin. Flumethrin is another synthetic pyrethroid chemical that is used in plant pest control. It is packaged for beekeepers in miticide impregnated plastic strips, Bayvarol® (Bayer). Bayvarol is currently used extensively in Europe, but it is not available in the United States. Like fluvalinate, it is highly effective on susceptible mite populations[30]. There is no withdrawal period for honey, and it can be used at any time when bees are not storing surplus honey for harvest. It is essential to locate strips in contact with the bee cluster. Strips are normally applied in autumn or early spring for six weeks. Flumethrin is similar to fluvalinate in its mode of action and chemical properties. If mite populations are not susceptible to fluvalinate, it is unlikely that flumethrin will control them.

Amitraz. Amitraz is a behavior-affecting compound in the formamidine group of chemicals. It was registered for use in the United States under the trade name of Miticur® by Hoechst-Roussel, but the product was withdrawn from the U.S.A. market due to beekeeper reports of colony injury and litigation. The target site for Amitraz is the octopamine receptor. Octopamine serves as a "fight or flight" neurohormone in arthropods. Varroa's response to amitraz is not immediate acute mortality. Mortality can be expected to occur over several days following treatment.

Amitraz is used in France in a miticide-impregnated strip, Apivar®. Strips must be positioned in contact with the bee cluster. The active ingredient is spread within the colony by direct contact with strips and by bees contacting other bees with the miticide on their bodies. Strips are applied in the autumn or early spring for six weeks. Amitraz is a lipophilic molecule. If residues are detected in hive products, they are more likely to be found in beeswax than in honey. To date, varroa that are resistant to Amitraz have not been detected.

Coumaphos. Coumaphos is an organophosphate compound. It has been used in Europe as Perizin® (Bayer). Perizin is an emulsion in water that is trickled over the bees. It was originally thought to be a systemic compound that was spread by food sharing[38]. More recent studies by van Buren and his colleagues[46] have demonstrated that only a small portion of the material reaches the bees blood and that direct contact with the material is necessary for mite control. Recent studies in the U.S.A. and Europe[13,29] have shown that coumaphos can be delivered effectively in a miticide-impregnated plastic strip. Currently (January 1999), coumaphos strips are available in the U.S.A. to beekeepers in several states under a Section 18 or "emergency use" registration. Bayer is completing residue studies on the strip formulation and will seek section 3 or "general use" registration when the required studies are completed.

The target site for coumaphos is synaptic transmission of nerve impulses. It inhibits the production of acetyl cholinesterase, a chemical that breaks down the neurotransmitter, acetylcholine. Coumaphos is a lipophilic molecule. If residues are detected in hive products, they are more likely to be found in beeswax than in honey. Coumaphos has the added advantage of effectively controlling the small hive beetle, *Aethina tumida*[2], an introduced beetle that feeds on honey, brood, and pollen. The beetle has caused extensive damage to colonies in coastal areas of the Southeast. It can be controlled by removing the corrugations from one side a four by four inch piece of cardboard, stapling a coumaphos strip cut into two equal parts to the exposed corrugations, and then placing the cardboard on the bottom board with the strip side down.

Cymiazole. Cymiazole is a modified heterocyclic compound, cymiazole hydrochloride. It is available as a powder that is dissolved in syrup and fed to bees, Apitol® (Ciba-Geigy). It is a systemic compound that is spread in the colony by food sharing. It is absorbed by varroa mites when they pierce and feed on adult bees. It is a water soluble molecule. If residues are detected in hive products, they are more likely to be found in honey than in beeswax. Cymiazole's hydrophilic nature and high price make it more attractive for package and queen production than for honey production. The mode of application (fed in syrup) makes it easy to incorporate into bee management. Toxicity to brood can be a problem if fed to the bees over a long time[10] also, residues in honey can be a persistent problem[6].

Rademacher[36] examined a modified version of Apitol called Apitol-Kombi. This product replaced 50% of the cymiazole with lactic acid. This change would reduce the costs and lower the risks of brood toxicity. However, she was only able to achieve 83% control in field tests.

Bromopropylate. Folbex-VA is a diphenylcarbinol acaricide (chemically related to DDT). It is packaged for beekeepers in a paper strip which contains potassium nitrate and bromopropylate, Folbex-VA® (Ciba-Geigy). Strips are ignited and left to smolder in hives. The potassium nitrate serves to make the strips smolder when they burn, and the material works as a fumigant. Bees must be confined to the hive and broodless for full efficacy. Rademacher and Geiseler[37] achieved 98% varroa control in broodless colonies.

Bromopropylate is a persistent lipophilic molecule. If residues are detected in hive products, they are more likely to be found in beeswax than in honey. While it is used in Europe, there has not been much interest in seeking registration in the U.S.A.

Essential oils. Currently, one essential oil-based product is available for varroa control in Europe, Api-LifeVAR®(LAIF)[21]. It is a porous vermiculite tablet impregnated with a blend of thymol (76%), eucalyptol (16.4%), menthol (3.8%), and camphor (3.8%). Thymol clearly exhibits varroacidal properties,[9] but the value and purpose of the other essential oil ingredients has not been clearly established. The compound works as a fumigant and is applied in saturated absorbent blocks placed over the brood combs. Its effectiveness is limited by temperature and it can exhibit bee toxicity at high temperatures[19].

Most essential oils are lipophilic compounds, but some exhibit weak polar affinities. If residues are detected in hive products, they are more likely to be detected in beeswax than honey. Some essential oils naturally occur in honey, and there are fewer barriers to registering them as miticides than are encountered in registering synthetic pesticides.

The mode of action of essential oils is unknown, and different essential oils may have different target sites[44]. Essential oils vary greatly in their toxicity to bees and mites. Beekeepers should be sure that any recommendations for their use are research-based and approved for use in bee hives. Some essential oils are highly toxic to bees and can injure colonies.

These naturally occurring compounds are an attractive class of compounds for developing novel varroacides due to their biodegradibility, selective toxicity to arthropods, and their use as flavoring and fragrance ingredients in food products. Currently, we know that some of them bind to target sites in varroa mites and are more toxic to mites than bees. At present, their efficacy is limited by their temperature sensitivity and the small margin of safety between the concentrations that will kill varroa and injure bees. Studies to identify their target site(s) and mode(s) of action are needed to develop them as varroacidal tools for beekeeping. Essential oils examined to date have not provided consistent control under a range of conditions[7]. Synthetic analogs of essential oils may offer the best opportunity to develop a new compound specifically to control varroa mites in beehives.

Formic acid. Formic acid efficacy against varroa was demonstrated by Ritter and Ruttner[39]. Subsequently, liquid formic acid has been shown to control varroa in a wide variety of situations[18,32,47]. Formic acid is a highly volatile compound. It interferes with basic metabolic and respiratory processes. The most widely recommended application rate is to apply 2 ml of 60% formic acid for each comb. The liquid is applied to pads or plates and placed above or below the brood nest. At high concentration, formic acid will kill mites in sealed brood. Three to four treatments are usually required to achieve a high degree of control.

Recently, Feldlaufer and his colleagues[15] developed a gel formulation of formic acid that is safer to the applicator and less likely to injure humans or bees. However, the degree of varroa control, 70%, was lower than beekeepers have come to expect with synthetic acaricides. Their gel-based product was approved for use in the U.S.A. in 1999.

Formic acid volatility and concentration in the hive are influenced by temperature, wind, hive size and condition, placement, and colony strength. Therefore, beekeepers should expect some inconsistency in performance. Under optimum research conditions, control can equal that achieved with synthetic pesticides. However, conditions are usually less than optimum in practical beekeeping.

Formic acid is water soluble, and residues are more likely to occur in honey than beeswax. Trace amounts of formic acid naturally occur in several food items, including honey, and residues tend to dissipate with time and exposure to heat.

Formic acid liquid and vapors can severely injure mammals, and it should be handled with care. Neoprene gloves and good ventilation are essential when handling. In some situations a gas mask with an organic vapor cartridge may be needed.

Lactic and oxalic acid. Lactic and oxalic acids have been tested in Germany for varroa control with reasonable success, however their application is very labor intensive. For lactic acid treatment, individual combs are removed and sprayed on both sides with five ml of a 15% solution[23]. As the treatment does not affect the mites in brood, it has to be repeated several times. In colonies free of brood, Kraus and Berg[24] were able to achieve control of most of the mites by treating twice in autumn at an outdoor temperature of at least 6°C. Similar results were achieved with oxalic acid by Fischermuhle[17]. Although both materials are natural products, recommendations are for use only when surplus honey supers are not on the colony. The labor required to use these products has limited their attractiveness to beekeepers.

Natural products smoke. Beekeepers routinely use smoke to calm their bees before opening the hive. Tobacco smoke increases mite fall and has been used for both detection[42] and control[41] of varroa. More recently, Eischen and Wilson[12] demonstrated that the creosote bush and grapefruit leaves produce a smoke that can knock down 90 percent of the mites in test cages. However, in these studies it was found that excessive exposure can harm bees. Also, mites are not usually killed by the smoke and may recover if not removed from the colony by sticky boards or other mite trapping devices. Mites in brood cells are not affected by natural product smoke. While natural product smoke is not an approved treatment for varroa, there is no legislation prohibiting their use as smoker fuel. With careful attention to bee safety, the smoke of some natural products may be helpful in retarding varroa population growth in colonies. Further details are given in a review article by Adams[1].

For additional reading on the chemical control of varroa refer to the Ministry of Agriculture, Fisheries and Food (UK) web site: <*http://www.airtime.co.uk/beekeeping/apiary/maff.htm*>[31]. Like all Internet web pages, it is subject to change, but as of January 1999, it provided an excellent review of the status of products used world-wide. Another review of the subject by Wolfgang Ritter is available in a book published by the International Bee Research Association[22].

Residues in hive products. Honey and beeswax rely on their image as pure and natural products to command prices considerably higher than prices paid for competing sweeteners and paraffin waxes. The need to preserve the purity of honey and beeswax cannot be overstated. Likewise, the need to control varroa cannot be overstated if beekeepers are to remain in business. When pesticides are registered for use to control bee pests, tolerance levels are set for residues in hive products. Pesticides that are not approved for use have a zero tolerance level. Prior to registration, studies must be done to show that use of the product in the prescribed manner will not result in residues that exceed the approved tolerance limit. Carefully following the instructions on the product label is the best way to maintain product integrity while controlling a pest that would devastate the hive if left unchecked.

Summary. Chemical acaricides have been the most important tool, worldwide, for managing varroa. Understanding miticide pharmacology will help beekeepers manage their selection and use of chemical tools wisely. Understanding how to apply products correctly will protect the integrity of hive products, and it will protect applicators from injury. Understanding the importance of resistance management measures will help preserve the efficacy of chemical tools. Varroa mites are capable of developing resistance to chemical tools, and there are a limited number of chemicals that will control varroa without harming bees.

Maintaining productive colonies with varroa present in an apiary requires a thorough understanding of varroa mite biology, detection, and control. For now, that includes an understanding of chemicals used to control the mite, and issues that surround their use.

References cited.

1. **Adams, S. 1997.** Smoking out bee mites. Agric. Res. 45(8): 19.

2. **Baxter, J. R., P. J. Elzen, D. Westervelt, D. Causey, C. Randall, F. A. Eischen & W. T. Wilson. 1999.** Control of the small hive bee-tle, *Aethina tumida*, in package bees. Am. Bee J. 139: 792-793

3. **Biove Laboratories. 1998.** Web site as of Jan. 1999: <http://www.apiservices.com/biove/index.htm>

4. **Brown, *A*. W. *A*. 1951.** Insect control by chemicals. Wiley. New York.

5. **Busvine, J. R. 1971.** Critical review of the techniques for testing insecticides. Commonwealth Agricultural Bureau. London, England.

6. **Cabras, P., M. G. Martini, I. Floris, & L. Spanedda. 1994.** Residues of cymiazole in honey and honeybees. J. Apic. Res. 33: 83-86.

7. **Calderone, N. W., W. T. Wilson & M. Spivak. 1997.** Plant extracts used for control of the parasitic mites *Varroa jacobsoni* (Acari: Varroidae) and *Acarapis woodi* (Acari: Tarsonemidae) in colonies of *Apis mellifera* (Hymenoptera: Apidae). J. Econ. Entomol. 90: 1080-1086.

8. **Chen, Y. S. & O. R. Moss. 1989.** Inhalation exposure systems (p.19-62). in R. O. McClellan and R.F. Henderson Eds. Concepts in Inhalation Toxicology. Hemisphere Publishing Corporation. New York.

9. **Chiesa, F. 1991.** Effective control of varroa using powdered thymol. Apidologie 22: 135-145.

10. **Dietz, *A*., D. S. Hurley, J. S. Pettis & F. *A*. Eischen. 1987.** Controlling *Acarapis woodi* (Rennie) in package bee colonies with

Apitol. Am. Bee J: 127: 843

11. **Eischen, F. A. 1998.** Varroa control problems: some answers. Am. Bee J: 138: 107-108.

12. **Eischen, F. A. & W. T. Wilson. 1998.** The effect of natural product smoke on *Varroa jacobsoni*: An update. Am. Bee J: 138: 293.

13. **Ellis, M. D., M. Spivak & M. Reed. 1998.** An evaluation of coumaphos impregnated plastic strips for varroa control in the Midwest. Am. Bee J: 138: 293-294.

14. **Elzen, P. J., F. A. Eischen, J. R. Baxter, J. Pettis, G. W. Elzen & W. T. Wilson. 1998.** Fluvalinate resistance in *Varroa jacobsoni* from several geographic locations. Am. Bee J: 138: 674-676.

15. **Feldlaufer, M., J. S. Pettis, J. P. Kochansky & H. Shiminuki. 1997.** A gel formulation of formic acid for the control of parasitic mites of honey bees. Am. Bee J. 137: 661-663.

16. **Finney, D. J. 1971.** Probit Analysis. Cambridge University Press. Cambridge, England.

17. **Fischermühle, H. 1994.** Oxalsäure - eine weitere organische Saure zur Varroa behandlung. Deutches Bienen Z. 2: 654-658.

18. **Fries, I. 1989.** Short-interval treatments with formic acid for control of *Varroa jacobsoni* in honeybees (*Apis mellifera*) colonies in cold climates. Swedish J. Agric. Res. 19: 213-216.

19. **Gal. H., Y. Slabezki & Y. Lensky. 1992.** A preliminary report on the effect of origanum oil and thymol applications in honey bee (*Apis mellifera* L.) colonies in a subtropical climate on population levels of *Varroa jacobsoni*. Bee Science 2: 175-179.

20. **Gage, J. C. 1970.** Experimental inhalation toxicity pp 258-278. *In* G. E. Paget [ed.] Methods in Toxicology. Blackwell Scientific Publications. Oxford.

21. **Imdorf A., S. Bogdanov, V. Kilchenmann & C. Maquelin. 1995.** Apilife Var: A new varroacide with thymol as the main ingredient. Bee World 76: 77-83.

22. **International Bee Research Association. 1993.** Living with *Varroa*. International Bee Research Association. Cardiff, UK.

23. **Kraus, B. 1991.** Preliminary report on lactic acid winter application as treatment of varroatosis. Apidologie 2: 473-475.

24. **Kraus, B. & S. Berg. 1994.** Effect of lactic acid treatment during winter in temperate climate upon *Varroa jacobsoni* Oud. and the bee (*Apis mellifera*) colony. Exp. Appl. Acarol: 18: 459-468.

25. **Larson, L. 1998.** Dow Elanco. Personal communication.

26. **Lee, S., R. Tsao, C. Peterson & J. R. Coats. 1997.** Insecticidal activity of monoterpenoids to western corn rootworm (Coleoptera: Chrysomelidae), two spotted spider mite (Acari:Tetranychidae) and house fly (Diptera: Muscidae). J. Econ. Entomol: 90: 883-892.

27. **Lodesani, M., M. Colombo & M. Spreafico. 1995.** Ineffectiveness of Apistan® treatment against the mite *Varroa jacobsoni* Oud. in several districts of Lombardy (Italy). Apidologie 26: 67-72.

28. **Lubinevski, Y., Y. Stern, Y. Slabezki, Y. Lensky, H. Ben-Yossef & U. Gerson. 1988.** Control of *Varroa jacobsoni* and *Tropilaelaps clareae* mites using Mavrik in *A. mellifera* colonies under subtropical and tropical climates. Am. Bee J: 128: 48-52.

29. **Milani, N. 1998.** Plastic strips containing organophosphorus acaricides to control *Varroa jacobsoni*: a preliminary experiment. Am. Bee J. 138: 612-615

30. **Milani, N. & R. Barbattini. 1989.** Treatment of varroatosis with Bayvarol strips (flumethrin) in Northern Italy. Apicoltura. 5: 173-192.

31. **Ministry of Agriculture, Fisheries and Food (UK). Web site as of Jan. 1999:** <http://www.airtime.co.uk/beekeeping/apiary/maff.htm>.

32. **Nelson, D., P. Mills, P. Sporns, S. Ooraikul & D. Mole. 1994.** Formic acid application methods for the control of honey bee tracheal mites. Bee Science. 3: 128-134.

33. **Nelson, G. O. 1971.** Controlled test atmospheres, Principles and techniques. Ann Arbor Science. Ann Arbor, MI.

34. **Pettis, J. S., H. Shiminuki & M. F. Feldlaufer. 1998.** An assay to detect fluvalinate resistance in varroa mites. Am. Bee J: 138: 538-541.

35. **Phalen, R. F. 1984.** Inhalation studies: Foundations and techniques. CRC Press. Boca Raton, FL.

36. **Rademacher, E. 1993.** Apitol-Kombi - A new product for controlling *Varroa jacobsoni* pp. 530-540. *In* L. Connor, T. Rinderer, A. Sylvester, and S. Wongsiri., Eds. Asian Apiculture. Wicwas Press. Cheshire, CT.

37. **Rademacher, E. & E. Geiseler. 1986.** Die *Varroa*tose der Bienen: Geschichte, Diagnose, Therapie. Schelzky und Jeep. Berlin, Germany.

38. **Ritter, W. 1986.** *Varroa*tosis in the honey bee, *Apis mellifera*, and its control with Perizin. Vet. Med. Rev. 1: 3-16.

39. **Ritter, W. & F. Ruttner. 1980.** Neue Wege in der Behandlung der Varroatose - Ameisensaure. Allgemeine. Deutsche Imkerzeitung 14: 151-159.

40. **Robertson, J. R. & H. K. Preisler. 1992.** Pesticide bioassays with Arthropods. CRC Press, Boca Raton, Florida.

41. **Ruijter, A. de. 1982.** Tobacco smoke can kill varroa mites. Bee World 63: 138.

42. **Ruijter, A. de & J. V. D. Eijnde. 1984.** Detection of varroa mite in the Netherlands using tobacco smoke. Bee World 65: 151-154.

43. **Shephard, H. H., ed. 1960.** Methods of testing chemicals on insects, II. Burgess Publishing, Minneapolis, MN.

44. **Tsao, R., S. Lee, P. J. Rice, C. Jensen & J. R. Coats. 1995.** Monoterpenoids and their synthetic derivatives as leads for new insect-control agents pp. 312-324. *In* Synthesis and Chemistry of Agrochemicals IV. American Chemical Society. Washington, D.C.

45. **USDA. 1997.** National Agriculture Statistics Service Commodity Report for Honey. Web site as of Jan. 1999. <http://www.usda.gov/nass/pubs/estindx2.htm#honey>.

46. **Van Buren, N. W. M., A. G. H. Marien & H. H. W. Velthuis. 1992.** The role of trophallaxis in the distribution of Perizin in a honeybee colony with regard to the control of the Varroa mite. Entomol. Exp. Appl. 65: 157-164.

47. **Wachendorfer, G., J. Fijalkowski, E. Kaiser, D. Seinsche & J.**

Siebentritt. **1985.** Laboratory and field tests with Illertisser Milbenplatte, a new application of formic acid to control varroatosis. Apidologie. 16: 291-305.

48. **Ware, G.W. 1975.** Pesticides. W.H. Freeman Co. San Francisco.

BIOTECHNICAL CONTROL OF VARROA MITES

Chapter 14

Roger Hoopingarner

*I*ntroduction. The descriptive term "biotechnical" refers to practices in which the beekeeper manipulates the environment of the hive, or conditions within the hive, such that the biology of the mite works against itself. In its general usage it does not mean using genetic selection to change the biology of either the host or the mite, but only the technical means of control. Genetic means of control are covered Chapter 15.

As we become more familiar with the life history of *Varroa jacobsoni,* it is possible that more emphasis on bio-technical control will be observed—especially in beekeeping operations with just a few hives where intensive labor manipulations are not an economic concern. It is also possible that as we learn more about the biology of the mite, we will use more than one of these techniques at one time, including genetic selection for resistance.

In this chapter I will cover those techniques that have been studied most extensively. I will then summarize by indicating some of the levels of control needed to create effective long-term solutions. A systems model was developed to compare different control techniques, and by what level of control must be obtained to have effective control by these methods. I will conclude with some speculations as to ultimate limits and a possible solution to the varroa problem by non-chemical means.

Trapping varroa with drone brood. It has been found that varroa mites prefer to reproduce in drone brood cells. The reason for this distinction may be twofold. First, the time period available for mites to enter into the brood cells before capping is about twice as long for drone brood as for worker brood[1]. Drone larvae also have certain chemicals that make them more attractive than worker larvae[8]. It is also possible that the mites find their preferred host (drone larvae) by other means such as cell height[3].

Varroa show a four-to-ten-times greater preference for the drone brood relative to worker brood. This preference is used for the drone brood trapping method. The technique uses at least two frames of drone comb for each colony. One is placed into the center of the broodnest. When the cells are sealed, and the mites are within the cells, the comb is removed and frozen. The second frame replaces the first within the broodnest. Since the time necessary for the cells to be sealed is 11 or 12 days (3 days for the egg plus 8 days for the larva), the process of removing and replacing combs is generally on a two-week timetable.

The success of this technique has been somewhat variable. This may be in part due to location, e.g., northern versus southern locations in Europe where it has been tried the most, or for other reasons such as stock, combs or rotation schedule[10]. However, if done with regular removal and with anywhere between 100-900 drone cells per kilogram of bees[12], the system seems to work quite well.

The criticism of the method is, first, that it is labor intensive by requiring the regular removal of the drone combs. Secondly, there is a fair amount of energy expended by the colony in raising the drone brood that is removed. The shortness of the drone production season also affects its success in controlling varroa, as well as the fact that usually not all the drone cells are found on the introduced drone combs.

One further problem with this method is that it exerts constant selection against the mites that prefer drone brood. This is not in the long-term best interest of a varroa reduction program. If beekeepers could select colonies that had mites that only developed on drones, then the problem of varroa would be reduced to insignificance. By selecting in just the opposite way beekeepers would be working against a good long-term solution.

Trapping varroa with worker brood. *Varroa* requires a developing pupa for reproduction, and disruption of the brood cycle limits its population growth. If the female mites were found only within a brood cell then the simple expedient of removing all the brood would eliminate the mites. However, there is a significant time period when the female mite feeds on an adult bee. This period is called the phoretic period. Trapping-comb techniques will only work if they are done long enough to allow the phoretic mites to enter brood cells.

The technique generally involves confining the queen to about three combs inside a queen-excluder chamber. The brood combs are then removed on either a 7- or a 9-day interval for about three cycles.

This method of control has been reasonably successful in Sweden and other northern countries[4]. The technique is obviously very labor intensive and thus could be used only with a few colonies. It also severely reduces the honey bee population at the same time as the mites are being reduced. Thus, the method should only be used when the honey bee population can afford the drastic reduction, e.g., at the end of the honey flow, but prior to the production of winter bees. The trapping comb technique has also been used in conjunction with drone trapping with good results.

Trapping varroa in manually uncapped brood. A variation of the above method uses the removal of the cell caps in order to increase the available time that mites can enter the cells. The technique requires carefully removing the cappings and then placing the comb within a screen cage so that the bees will not replace the caps. When some additional time has elapsed with the trap-comb in the cage, the comb is removed with the mites and the brood and mites are frozen to destroy them.

The cappings can be removed with a textile, or plastic sheet the size of the frame, which has been dipped into melted beeswax and then quickly placed on the comb. This melts the cappings onto the material. After it has cooled it is carefully removed, so that the cappings are removed also.

Like the previous method this technique requires a large amount of labor and controlled timing. It also removes a significant amount of brood, though it could be less if the extra time of exposure to the mites traps significantly more mites per comb, and thus you would have to use fewer combs. This latter point has not been sufficiently proven.

Thermal treatment. Research has shown that varroa mites can be killed at a sufficiently high temperature, but one that does not kill the bees. The method is especially effective with caged (package) bees where a temperature of 40-42° C. (104-108° F.) for at least 4 hours kills most of the mites[6]. When this control has been tried with whole colonies or with brood combs, the treatment has not been as successful because the colony exerts its own control over temperature extremes. In tests with colonies and brood the level of mite control has been in the range of 35-50%.

It is possible that there is a time-temperature relationship that would work to better advantage. Automatic systems could be developed to regulate time and temperature exposures. Some attempts have been made in Europe to automate heat control by putting colonies on a conveyer into an oven. Package-bee shippers should be able to use heat to effectively control mites.

Cell size modifications. Studies of cell size and modifications of the shape of the cell have been examined as much as any method for the control of varroa mites. For example, the difference in size of the worker and drone cells, along with the fact that varroa prefers drone cells for reproduction, is the reason for many of the research projects[5]. However, the main thrust in this section is the effect of worker cell size on reproduction of the mite, even though the sex of the bee larva has a great influence, regardless of the cell in which it is grown[7].

The smaller cell size of Africanized bees, along with the fact that these bees have fewer mites than European bees within the same setting, has led to the idea that possibly a small cell would limit mite reproduction. Just the opposite seems to be true. Larger cell sizes have fewer mites[11]. There also seems to be a strong correlation between the height of the cell and number of mites within those cells; the cells with greater distance between the larva and the rim having fewer mites.

The idea of cell shape has been used in the plastic ANP® combs where there is greater distance between the larva and the cell wall, especially at the base of the cell. These combs also seem to have fewer mites when there is a choice between combs[13] . This may be in part because the mites seem to have less time to enter these cells for reproduction.

Wire-screened bottom boards. This is an area of research that has just now started to be studied in any detail. I suggested the idea to some beekeepers a few years ago that varroa mites may be falling off the adult bees, by accident or by grooming, more often than we realized[2, 9]. When the mites fall to the bottom board and are not damaged by the grooming behavior, they may just scramble onto the next passing bee. However, if the bottom were screened with an 8-mesh hardware cloth, the mites would fall through and not be able to get back onto a bee. Bottom boards modified such that most of the bottom was screened were tried by a couple of beekeepers with some reasonably good empirical results. Scientific studies are now just being started. It is possible that a simple modification such as this could reduce the mite number significantly, and along with other techniques would aid in the survival of honey bee colonies.

Computer simulations. My former graduate student, Ahmad Al Ghamdi, and I developed a computer model of the honey bee colony and varroa mite populations. The idea was to test various control strategies to find the best time or conditions in which to control the mite. In our computer simulations almost no biotechnical control method was very effective in preventing the death of a colony in the long term. Some control programs would delay the decline and death until maybe the third year, but still could not prevent the collapse. The problem lies in the fact that these techniques do not reach the level of control necessary to prevent the rise in varroa populations to the critical level. In our model, the level of control has to be about 95% in order to effectively limit the growth of the mite population. We have not found a single biotechnical method that could reach this level of control. However, none of the simulations to date have combined more than two systems of control. It may be possible that by incorporating several schemes into a beekeeping management program that varroa may be controlled without use of chemicals. Most biotechnical control programs would require the use of a pesticide treatment at least in the third year to reduce the varroa population to a low level. Once the varroa population has been reduced by chemicals, then biotechnical control could resume for another two or three years before pesticides would have to be again applied.

Summary. The biotechnical control of varroa mites has been studied in many different places with varying degrees of success. Most systems depend upon the fact that the mites must enter a brood cell within which to reproduce. *Varroa* mites prefer drone cells since the potential number of offspring is much greater because of the longer pupal period of the drone. Drone-trapping techniques generally insert drone combs into the colony at about two-week intervals and then remove the sealed brood and trapped mites within and freeze them to kill the mites. Since between 70- and 80-percent of the mites are in brood cells, the system does reduce the number of mites. Repeat treatments are necessary because of the number of phoretic mites that remain on the adult bees.

Similar strategies using all of the brood combs as trapping combs have also been reasonably successful in reducing the mite populations. The timing of these procedures is very critical to its success.

The use of special combs has also been given as a means of control, as well as many other bio-technical methods. However, by using computer simulation studies it has been shown that most of these techniques will fail after three to five years for the simple reason that the level of control is not sufficient. To be successful a technique (or more than one method in combination) would have to reach a level of control near 95 percent to be effective in the long term. Further studies may provide a proper series of methods that would provide this level of control.

An area of study that apparently has not been developed in control of varroa has been non-insecticidal dusts. Such dusts have been used on some other arthropods with some reasonable success, but as far as I can determine they have not been used to any great degree to control varroa. Since many small arthropods are very susceptible to cuticle abrasion and desiccation, dusts and abrasive dusts might be effectively used. This treatment could be especially effective along with a screened bottom board.

References cited.

1. **Boot, W. J., J. N. M. Calis & J. Beetsma. 1992.** Differential periods of *Varroa* mite invasion into worker and drone cells of honey bees. Exp. Appl. Acar. 16: 293-301.

2. **Büchler, R. 1993.** Rate of damaged mites (*Varroa jacobsoni*) in natural mite fall with regard to seasonal effects and infestation development. Apidologie 24: 492-493.

3. **De Jong, D. & R. A. Morse. 1988.** Utilisation of raised brood cells of the honey bee, *Apis mellifera* (Hymenoptera: Apidae), by the bee mite, *Varroa jacobsoni* (Acarina: Varroidae). Entomol. Gen. 14: 103-106.

4. **Fries, I. & H. Hansen. 1993.** Biotechnical control of varroa mites in cold climates. Am. Bee J. 133: 435-438.

5. **Fuchs, S. 1990.** Preference for drone brood cells by *Varroa jacobsoni* Oud. in colonies of *Apis mellifera* carnica. Apidologie 21: 193-199.

6. **Harbo, J. R. & R. A. Hoopingarner. 1997.** Honey bees (Hymenoptera: Apidae) in the United States that express resistance to *Varroa jacobsoni* (Mesostigmata: Varroidae). J. Econ. Entomol. 90: 893-898.

7. **Issa, M. R. C., D. De Jong & L. S. Gonçalves. 1993.** Reproductive strategies of the mite *Varroa jacobsoni* (Mesostigmata, Varroidae): influence of larva type and comb size on honey bee brood infestation rates. Revista Brasil. Genet. 16: 219-224.

8. **Le Conte, Y., G. Arnold, J. Trouiller, C. Masson, B. Chappe & G. Ourisson. 1989.** Attraction of the parasitic mite *Varroa* to the drone larvae of honey bees by simple aliphatic esters. Science 245: 638-639.

9. **Leibig, G. 1994.** Entstehung und Zusammensetzung des natürlichen Milben(ab)falls. [Occurrence and composition of natural mite fall.]. Deutsches Bienen J. 2: 21-23.

10. **Marletto, F., A. Patetta & A. Manino. 1991.** Ulteriori prove di lotta alla varroasi mediante periodica asportazione di covata maschile. [Further tests on *Varroa* disease control by means of periodical drone brood removal.]. Apic. Mod. 82: 219-224.

11. **Ramon, H. & O. Van Laere. 1993.** Size of comb cell and reproduction of *Varroa jacobsoni.* pp. 521-529. *In* L. J. Connor, T. E. Rinderer, H. A. Sylvester & S. Wongseri, eds. Asian Apiculture. Wicwas Press, Cheshire, Connecticut.

12. **Schmidt-Bailey, J., S. Fuchs & R. Büchler. 1996.** Effectiveness of drone brood trapping combs in broodless honey bee colonies. Apidologie 27: 293-295.

13. **Wieting, J. & H. J. Ferenz. 1991.** Behavioral study on the invasion of honeybee brood by the mite *Varroa jacobsoni* on wax combs and ANP combs. Am. Bee J. 131: 117-118.

HONEY BEE RESISTANCE TO VARROA MITES

Marla Spivak
Otto Boecking

*I*ntroduction. Breeding the western honey bee (*Apis mellifera* L.) for resistance to the parasitic mite *Varroa jacobsoni* Oud. is the most sustainable yet difficult solution to the problems caused by this destructive mite pest. Treating infested colonies with acaricides is an effective short-term solution, but long-term acaricide use may contaminate bee products with chemical residues and select for mites that are resistant to the treatments. Currently, there is evidence of mite resistance to fluvalinate in Europe, Florida (USA) and Argentina[25,27,53] (and see Chapter 17).

Commercially available lines of honey bees that demonstrate resistance to varroa would alleviate the need for frequent and expensive acaricide use; however, there are difficulties inherent in breeding bees for resistance. The first difficulty is in identifying the mechanisms and characteristics of the bees that confer resistance. The second is in ensuring that these characteristics have a genetic basis (are heritable). Another difficulty is in the propagation, maintenance, and commercial distribution of lines of bees bred for resistance. Finally, there is ambiguity in the definition of resistance and in the goals for breeding resistant bees. It is not possible to breed bees that completely resist varroa infestation. Wherever honey bees and mites are found in the same locations, the mites will invade bee colonies. For this reason, many researchers prefer to use the term "tolerance" instead of resistance to signify that the colonies are infested but, nevertheless, are able to survive. Theoretically, with consistent selection pressure, lines of bees could be bred that could survive mite infestation without acaricide treatment. The most realistic goal, however, is to breed lines of bees with heritable defenses against the mites that allow them to survive mite infestation for a longer time than unselected stocks. These colonies would require less frequent acaricide treatments, but, if left unattended, might eventually succumb to parasitism. As a logical requirement, selection for resistance in the bees should not compromise honey production.

For bee colonies to survive any extended period of time without treatment, the bees must have mechanisms that limit the survivorship and/or reproductive success of the mites. In general, the population growth of varroa is influenced by the following factors[28]: (1) the successful entry of a mated female mite into a brood cell containing a fifth instar larva; (2) the successful reproduction of the mite within the cell (production of at least one mated female offspring); (3) the probability that the same mite will survive to enter another brood cell; and (4) the number of complete reproductive cycles a mite can complete within a season. .

In breeding bees for resistance to varroa, it is important to differentiate between the effects of genetics and of the environment on both the bee and the mite. For example, honey bee colonies in a particular environment may survive mite infestation without treatment, but the same colonies in a different environment may require periodic treatments. Or, colonies that appear resistant in one country may be so only because the mites there are less fertile than the mites in a different country. Mite fertility may be a function of mite genetics, but it could also be due to environmental factors associated with the bee colony (e.g., nutritional state) and/or genetic factors associated with the bee. Environmental effects on bees or mites may temporarily influence the reproductive success of the mites, but will not lead to sustainable resistance. Only bees that have genetic mechanisms of increasing the mortality and/or decreasing the fertility of the mites will demonstrate some degree of resistance.

This chapter will be divided into the following sections: (1) mite environment; (2) mite genetics; (3) bee environment; (4); bee genetics; and (5) current breeding programs. It is in no way intended to be a thorough review of all the research that has been done on these topics. Our aim is to highlight some of the key research findings in each topic to help focus attention on areas where more research is needed. We also recommend other review articles with somewhat different emphases[10,16].

Mite environment. Because varroa is an obligate parasite of the honey bee, the environment of the mite is restricted to the honey bee colony. In the section on Bee Environment (below) examples will be presented of how climatic and resource conditions that affect the entire bee colony may also affect the reproductive success of the mites within the colony. In this section, the discussion will be limited to the more immediate environment of the mite: the adult bees on which the mites are phoretic ("hitchhike"), and the developing larvae and pupae within the cells on which the mites reproduce. Genetic and environmental factors that influence the physiology of the individual adult and/or immature bee may also affect the physiology, and therefore the fertility of the mite. The behaviors and life-history of successfully reproducing varroa have been the subject of considerable research[4,16,21,22,23,24,48,50]. Of interest in breeding for resistance to varroa are the factors that limit the reproductive success of the mites.

Several researchers have asked whether increasing the phoretic period of the mites on adult bees decreases the mite's reproductive success (reviewed in Büchler[12]). For example, in winter, or when no brood is available in the nest, the mites are restricted to adult bees. Mites collected from adult bees during the winter were less fertile when introduced into brood cells containing fifth instar larvae than mites transferred during summer months[38]. When mites were forced to remain phoretic for six weeks during the summer and there were no young nurse bees in the colony, the reproductive success of the mites was diminished[71], although some mites continued to reproduce successfully despite the unfavorable colony conditions imposed by the experimental procedure. When mites were forced to be phoretic for a shorter period of time in summer, 10, 16, and 20 days, the proportion of successfully reproducing mites was not affected by the time spent on adult bees[11].

Other researchers have asked what inhibits the initiation of oviposition once a mite enters a cell containing a fifth instar larva. A fertile female mite will initiate egg-laying approximately 60 hours after the cell is capped. In cases where the mites do not initiate oviposition, it is unclear whether it is due to the status of the mite or to some factor within the brood cell. Hänel and Koeniger[38] hypothesized that mites do not initiate oviposition on *A. cerana* worker brood because the "trigger" signal from worker brood has a lower stimulus intensity than does the signal from drone brood. The nature of the "trigger" signal remains unknown. It was first postulated that the induction of oogenesis (egg development) by the mite within brood cells was regulated by juvenile hormone (JH III) from the bee larva[37,38]. When JH was applied to worker larvae, the reproductive rate of mites collected from bees during the winter increased. However, in subsequent studies, JH titers were radioimmunosassayed from fifth instar larvae of *A. m. carnica*, *A. m. lamarckii*, and Africanized bees in temperate and tropical climates[72], and from fifth instar larvae of *A. cerana* and *A. mellifera* in the same location[73] . In both studies no differences in hormone titres were found among the different bees and it was concluded that JH III could not be the trigger for mite oogenesis.

In a separate study in which comb sections containing brood from six different bee races and four hybrids were introduced into one infested colony, Fuchs[31] found that the genetic source of the larva did not influence the initiation of oviposition. Additionally, the number of mites that infested an individual cell did not limit the initiation of oviposition, as each female produced a male offspring (the first egg laid in the cell by each female); however, the successful development of the subsequent female offspring was reduced in cells infested by multiple mites[32,49]. Fuchs[31] concluded that the initiation of oviposition is mostly influenced by "unknown colony factors influencing the reproductive state of varroa when they enter cells for reproduction." Nazzi and Milani[59] speculated that there may be an inhibitor of reproduction released into infested cells such that the fertility of subsequent mites that invade the cells is reduced. In this study, infested pupae were introduced into artificial cell cups in the laboratory; the presence of such an inhibitor has not been confirmed in natural conditions.

Of the mites that do initiate oviposition, successful reproduction may be limited if the eggs laid are not viable, or if viable female offspring are not produced. Recently, Martin and others[51] found that some females only produced male offspring, and that premature death of male offspring within other cells led to unfertilized adult female offspring. These unmated females could not subsequently produce haploid male offspring, although they did enter cells in an attempt to reproduce. Harris and Harbo[42] found that non-reproductive female mites had few or no spermatozoa in their seminal receptacles, which was probably related to inadequate fertilization of the female mites. Successful reproduction may be limited by the nutritional or hormonal state of the pupae during the development of female mites within a cell, which in turn may influence their fertility as adults. However, the nutritional state of the pupae may be influenced by the nutritional state of the colony (bee environment), genotype of larva (bee genetics), and/or genotype of the mite (mite genetics). Continued research, is critical to determine what factors regulate the initiation and successful reproduction of varroa on worker and drone brood. It also is necessary to determine if the high proportion of mites with low reproductive success in worker brood observed in some locations is stable over time, or if it is environmentally labile.

Mite genetics. Recent observations[1,2,3] of varroa infestation on *Apis cerana* Fabr. and *Apis mellifera* in Papua New Guinea and islands in Indonesia (Java, Irian Jaya, Biak and Yapen) have yielded some interesting new insights into the bee-mite interaction. *Varroa* mites reproduce successfully on drone brood but not on worker brood of *A. cerana*, which is typical of varroa infestations on this species of honey bee throughout most of its distribution in Asia. During 1992-1995 in Papua New Guinea and Irian Jaya, Anderson and coworkers observed that although the *A. mellifera* colonies in the same areas were infested with varroa, the mites were not reproducing on either the drone or worker brood. The lack of reproduction was observed also in Java during 1991 and 1992, but in subsequent years (1993-1995), mites were found reproducing in sealed worker and drone brood of *A. mellifera*. Anderson and Sukarsih[2] speculated that the observed change in varroa reproductive behavior in *A. mellifera* colonies in Java may be due to a new "strain" of varroa introduced to Java after January, 1992. Recent experiments and DNA analyses of the mite indicates that in fact there now may be two types of varroa in this area[3].

Research on molecular genetic differences among mites from different locations (reviewed in de Guzman and Rinderer [18]) suggests that the varroa of the United States, Morocco, Germany, Italy, Spain, and Portugal are Russian in origin (via Europe), while mites of Brazil and Puerto Rico may be Japanese in origin. In a different study, genetic differences were found between mites collected from *A. mellifera* in the USA and mites in Germany, and these differences were more pronounced when compared to mites collected from *A. cerana* in Malaysia[44]. Current research is underway to determine the extent of these genetic differences among mites from different areas. Continued research is necessary to determine whether the genetic differences are related to differing reproductive success of the mites on the bee populations where they are found. (See also Chapters 1 and 8.)

Bee environment. There are seasonal, climatic, and internal colony conditions that influence the proportion of non-reproducing varroa in all colonies of *A. mellifera*[33,45,46,60]. Some interesting examples of how the environment may affect the bee-mite interaction are found in Brazil on Africanized bees. When varroa-resistant Africanized bees are moved from warmer to cooler climates in Brazil, such as from the lowlands in São Paulo to higher elevations in Santa Catarina, the infestation of varroa on worker brood increases[20,54]. In addition, a positive correlation was found between the amount of pollen stored in the nest and the percent of mites that reproduced on worker brood in lowlands of Brazil[55]. Colony factors that do not appear to affect the reproductive success of varroa include the size of worker cells[52], and colony temperature[5,70]. Although it is unclear how a cooler climate or the amount of stored pollen could affect the fertility of the mites, these observations emphasize the importance of testing "resistant" bee stocks in different environmental conditions to ensure that the observed resistance in one location is maintained in different geographic regions and resource conditions.

Bee genetics. Certain races and lines of bees appear to have genetic mechanisms that enable them to actively or passively defend themselves against the mites, although there is limited information on the nature of the mechanisms. There are reports that indicate the possibility of varroa resistance in Africanized bees from Brazil[69], European honey bees from Uruguay[69], and *A. mellifera intermissa* from Tunisia[68]. In these areas, varroa is reported to have low reproductive success on worker brood (but high reproductive success on drone brood).

Although some *A. m. intermissa* colonies in Tunisia have survived high varroa infestations without treatment for several years, the low reproductive success of varroa on worker brood does not seem to be a stable phenomenon (Ritter and Boecking, unpublished observations). In Uruguay, no treatment for varroa has been necessary over the last 15 years. Observations by Ruttner et al.[76] could not be substantiated that the resistance was due to a high percentage of mites with reduced fertility. European queens from Uruguay, purported to be resistant, were imported into France and Poland (N. Koeniger, unpublished data). There, the number of reproductive mites was the same as in susceptible colonies from Europe. One interpretation is that the colonies with queens from Uruguay had larger brood areas in Europe, which stimulated the growth of mite populations.

The situation in Brazil, however, continues to be intriguing. The reproductive success of varroa on worker brood of Africanized bees appears to be much lower than on worker brood of European bees situated in the same area. Chemical treatments of infested Africanized colonies have not been applied and are not necessary in Brazil[69].

In Mexico, where Africanized bees have been present for a much shorter time than in Brazil, tests revealed that European brood was twice as attractive to varroa as was Africanized brood (reviewed by Guzman-Novoa & others[36]). However, the reproductive success of varroa was the same in worker brood of Africanized and European colonies and was significantly higher on worker brood of reciprocal F1 hybrids. Vandame & others[85] compared varroa population dynamics between 10 European (EHB) and 10 Africanized (AHB) honey bee colonies in a tropical climate of Mexico over 18 months. As in temperate climates, EHB was susceptible to varroa. AHB showed some resistance but not to the same degree as in Brazil since up to 2500 mites per hive were encountered (corresponding to 20% brood infestation rate) and the percentage of fertile mother mites was high (about 85%). Thus, mite infertility did not prove to be the main mechanism of resistance in Mexico. Further experiments revealed that post-capping duration and grooming behavior did not explain the observed resistance either; however, brood attractivity and removal behavior appeared to have some importance.

Continued research is necessary to determine whether the differences in fertility in Brazil are due to the genetics of the mite or the bee, and the extent that the reproductive differences are influenced by environmental conditions and colony characteristics. The low reproductive success of mites in worker brood compared to the high reproductive success in drone brood may alone explain varroa resistance in Africanized *A. mellifera* colonies in Brazil[30], since the worker force would not be affected as much by the parasitism. In addition, the intense tendency to swarm and the high density of feral colonies may contribute to the rapid development of natural resistance[26]. Defense mechanisms, such as grooming and brood removal behavior (see below), may provide additional explanations for resistance of *A. mellifera* colonies in Brazil, Mexico and Tunisia.

Bee post-capping duration. An example of a heritable physiological mechanism that may affect the reproductive rate and population growth of the mite is the duration of the post-capping, or pre-pupal and pupal stages of the bees. The Cape bee from South Africa, *A. m. capensis*, has a shorter duration of the post-capping stage which may result in lower mite population growth in these colonies[57]. Although others[14,47,56,58,77] have speculated that post-capping duration is a significant factor in limiting mite reproduction, at present, no one has provided data from *A. mellifera* that supports the hypothesis that there is a correlation between the duration of the capped bee brood stage and the reproduction success rates of the mite. In Brazil and in Mexico it was determined that post-capping duration was found not to be responsible for the resistance of Africanized bees to varroa[70,85].

Bee behavioral defenses. Two genetically determined behaviors of honey bees, grooming behavior and removal behavior, may also limit the survivorship and reproductive success of varroa.

Grooming. In grooming behavior, an adult bee removes the mites from herself (auto-grooming), or from infested nestmates (allo-grooming) (reviewed by Boecking & Spivak[10] and Rath[64]). The survivorship of the mite decreases if the bee successfully damages the mite with her mouthparts during the grooming process. If the mites are simply disturbed during grooming and fall to the bottom of the colony without being damaged, they are able to subsequently reproduce.

The first study of grooming behavior was conducted by Peng & others[61] in China. Observation hives containing *A. cerana* and *A. mellifera* were inoculated with mites collected from *A. mellifera* colonies. Of the introduced mites in the *A. cerana* colonies, 98% were either removed by the bees by auto- or allo-grooming or moved onto another bee, only 3% of the mites were groomed or moved to another bee in the *A. mellifera* colonies. Other researchers have confirmed that *A. mellifera* does exhibit grooming behavior, but to a lesser extent than *A. cerana* (reviewed in Boecking & Spivak[10] and Rath[64]). More recent investigations by Fries & others[29] indicate that grooming behavior in *A. cerana* may be less effective in combating the mites than previously reported. When mites were introduced into field colonies of *A. cerana* and *A. mellifera*, the percent of live mites with visible damage as a consequence of grooming was about 30% in *A. cerana* compared to 12.3% in *A. mellifera* colonies. In observation hives, 12.5% of the recovered mites were damaged by *A. cerana* and none were damaged by *A. mellifera*. Fries & others[29] tabulated only incidents of successful grooming that resulted in damage to the mite, in contrast to the studies by previous researchers[15,61] who included as grooming events the movement of mites from one bee to another bee and the loss of mites from the observation area by the observer.

Although the proportion of damaged mites may vary widely from colony to colony, the overall effect of grooming behavior on the reduction of the mites within bee colonies remains unclear.

Removal behavior. In removal, or hygienic, behavior, an adult bee detects, uncaps, and removes an infested pupa from the cell[10](Fig.15.1). The removal of infested pupae may theoretically limit the growth of a varroa population in three ways: (1) immature mites which have begun to develop in brood cells are killed, decreasing the average number of offspring per mother mite; (2) the mother mites may be damaged during the removal process, and (3) the phoretic period of a mother mite is extended if she escapes during the removal process[28].

Peng & others[62] were the first to describe removal behavior in colonies of *A. cerana* in China. A significant correlation was found between the infestation level of the observation hives containing *A. cerana* or *A. mellifera* and the degree of removal of infested pupae by the bees. Subsequently, Rath & Drescher[65] found that *A. cerana* detected and removed 98.8% of the worker pupae experimentally infested with varroa. Investigations by Rosenkranz & others[74] indicated that the amount of brood removed by *A. cerana* after experimental infestation with live mites may be lower than previously reported[62,65] because the

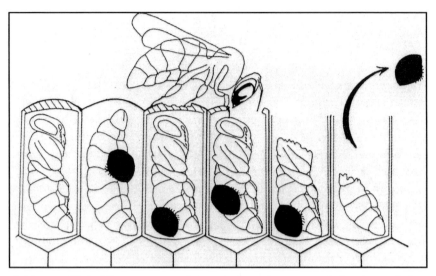

▲Figure 15.1   The process of removal, or hygienic, behavior. A bee detects a cell containing a parasitized pupa. She uncaps the cell, and the pupa is removed from the cell. The mother mite may escape from the cell, but her offspring would be destroyed by the bees during the removal process. Drawing by O. Boecking.

source of mites used for experimental infestation influences the removal behavior of the bees.

Because varroa has limited or no reproduction in worker cells of *A. cerana*, the successful reproduction of the mite is limited to its seasonal occurrence of drone brood (reviewed in Rath[64]). *A. cerana* workers do not remove mite-infested drone brood due to the thick cell capping over the drone cell, a structure unique to this species[64,65]. Drones which are infested with multiple mites become weakened and are not able to open their cell caps and they die together with the mites inside such cells[43,63]. Thus, drone brood in *A. cerana* colony acts as a varroa trap. The combination of non-reproduction in worker cells and the drone cell capping result in low overall rates of parasitism in *A. cerana*.

A. mellifera from North American and European stocks also display removal behavior of varroa mites from capped, infested worker brood cells, but to a limited extent compared to *A. cerana* (reviewed by Boecking & Spivak[10]). When varroa was experimentally introduced into *A. m. carnica* colonies in Germany, Boecking & Drescher[8] found that the mean rate of removal by the Carniolan bees on day 10 after infestation was 29.3% when one mite per cell was introduced, but 55.1%

when two mites per cell were introduced. A positive correlation was found between the removal rates of mite-infested brood and the removal of freeze-killed brood, a commonly used assay to test for hygienic behavior.

Spivak[78] used a similar approach in the USA to test *A. mellifera* colonies of Italian origin for their ability to remove infested pupae. The colonies tested had been bred *a priori* for two generations for hygienic behavior with the goal of breeding colonies resistant to chalkbrood disease[34,35,79]. A freeze-killed brood assay was used to select colonies for hygienic behavior[82]. Daughter queens were raised from the hygienic colonies and were instrumentally inseminated with semen from drones from other hygienic colonies. A non-hygienic line of bees was also bred as a control. Following the methods of Boecking & Drescher[7,8], cells containing recently sealed fifth-instar larvae within the hygienic and non-hygienic colonies were inoculated with one varroa per cell. In three of four years (1994, 1996, 1997), an average of 60.6% of the infested pupae were removed by the hygienic colonies 10 days after the cells were experimentally infested compared to 13.8% uninfested (but manipulated) pupae within the control cells (Fig. 15.2). The non-hygienic colonies over the three years removed an average of 20.9% of the infested pupae and 7.7% of the controls. In 1995, there was a significant difference in the percent infested pupae removed between the hygienic and non-hygienic colonies only when two mites per cell were introduced. The results of these experiments are discussed in detail in Spivak[78] and Spivak & Gilliam[81].

During the removal process, the female mite that parasitized the larva may escape and re-enter a different brood cell. Experiments by Boecking[6] and Boecking & Drescher[9] revealed that most of the adult female varroa that escaped the brood cells after removal could invade other brood cells (mean = 61.3%). Some mites attached themselves to adult bees (14.6%), and a small percentage were killed by bees (10.9%). If a cell containing an infested pupa is detected by the bees after the female mite has oviposited, her offspring are killed by the bees during the removal of the pupa.

As with grooming behavior, the effect of hygienic behavior on the population regulation of varroa within bee colonies remains unclear. However, because hygienic colonies demonstrate resistance to brood diseases such as American foulbrood and chalkbrood, the trait may be worthwhile to incorporate into honey bee stocks (reviewed in Spivak & Gilliam[80,81]).

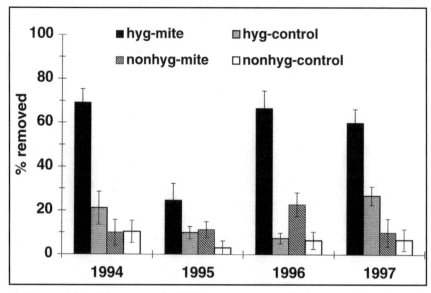

▲*Figure 15.2 The mean (±SE) percent removal of mite-infested pupae by hygienic and non-hygienic colonies 10 days after introduction of the mites through cell bases (methods in Spivak[78]). In 1994, 1996, and 1997, the hygienic colonies (n = 4, 10, and 6 respectively) removed significantly more pupae infested with one mite per cell than did the non-hygienic colonies (n = 3, 6, and 6) (P <0.01; split-plot 2-way ANOVA for each year). There also was a significant difference between the removal of infested pupae and controls (P < 0.05) in those years. Tests in 1995 (n = 7 hyg, 4 non-hyg) revealed a significant difference only when two mites per cell were introduced (treatment effect: P < 0.01).*

Current breeding programs. There are a variety of beekeepers and researchers in Europe and the USA who are attempting to breed bee colonies that demonstrate resistance to varroa. Some have selected for colonies that display a specific trait such as grooming behavior[75] and hygienic behavior[78]. Others have imported stock that demonstrates some resistance in the country of its origin (e.g., bees from far-eastern Russia imported into the U.S.[67]), or bred from colonies that have survived longer with higher infestation levels than other colonies in the same apiaries, e.g. the "Yugo" strain of *A. m. carnica* imported into the U.S. from Yugoslavia[19,66]. Groups of beekeepers have formed cooperatives to breed from colonies that survive without treatment, e.g.

"Honey Bee Improvement Program" (J. Griffes, unpublished data).

In recent years, some researchers have developed comprehensive approaches to breeding for resistance. In Kirchhain Germany, 200 colonies have been evaluated for mite resistance and performance in a closed experimental population since 1990[13]. At the beginning of the evaluation (in December), each colony is infested with 70 varroa, and a final mite count is taken after a treatment in July to calculate the mite population increase and the proportion of brood and adult bees that are infested. The degree of grooming and hygienic behaviors are evaluated by repeated tests during the season. For selection, the colonies are scored such that the degree of varroa resistance accounts for 50% of the total selection index. Honey yield accounts for 25% of the total, gentleness for 12.5%, and calmness of the comb surface 12.5%. Different breeding lines have demonstrated significantly different degrees of susceptibility and performance using this approach.

Another comprehensive approach was taken by Spivak & Reuter[83]. In this study, colonies with hygienic queens were compared to colonies with Italian queens not selected for the behavior. This was the first study in the USA to evaluate hygienic stock in large field colonies with naturally-mated queens. The results of tests conducted in 1995 and 1996 revealed that the hygienic colonies removed significantly more freeze-killed brood than the commercial colonies, had significantly less chalkbrood, had no American foulbrood (AFB), and produced significantly more honey than the commercial colonies. No treatments were applied to the colonies to control for mites for one year. Estimates of the number of varroa on adult bees at the end of one year indicated that the hygienic colonies had fewer mites than the commercial colonies in three of four apiaries, although the numbers of mites within all of the colonies were very low.

The experiment was repeated in 1997 comparing the hygienic colonies to a line of bees renowned for honey production (Starline bees)[84]. The same procedures were followed, but the colonies were left untreated for a longer period. The hygienic colonies had significantly less chalkbrood, no AFB, and produced as much honey as the Starline colonies. Although the infestation levels of varroa were considerably higher after the first year than they were in the previous test, the hygienic colonies had significantly fewer mites than the Starline colonies across all apiaries one year after treatment.

These results demonstrated that colonies with naturally-mated queens from a selected line of hygienic bees have less disease and fewer mites than colonies not selected for the behavior. The fact that the hygienic colonies produced as much, if not more, honey than the unselected colonies indicates it is possible to select for hygienic behavior without compromising honey production. The reduction in diseases and parasite pressure may lead to increased colony populations and hence, to more foragers. No negative characteristics were apparent in the hygienic colonies; however, there could be negative fitness effects associated with removing diseased brood that have yet to be substantiated[10,79].

Harbo developed a 10 week procedure for evaluating the population growth of mites and correlating mite population growth with resistance mechanisms in the bee[39,40]. The procedure involves introducing queens from various sources into colonies that originated from a common source of bees of known infestation level. During the 10 weeks, the following parameters are measured: initial and final mite populations (mite population increase); proportion of brood that is infested; ratio of mites on adults to mites within brood cells; degree of non-reproduction of mites in worker brood cells; post-capping duration of the brood; and degree of grooming and hygienic behaviors. Tests on queens introduced into colonies in Michigan and Baton Rouge in 1996 revealed that three of 43 test colonies had fewer mites at the end of the experiment than they had at the beginning[41]. Non-reproduction of mites was the most significant factor related to the reduction in mite population growth, but had little effect when it occurred at levels <30%. Post-capping period also had a minor effect. Findings on the mechanism of suppression of mite introduction indicated that the non-reproductive female mites had few or no spermatozoa in their seminal receptacles, which was related to the reduced or lack of fertilization of the mite[42]. Hygienic behavior, grooming behavior, and post-capping duration also may be important mechanisms of resistance[17], but, as with suppression of mite reproduction, the traits may only be effective if expressed at a very high level in the bee colony.

Conclusions. To understand the factors responsible for honey bee resistance to varroa infestation, continued research and breeding programs are critical. If colonies are bred from the survivors of untreated colonies, some degree of resistance in the progeny may be obtained, but it is important to understand the reasons why some colonies survive.

The most efficient breeding program should be based on selection for characteristics that have the greatest impact on reducing mite survival and reproductive success, and those characteristics should be heritable.

Despite some claims to the contrary, there are no beekeepers or researchers who have successfully bred a line of bees that is varroa resistant or tolerant such that they can survive without treatment. Even within the breeding programs for stocks resistant to varroa in North America and Europe, treatments are absolutely necessary at present to keep the colonies alive. In the search for bee colonies that are resistant to varroa, the goals of the breeding program should be clear: How long should colonies be expected to survive without chemical treatment? Is it realistic to attempt to breed lines of bees that never require the application of miticides? Is it sufficient to breed lines of bees which survive without treatment for one or two years? In either case, it is important to search for the most critical, heritable factors that limit the survivorship and reproductive success of varroa within honey bee colonies.

Summary. Breeding honey bees for resistance to *Varroa jacobsoni* is the most sustainable yet difficult long-term solution to the mite problem. When breeding honey bees, it is important to select for genetic characteristics of the bee that have the greatest impact on reducing mite survivorship and reproductive success. To find heritable characteristics, the effects of genetics and of the environment on both the bee and the mite must be clearly defined. For example, bee colonies in Brazil do not require treatment to survive mite infestation. However, is the resistance because the mites are a different genotype and possibly less virulent? Or, is the resistance because the Africanized bees in Brazil have genetic mechanisms of defense against the mites? How does the climate or resources in Brazil affect the reproductive success of the mites, particularly on Africanized bees? In this chapter, we highlight some key research findings on mite genetics, mite environment, bee genetics, and bee environment to point out where further research is needed in each of these areas.

Acknowledgments. We thank John Harbo, Greg Hunt, and Rebecca Melton Masterman for reviewing this manuscript. This is contribution 99-1-17-0007 of the Minnesota Agriculture Experiment Station.

References cited.

1. **Anderson, D. L. 1994.** Non-reproduction of *Varroa jacobsoni* in *Apis mellifera* colonies in Papua New Guinea and Indonesia. Apidologie 25: 412-421.

2. **Anderson, D. L. & Sukarsih. 1996.** Changed *Varroa jacobsoni* reproduction in *Apis mellifera* colonies in Java. Apidologie 27: 461-466.

3. **Anderson, D. L. & S. Fuchs. 1998.** Two genetically distinct populations of *Varroa jacobsoni* with contrasting reproductive abilities on the European honey bee, *Apis mellifera.* J. Apic. Res. 37: 69-78.

4. **Beetsma, J., W. J. Boot & J. Calis. 1999.** Invasion behaviour of *Varroa jacobsoni.* Oud.: From bees into brood cells. Apidologie 30: 125-140.

5. **Bienfeld, K., J. Radtke & F. Zautke. 1995.** Influence of thermoregulation within honeybee colonies on the reproduction success of *Varroa jacobsoni* Oud. Apidologie 26: 329-330.

6. **Boecking, O. 1992.** Removal behaviour of *Apis mellifera* colonies towards sealed brood cells infested with *Varroa jacobsoni*: techniques, extent and efficacy. Apidologie 23: 371-373.

7. **Boecking, O. & W. Drescher. 1991.** Response of *Apis mellifera* L. colonies to brood infested with *Varroa jacobsoni.* Oud. Apidologie 22: 237-241.

8. **Boecking, O. & W. Drescher. 1992.** The removal response of *Apis mellifera* L. colonies to brood in wax and plastic cells after artificial and natural infestation with *Varroa jacobsoni* Oud. and to freeze-killed brood. Exp. Appl. Acarol. 16: 321-329.

9. **Boecking, O. & W. Drescher. 1993.** Preliminary data on the response of *Apis mellifera* to brood infested with *Varroa jacobsoni* and the effect of this resistance mechanism. pp. 454-462. *In* Connor, L. J., T. Rinderer, H. *A.* Sylvester, and S. Wongsiri, [eds]. Asian Apiculture. Wicwas Press, Cheshire, USA. 704 p.

10. **Boecking, O. & M. Spivak. 1999.** Behavioral defenses of honey bees against *Varroa jacobsoni* Oud. Apidologie 30: 141-158.

11. **Boot, W. J., J. N. M. Calis & J. Beetsma. 1995.** Does time spent on adult bees affect reproductive success of *Varroa* mites. Entomol.

Exp. et Applicata 75: 1-7.

12. Büchler, R. 1994. *Varroa* tolerance in honey bees - occurrence, characters and breeding. Bee World 75: 54-70.

13. Büchler, R. 1997. Aktuelle ergebnisse zur selektion auf *Varroa*toleranz. Allg. Deut. Emkerzeitung 31: 10-15.

14. Büchler, R. & W. Drescher. 1990. Variance and heritability of the capped developmental stage in European *Apis mellifera* L. and its correlation with increased *Varroa jacobsoni* Oud. infestation. J. Apic. Res. 29: 172-176.

15. Büchler, R., W. Drescher & I. Tournier. 1992. Grooming behaviour of *Apis cerana*, *Apis mellifera* and *Apis dorsata*, reacting to *Varroa jacobsoni* and *Tropilaelaps clareae*. Exp. Appl. Acarol. 16: 313-319.

16. Calis, J. N. M., I. Fries & S. C. Ryrie. 1999. Population modeling of *Varroa jacobsoni*. Apidologie 30: 111-124.

17. Danka, R. G., J. D. Villa, J. R. Harbo & T. E. Rinderer. 1997. Initial evaluation of industry-contributed honey bees for resistance to *Varroa jacobsoni*. Amer. Bee J. 137: 221-222.

18. De Guzman, L. I. & T. E. Rinderer. 1999. Identification and comparison of *Varroa* species infesting honey bees. Apidologie 30: 85-95.

19. De Guzman, L. L., T. E. Rinderer, G. T. Delatte & R. E. Macchiavelli. 1996. *Varroa jacobsoni* Oudemans tolerance in selected stocks of *Apis mellifera* L. Apidologie 27: 193-210.

20. De Jong, D., L. S. Gonçalves & R. A. Morse. 1984. Dependence on climate of the virulence of *Varroa jacobsoni*. Bee World 65: 117-121.

21. De Ruijter, A. 1987. Reproduction of *Varroa jacobsoni* during successive brood cycles of the honeybee. Apidologie 18: 321-326.

22. Donzé, G, & P. M. Guerin. 1994. Behavioral attributes and parental care of *Varroa* mites parasitizing honeybee brood. Behav. Ecol. Sociobiol. 34: 305-319.

23. Donzé, G, & P. M. Guerin. 1997. Time-activity budgets and space structuring by the different life stages of *Varroa jacobsoni* in capped brood of the honey bees *Apis mellifera*. J. Insect Behav. 10: 371-393.

24. Donzé, G., M. Herrmann, B. Bachofen & P. M. Guerin. 1996. Effect of mating frequency and brood cell infestation rate on the reproductive success of the honeybee parasite *Varroa jacobsoni.* J. Ecol. Entomol. 21: 17-26.

25. Elzen, P. J., F. A. Eischen, J. R. Baxter, J. Pettis & W. T. Wilson. 1998. Fluvalinate resistance in *Varroa jacobsoni* for several geographic locations. Am. Bee J. 138: 674-676.

26. Engels, W., L. S. Gonçalves, J. Steiner, A. M. Buriolla & M. R. Cavichio Issa. 1986. *Varroa*-Befall von Carnica-Völkern in Tropenklima. Apidologie 17: 203-216.

27. Fernandez, N. A. & O. García. 1997. Decrease in the efficacy of fluvalinate in the control of the mite *Varroa jacobsoni* in Argentina. Buletín del Colmenar 4(25): 14-18.

28. Fries, I., S. Camazine & J. Sneyd. 1994. Population dynamics of *Varroa jacobsoni*: a model and a review. Bee World 75: 5-28.

29. Fries, I., H. Wei, W. Shi & S.X. Huazhen. 1996. Grooming behavior and damaged mites (*Varroa jacobsoni*) in *Apis cerana cerana* and *Apis mellifera ligustica.* Apidologie 27: 3-11.

30. Fuchs, S. 1992. Choice in *Varroa jacobsoni* Oud. between honey bee drone or worker brood cells for reproduction. Behav. Ecol. Sociobiol. 31: 429-435.

31. Fuchs, S. 1994. Non-reproducing *Varroa jacobsoni* Oud. in honey bee worker cells - status of mites or effect of brood cells? Exp. Appl. Acarology. 18: 309-317.

32. Fuchs, S. & K. Lagenbach. 1989. Multiple infestation of *Apis mellifera* L. brood cells and reproduction in *Varroa jacobsoni* Oud. Apidologie 20: 257-266.

33. García-Fernández, P., R. Benítez Rodriguiez & F. J. Oranges-Bermejo. 1995. Influence du climat sur le développement de la population de *Varroa jacobsoni* Oud. dans des colonies d' *Apis mellifera* iberica (Goetze) dans le sud de l'Espagne. Apidologie 26: 371-380.

34. Gilliam, M., S. Taber III & G. V. Richardson. 1983. Hygienic behavior of honey bees in relation to chalkbrood disease. Apidologie 14: 29-39.

35. Gilliam, M., S. Taber III, B. J. Lorenz & D. B. Prest. 1988. Factors affecting development of chalkbrood disease in colonies of honey bees, *Apis mellifera*, fed pollen contaminated with *Ascosphaera apis*. J. Invertebr. Pathol. 52: 314-325.

36. Guzman-Novoa, E., R. Vandame & M. E. Arechavaleta. 1999. Susceptibility of European and Africanized honey bees (*Apis mellifera* L.) to *Varroa jacobsoni* Oud. in Mexico. Apidologie 30: 173-182.

37. Hänel, H. 1983. Effect of JH-III on the reproduction of *Varroa jacobsoni*. Apidologie 14: 137-142.

38. Hänel, H. & N. Koeniger. 1986. Possible regulation of the reproduction of the honey bee mite *Varroa jacobsoni* (Mesostigmata: Acari) by a hosts hormone: Juvenile hormone III. J. Insect Physiol. 32: 791-798.

39. Harbo, J. R. 1996. Evaluating colonies of honey bees for resistance to *Varroa jacobsoni*. Bee Science 4: 100-105.

40. Harbo, J. R. & J. W. Harris. 1999. Selecting honey bees for resistance to *Varroa jacobsoni*. Apidologie 30: 183-196.

41. Harbo, J. R. & R. A. Hoopingarner. 1997. Honey bees (Hymenoptera: Apidae) in the United States that express resistance to *Varroa jacobsoni* (Mesostigmata: Varroidae). J. Econ. Entomol. 90: 893-898.

42. Harris, J. W. & J. R. Harbo. 1998. Low sperm counts and reduced fecundity of mites in colonies of honey bees (Hymenoptera: Apidae) that are resistant to *Varroa jacobsoni*. J. Econ. Entomol. 92: 83-90.

43. Koeniger, N., G. Koeniger & M. Delfinado-Baker. 1983. Observations on mites of the Asian honeybee species. Apidologie 14: 197-204.

44. Kraus, B. & G. Hunt. 1995. Differentiation of *Varroa jacobsoni* Oud. populations by random amplification of polymorphic DNA (RAPD). Apidologie 26: 283-290.

45. Kraus, B. & H. H. W. Velthuis. 1997. High humidity in the honey bee (*Apis mellifera* L.) brood nest limits reproduction of the para-

sitic mite *Varroa jacobsoni Oud.* Naturwissenschaften 84: 217-218.

46. Kulinçeviç, J. M., T. E. Rinderer & D. J. Uroseviç. 1988. Seasonality and colony variation of reproducing and non-reproducing *Varroa jacobsoni* females in western honey bees (*Apis mellifera*) worker brood. Apidologie 19: 173-179.

47. Le Conte, Y., C. Bruchou, K. Benhamouda, C. Gauthier, & J. M. Cornuet. 1994. Heritability of the queen brood post-capping stage duration of *Apis mellifera mellifera L.* Apidologie 25: 513-519.

48. Martin, S. J. 1994. Ontogenesis of the mite *Varroa jacobsoni* Oud. in worker brood of the honeybee *Apis mellifera* L. under natural conditions. Exp. Appl. Acarol. 18: 87-100.

49. Martin, S. J. 1995. Reproduction of *Varroa jacobsoni* in cells of *Apis mellifera* containing one or more mother mites and the distribution of these cells. J. Apic. Res. 34: 187-196.

50. Martin, S. J. & D. Kemp. 1997. Average number of reproductive cycles performed by *Varroa jacobsoni* in honey bee (*Apis mellifera*) colonies. J. Apic. Res. 36: 113-123.

51. Martin, S., K. Holland & M. Murray. 1997. Non-reproduction in the honeybee mite *Varroa jacobsoni*. Exp. Appl. Acarol. 21: 539-549.

52. Message, D. & L. S. Gonçalves. 1995. Effect of the size of worker brood cells of Africanized honey bees on infestation and reproduction of the ectoparasitic mite *Varroa jacobsoni* Oud. Apidologie 26: 381-386.

53. Milani, N. 1999. The resistance of *Varroa jacobsoni* Oud. to acaracides. Apidologie 30: 229-234.

54. Moretto, G., L. S. Gonçalves, D. De Jong & M. Z. Bichuette. 1991. The effects of climate and bee race on *Varroa jacobsoni* Oud. infestations in Brazil. Apidologie 22: 197-203.

55. Moretto, G., L. S. Goncalves & D. De Jong. 1997. Relationship between food availability and the reproductive ability of the mite *Varroa jacobsoni* in Africanized bee colonies. Am. Bee J. 137: 67-69.

56. Moritz, R. F. A. 1985. Heritability of the postcapping stage in *Apis mellifera* and its relation to varroatosis resistance. J. Heredity 76: 267-270.

57. **Moritz, R. F. A. & H. Hänel. 1984.** Restricted development of the parasitic mite *Varroa jacobsoni* Oud. in the Cape honey bee *Apis mellifera capensis* Esch. Z. angew. Ent. 97: 91-95.

58. **Moritz, R. F. A. & D. Mautz. 1990.** Development of *Varroa jacobsoni* in colonies of *Apis mellifera capensis* and *Apis mellifera carnica.* Apidologie 21: 53-58.

59. **Nazzi, F. & N. Milani. 1996.** The presence of inhibitors of the reproduction of *Varroa jacobsoni* Oud. (Gamasida: Varroidae) in infested cells. Exp. Appl. Acarol. 20: 617-623.

60. **Otten, C. & S. Fuchs. 1990.** Seasonal variations in the reproductive behavior of *Varroa jacobsoni* in colonies of *Apis mellifera carnica, A. m. ligustica* and *A. m. mellifera.* Apidologie 21: 367-368.

61. **Peng, Y. S., Y. Fang, S. Xu & L. Ge. 1987.** The resistance mechanism of the Asian honey bee, *Apis cerana* Fabr., to an ectoparasitic mite *Varroa jacobsoni* Oudemans. J. Invertebr. Pathol. 49: 54-60.

62. **Peng, Y. S., Y. Fang, S. Xu, L. Ge & M. E. Nasr. 1987.** Response of foster Asian Honey bee (*Apis cerana* Fabr.) colonies to the brood of European honey bee (*Apis mellifera* L.) infested with parasitic mite *Varroa jacobsoni* Oudemans. J. Invertebr. Pathol. 49: 259-264.

63. **Rath, W. 1992.** The key to *Varroa*: The drones of *Apis cerana* and their cell cap. Am. Bee J. 132: 329-331.

64. **Rath, W. 1999.** Co-adaptation of *Apis cerana* Fabr. and *Varroa jacobsoni* Oud. Apidologie 30: 97-110.

65. **Rath, W. & W. Drescher. 1990.** Response of *Apis cerana* Fabr. towards brood infested with *Varroa jacobsoni* Oud. and infestation rate of colonies in Thailand. Apidologie 21: 311-321.

66. **Rinderer, T. E., L. I. de Guzman, J. M. Kulinçeviç, G. T. Delatte, L. D. Beaman & S. M. Buco. 1993.** The breeding, importing, testing and general characteristics of Yugoslavian honey bee bred for resistance to *Varroa jacobsoni.* Am. Bee J. 133: 197-200.

67. **Rinderer, T.E., V. N. Kuznetsov, R. G. Danka & G. T. Delatte. 1997.** An importation of potentially *Varroa*-resistant honey bees from far-eastern Russia. Am. Bee J. 137: 787-789.

68. **Ritter, W. 1990.** Development of the *Varroa* mite populations in

treated and untreated colonies in Tunisia. Apidologie 21: 368-370.

69. **Rosenkranz, P. 1999.** Honey bee (*Apis mellifera* L.) tolerance to *Varroa jacobsoni* Oud. in South America. Apidologie 30: 159-172.

70. **Rosenkranz, P. & W. Engels. 1994.** Infertility of *Varroa jacobsoni* females after invasion into *Apis mellifera* worker brood as a tolerance factor against varroatosis. Apidologie 25: 402-411.

71. **Rosenkranz, P. & H. Bartlaszky. 1996.** Reproduction of *Varroa* females after long broodless periods of the honey bee colony during summer. German Bee Research Institutes Seminar. Apidologie 27: 288-289.

72. **Rosenkranz, P., A. Rachinsky, A. Strambi, C. Strambi & P. Röpstorf. 1990.** Juvenile hormone titer in capped worker brood of *Apis mellifera* and reproduction in the bee mite *Varroa jacobsoni*. Gen. Comp. Endocrinol. 78: 189-193.

73. **Rosenkranz, P., N. C. Tewarson, A. Rachinsky, A. Strambi, C. Strambi & W. Engels. 1993.** Juvenile hormone titer and reproduction of *Varroa jacobsoni* in capped brood stages of *Apis cerana indica* in comparison to *Apis mellifera ligustica*. Apidologie 24: 375-382.

74. **Rosenkranz, P., N. C. Tewarson, A. Singh & W. Engels. 1993.** Differential hygienic behaviour towards *Varroa jacobsoni* in capped worker brood of *Apis cerana* depends on alien scent adhering to the mites. J. Apic. Res. 32: 89-93.

75. **Ruttner, F. & H. Hänel. 1992.** Active defense against *Varroa* mites in Carniolan strains of honey bees. Apidologie 23: 173-187.

76. **Ruttner, F., H. Marx & G. Marx. 1984.** Beobachtungen über eine mögliche Anpassung von *Varroa jacobsoni* an *Apis mellifera* L. in Uruguay. Apidologie 15: 43-62.

77. **Schousboe, C. 1986.** The duration of sealed cell stage in worker honeybee brood (*Apis mellifera* L.) in relation to increased resistance to the *Varroa* mite (*Varroa jacobsoni* Oud.). Tidsskrift for Planteavl 90: 293-299.

78. **Spivak, M. 1996.** Hygienic behavior and defense against *Varroa jacobsoni*. Apidologie 27: 245-260.

79. **Spivak, M. & M. Gilliam. 1993.** Facultative expression of hygienic behaviour of honey bees in relation to disease resistance. J. Apic. Res. 32: 147-157.

80. **Spivak, M. & M. Gilliam. 1998.** Hygienic behaviour of honey bees and its application for control of brood diseases and varroa mites. Part I. Hygienic behaviour and resistance to American foulbrood. Bee World 79: 124-134.

81. **Spivak, M. & M. Gilliam. 1998.** Hygienic behaviour of honey bees and its application for control of brood diseases and varroa mites. Part II. Studies on hygienic behaviour since the Rothenbuhler era. Bee World 179: 169-186.

82. **Spivak, M. & D. Downey. 1998.** Field assays for hygienic behavior in honey bees (Apidae: Hymenoptera). J. Econ. Entomol. 91: 64-70.

83. **Spivak, M. & G. S. Reuter. 1998.** Performance of hygienic colonies in a commercial apiary. Apidologie 29: 285-296

84. **Spivak, M. & G. S. Reuter. 1998.** Hygienic honey bees and resistance to varroa and brood diseases. Am. Bee J. 138: 299.

85. **Vandame, R., M. E. Colin, & G. Otero-Colina 1997.** Africanized honey bees tolerance to *Varroa* in Mexico: mite infertility is not the main tolerance factor. XXXVTH Intern. Apimondia Congress in Antwerp, Belgium. Sept. 1997.

TREATMENT THRESHOLDS FOR VARROA MITES

W. Michael Hood
Keith S. Delaplane

*I*ntroduction. Beekeepers must accept the fact that varroa mite eradication is not possible, therefore, we must aim at avoiding pest damage levels using highly effective means of control. Chemical acaricides have been used universally in most successful varroa mite control programs. The goal should be to avoid treatments at low tolerable mite levels, and to interject with a treatment only when higher pest levels are reached.

A crucial problem in successful varroa mite management is the proper timing of acaricide treatments. The treat when necessary program is much preferable to the calendar recommended treatment or constant treatment practiced by some beekeepers. In reality, however, it is perhaps fair to say that in the past most beekeepers prefer to treat for varroa on a routine basis rather than go to the time consuming trouble of measuring mite levels through careful sampling prior to treatment. This is not surprising, for in the past typical honey bee maladies such as foulbrood and nosema have been effectively controlled with routine

preventive measures or treatments foregoing the necessity of time consuming inspections or surveys. The "preventive treatment is preferred
over the necessary control treatment" idea is pervasive throughout the
beekeeping industry and will be difficult to overcome. Risk-averse beekeepers may be reluctant to forego treatments of an acaricide for fear of
the uncertainty of the efficacy of a minimum treatment system.

The development of varroa mite resistance to fluvalinate in recent
years[3,9,11] has created much concern throughout the beekeeping industry
(Chapter 17). Cherrett & others[2] noted that the continual use of one
chemical or closely related chemicals to control a single pest will ulti-
mately lead to resistance, therefore a "need for monitoring the development of resistance" should be stressed to minimize this problem.

A more judicious system of properly timed treatments may have
prolonged the useful life of fluvalinate in areas where resistance to the
acaricide has been reported. The resistance problem has led to a vicious
cycle where all the spinoffs are negative such as:

* increased use of illegal, unregistered chemicals for varroa control
* increased danger to the honey bees from chemical overexposure
* increased danger to the beekeeper while experimenting with
  other chemicals
* increased chance of honey contamination
* increased management costs for chemicals and labor
* increased chemical use which may cause residue buildup in comb
* increased chance of chemical cross resistance.

The magnitude of these spinoffs is difficult to estimate, and the additional costs to the beekeepers as a result of acaricide resistance are
unknown.

Defining treatment thresholds. Optimal use of acaricides is highly recommended to protect the integrity of products, given that varroa mite
resistance to a pesticide has developed in some parts of the world. On
the other hand, beekeepers must avoid delaying treatment to the colony
collapse level, which can be defined as the lowest varroa mite density
which causes colony mortality regardless of treatment. This mite level
can vary considerably from region to region, depending on climate and
other factors which affect bee colony health. The mite damage to the
colony below this level is tolerable, but beekeepers should treat well
below the colony collapse level to maintain productive colonies.

The key to this pest management dilemma is the development of suitable guidelines for treatment recommendations commonly referred to as treatment thresholds. Treatment threshold here is defined as "the varroa mite density at which control measures should be applied to prevent an increasing pest population from reaching the colony collapse level." The treatment threshold always represents a varroa mite level lower than that of the colony collapse level in order that the beekeeper may take action before the varroa density reaches the colony collapse level. These relationships are illustrated in Fig. 16.1. By delaying treatment beyond the treatment threshold, the beekeeper risks increased bee mortality, brood pathology and colony mortality. On the other hand, if a beekeeper treats far below the treatment threshold as an "insurance treatment", he/she has increased management costs and other negative

One Annual Varroa Mite Treatment

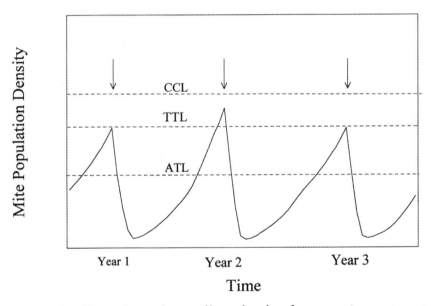

Figure 16.1 Honey bee colony collapse level and varroa mite treatment threshold level. CCL, colony collapse level; TTL, treatment threshold level; ATL, average tolerable mite level. Arrows indicate acaricide treatments.

side effects as mentioned earlier. The "average tolerable varroa level" is an average level of varroa mites over a long period of time. The mite population density level fluctuates about this average level as a result of variations in bee brood level, mite emigration, effectiveness of acaricide treatments, etc. The goal is to identify, based on adequate and reliable sampling data, that level of varroa mites that should be treated to maintain productive colonies and thus minimize treatments. Unfortunately, research-based treatment thresholds must be developed for different regions of the world because of variable conditions that affect mite levels such as season length, bee and mite population growth parameters, and sampling method sensitivity. In each region, treatment thresholds must be revalidated periodically to prevent treatment at lower mite densities than necessary.

Objectives of research in treatment threshold development. The primary objective of a treatment threshold system is to reduce the number of acaricide applications and still maintain strong, productive colonies. This may result in an immediate cost savings to the beekeeper. A timely application of a highly efficient varroa mite control product is recommended to lengthen the interval between applications to conserve susceptible genes in the mite population. If a less effective control product is used, the varroa mite population density will build back quickly and reduce the time interval between applications.

The treatment threshold system should identify, for a given region, the mite level/time of year at which acaricide treatments give satisfactory results relative to some future date. This permits a beekeeper to (1) anticipate at what time of year treatment may be necessary and (2) make an informed treatment decision if sampled mite levels at that time meet or exceed an established threshold.

Mite survey sampling techniques must be simple and quickly administered if beekeepers are to adopt a threshold regimen. The ether roll or mite sticky board techniques are examples of sampling methods that have been used in the past in treatment threshold development[4,6,11].

Constraints to the development and use of treatment thresholds. Preventive or calendar varroa mite treatments may be widely practiced and unavoidable to maintain strong honey bee colonies under some conditions:

* in regions where there are an absence of qualified personnel

available or willing to develop and periodically validate adequate
and reliable treatment threshold regimes
* where beekeepers cannot be relied upon to accurately and
promptly sample mite levels prior to treatment
* where beekeepers allow other contributing disorders to stress
colony health
* when distance or time does not allow follow up monitoring of
mite levels.

These treatments will many times be premature or too late and lead
to problems for the beekeeper and the beekeeping industry in the long
run. But, the dominant consideration is that beekeepers will prefer to
treat well below a suspected treatment threshold rather than risk potential colony loss by treating too late.

Treatment threshold development. Varroa mite treatment threshold
development should be based on the recognition of natural confound-
ing variables such as time of year and bee population, time of year and
brood area, brood area and mite population, etc. Treatment recommendations are based on the identification of mite levels that are detrimental and levels that are tolerable for a given region. These recommendations will vary by region[1], owing in part to differences in the
length of the brood rearing season, one of the most important regulators of mite population dynamics[7]. Thresholds may also vary depending
on the risk of mite emigration[8] and on management history of colonies.

Example 1. A practical example of how to calculate a research based
varroa mite treatment threshold has been given by Delaplane and
Hood[4] in the southeastern United States. Seventy-two colonies of
newly installed package bees were set up in April in Georgia and South
Carolina, USA (2 states, 6 apiaries per state and 6 colonies per apiary).
Bee packages were obtained from one supplier to give a high degree of
colony uniformity. All colonies were given disease and tracheal mite
preventive treatments and managed optimally for honey production.
Within each state, each apiary was randomly assigned one of the following treatments:
* acaricide treatment in June only
* acaricide treatment in August only
* acaricide treatment in October only
* no treatment (control)

The objective of this research project was to discover the varroa mite treatment threshold using a single acaricide as a comparison over a one year period. By December, colony bee populations were optimum for apiaries treated in August. Data suggested that late season acaricide treatments in first year colonies in the southeastern USA piedmont are justified at colony mite populations of 3,172 ± 324, 300 bee ether roll mite levels of 15 ± 1.4, and overnight adhesive bottom board insert (sticky board) mite levels of 117 ± 15 in colonies with 24,808 ± 2,245 bees and 1,825 ± 327 cm^2 sealed brood; these conditions occurred in mid August.

Application. Beekeepers in the southeastern USA may apply this information to their varroa mite management plans for newly installed package bee colonies. *Varroa* mite samples should be taken in August to determine mite levels relative to the research based treatment thresholds of about 15 mites using a 300 bee ether roll or 117 mites using an overnight bottom board insert. The following actions should be taken:

(1) If mite levels detected meet or exceed the treatment threshold level, then immediate treatment with an acaricide is recommended to prevent the mite population from reaching the colony collapse level. Treated colonies should winter well with adequate number of bees and a tolerable number of varroa mites.

(2) If the mite level is well below the treatment threshold in August, the beekeeper should sample again at 4 week intervals, and treat only when the threshold is triggered.

(3) If the mite level is much greater than the treatment threshold, the beekeeper may treat but expect to lose the colony.

Example 2. Martin[10] reports preliminary data to suggest that a colony will not collapse from varroa mite problems during the following winter when the peak varroa population is found to be below 2,500 mites in August or September in Great Britain. The chance of colony collapse increases as the mite population exceeds this threshold. A research based computer simulation model was used to calculate the lowest mite level necessary throughout the year that will ensure the peak population will not exceed this threshold the remainder of the year (Table 16.1).

The model can be used to assess present conditions of colony mite problems and to forecast future infestation levels. Treatment thresholds were developed using two methods of estimating mite population within a colony, a natural mite fall bottom board insert and a sampling method using sealed brood and adult bees.

The method of estimating the total mite infestation level within a colony by using sealed brood and adult bees is used widely in Great Britain. A pictorial guide by Martin[10] is given to make this estimate. The larger the sample, the more accurate the assessment. A correction factor is used for different parts (drone brood, worker brood and adult bees) of the bee colony because the mites are not evenly distributed throughout the colony. The mite estimation method using the natural mite fall is most accurate during months when the colony is either broodless or when the colony has 10,000+ brood cells. This method is less accurate during other times of the year and is unreliable when the colony is small (less than 5,000 brood cells), when the colony is collapsing, or when the colony is fluctuating in size such as swarming.

There are several considerations. Falling mites should be collected on a varroa floor, or a tray which covers the hive floor and is protected by a mesh screen. During the summer, mites falling over a period of approximately two weeks should be collected. During the winter fewer mites will be falling, so a longer collection period of about 1 month is advisable. Mites can either be counted on the floor or separated from the debris before counting. To obtain the daily mite drop, divide the number of days on which mites were collected.

Table 16.1 Estimated varroa mite population level below which no control measures are needed during the current year, but monitoring must be undertaken the following year[10].

Month colony monitored	Estimated number of mites in colony
January to May	below 170
June	below 300
July	below 500
August	below 1000
September	below 2000
October to December	below 2500 (if below 200, no control is needed during the following year; if between 200 and 2500, control is required the next year.)

The colony mite population is calculated by using a multiplication factor to convert daily mite fall into an estimate of the total mites in the colony. This conversion procedure is valid for most healthy colonies because the values are not colony size dependent. The multiplication factor for the months of November, December, January and February is 400; the multiplication factor for May, June, July and August is 30. The author notes that the multiplication factor for the months of March, April, September and October is 100, but is not as reliable because the brood nest may be rapidly changing.

Application. Beekeeper No. 1 in Great Britain finds 80 varroa mites using the natural mite fall method during a 14 day period in May. (80 mites / 14 days X 30 multiplication factor = 172 mites). The treatment threshold level for the month of May is 170 mites (Table 16.1), therefore the beekeeper should treat immediately to save the colony.

Beekeeper No. 2 finds 150 varroa mites using the natural mite fall method during a 30 day period in November. (150 mites / 30 days X 400 = 2,000 mites). The treatment threshold level for the month of November is 2,500 mites (Table 16.1), therefore a treatment is unnecessary, but control will be required the next year.

Limitations to treatment thresholds. *Varroa* mite treatment thresholds should not be universally accepted outside the region from which they were developed. Treatment thresholds will vary by region[1], owing to such differences as brood rearing and possibly unknown genetic differences in bee and mite populations. Treatment thresholds are not valid when used outside the parameters with which they were developed such as time of year (month and approximate bee and brood level). Extreme colony conditions such as swarming or a period following a pesticide kill may result in erroneous conclusions.

A research based treatment threshold system is not a long-term prescription for good bee health without other adequate disease and pest management practices by the beekeeper. Treatment thresholds will have to be revalidated periodically, therefore the beekeeper should pay close attention to when thresholds were last updated.

Conclusions. Past experience in the use of agricultural pesticides in controlling mites suggests that resistance should be anticipated as a possible outcome of repeated applications of a single pesticide to control varroa. The industry adoption of the use of "necessary application" of a pesticide over the "calendar treatment" will no doubt slow the development of mite resistance to pesticides.

The recent news of varroa mites developing resistance to a pesticide in some parts of the world, the increased cost of varroa mite management by the beekeeper, the increased cost of discovering and developing new pesticides, and the continued fear of honey and comb contamination have all contributed to arguments for use of treatment threshold systems. Due to the limited options available to beekeepers in controlling varroa mites, the advent of treatment thresholds is warranted.

The varroa mite treatment threshold system is based on the principal that pesticides should be used only when the mite population reaches a certain critical level. Much time and effort are required to develop research based treatment thresholds that must be revalidated periodically. The greatest benefit will be realized if a threshold based control system is adopted by most beekeepers on a regional basis.

Widespread adoption and use of treatment threshold in a region will further enhance the effectiveness and prolong the useful life of an acaricide. The inability of an acaricide to sustain acceptable control of varroa will be a major cost to the beekeeper in the long run because of increased colony losses, especially if other effective controls are not available. A national initiative to develop and implement varroa mite treatment thresholds will prolong the useful life of acaricides.

For a different perspective, Dinar & Efrat[5] have developed an economic threshold for varroa mites based mainly on rate of interest, the size of the apiary, the initial population of varroa, and especially the length of the time horizon. They used a long run economic decision model to determine optimal varroa treatment regimes. Although the model was developed using conditions prevailing in Israel, the authors note the model may be modified to different economic and biological conditions.

Summary. Beekeepers should carefully consider the timing of acaricide treatments for the control of varroa mites. Unnecessary treatments may lead to increased risks of honey and wax contamination, accelerated mite resistance to the acaricide, and extra expense and labor to the beekeeper. The goal should be to avoid treatment at low tolerable mite levels, and to interject with an acaricide only when higher pest levels are reached. The optimum treatment time is when the varroa mite infestation reaches the "treatment threshold." This is the density at which control measures should be applied to prevent the mite population from reaching the colony collapse level. If the beekeeper delays treatment well beyond the recommended treatment threshold, the colony may die regardless of treatment. We present the results of our studies that have determined the varroa mite treatment threshold for colonies kept in the southeastern United States. Two examples are given and explained. Widespread use of treatment thresholds by beekeepers will prolong the life of the acaricides now in use, by slowing the development of mites resistant to those chemicals.

References cited.
1. Bach, J. C., R. G. Danka, M. D. Ellis, E. C. Mussen, J. S. Pettis & M. T. Sanford. 1998. Protecting honey bees from *Varroa jacobsoni.* American Association of Professional Apiculturists, Lincoln, Nebraska, USA.

2. Cherrett, J. M., J. B. Ford, I. V. Herbert & A. J. Probert. 1971. The control of injurious animals. The English Universities Press Limited, London.

3. Colin, M. E., R. Vandame, P. Jourdan & S. Di Pasquale. 1997. Fluvalinate resistance of *Varroa jacobsoni* Oudemans (Acari: Varroidae) in Mediterranean apiaries of France. Apidologie 28: 375-384.

4. Delaplane, K. S. & W. M. Hood. 1997. Effects of delayed acaricide treatment in honey bee colonies parasitized by *Varroa jacobsoni* and a late season treatment threshold for the southeastern USA. J. Apic. Res. 33: 155-159.

5. Dinar, A. & C. Efrat. 1990. Economic threshold for a pathogenic disease: the case of varroasis in bees. Agricultural Systems 32: 13-25. Elsevier Science Publishers Ltd, England.

6. Ellis, M. D. & F. P. Baxendale. 1994. Comparison of formic acid sampling with other methods to detect varroa mites (*Varroa jacob-*

soni Oud.) and mite distribution within colonies in Nebraska. Bee Science 3: 139-144.

7. **Fries, I., S. Camazine & J. Sneyd. 1994.** Population dynamics of *Varroa jacobsoni*: a model and a review. Bee World 75: 5-28.

8. **Greatti, M., N. Milani & F. Nazzi. 1992.** Reinfestation of an acari-cide treated apiary by *Varroa jacobsoni* Oud. Exp. Appl. Acarol. 16: 279-286.

9. **Lodesani, M., M. Colombo & M. Spreafico. 1995.** Ineffectiveness of *Apis*tan treatment against the mite *Varroa jacobsoni* Oud. in several districts of Lombardy (Italy). Apidologie 26: 67-72.

10. **Martin, S. 1998.** *Varroa jacobsoni* : monitoring and forecasting mite populations within honey bee colonies in Britain. Ministry of Agriculture, Fisheries and Food in association with the Central Science Laboratory. Leaflet PB 3611; York, England: 12 pp.

11. **Sanford, M. T. 1998.** *Varroa* certification changes in Florida. Apis 16(2), University of Florida, Gainesville, Florida, USA.

Chapter 17

MANAGEMENT OF THE RESISTANCE OF VARROA MITES TO ACARICIDES

Norberto Milani

I n most areas of the temperate zones, the control of *Varroa jacob-soni* requires regular chemical treatments. A few products based on pyrethroid acaricides and formulated in plastic strips (Apistan®, Bayvarol®, etc.), introduced at the end of the 1980s, showed high efficacy even when capped brood is present in the hive. They became the preferred treatment in most countries and were often considered the ideal solution to the varroa problem.

However, as early as 1992, after about four years of use, Apistan failed to control varroa in Lombardy, a region in Northern Italy where all the beekeepers had received free Apistan strips from the veterinary services, and in other Italian regions. The inefficacy was confirmed by field trials[5], and a laboratory assay[6] showed that it was due to the resistance of the mite against fluvalinate, the active ingredient in Apistan. The consequences were disastrous colony losses, often exceeding 70% of the colonies. Such losses were unexpected since no abnormal increase in the varroa infestation nor acaricide inefficacy had been noted in previous years. Initial denial of the presence of resistant strains by the manufacturer of Apistan, on the basis of inadequate tests, made things even worse. Although aware of the risk of varroa becoming resistant, we were not prepared for it. Resistance was later detected in other European countries (Fig. 17.1); apparently it spread from a single center rather than originating independently in several areas[8].

The origin of resistance. Resistance to pesticides is a frequent problem in crop protection and is usually overcome by changing the active ingredient used for control of the pest. In the case of varroa, the problem is more serious since there are relatively few unrelated chemicals available for control.

According to a simplified definition, resistance of an insect or mite against a pesticide means its capability to withstand a dose that would ordinarily kill the majority of individuals in the population, i.e., its

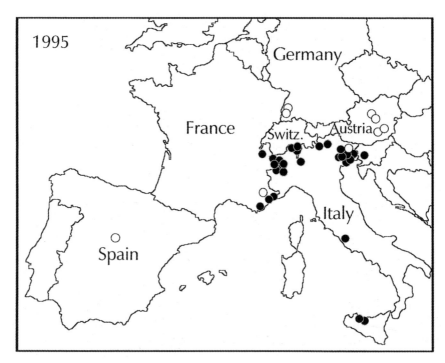

▲▶ *Figure 17.1 Spread of the fluvalinate resistant varroa mites in Europe in 1995-1997, monitored with the bioassay mentioned in the text. Open circles: no resistant mites found; black circles: resistant mites present. Redrawn from Trouiller[8], courtesy of Elsevier.*

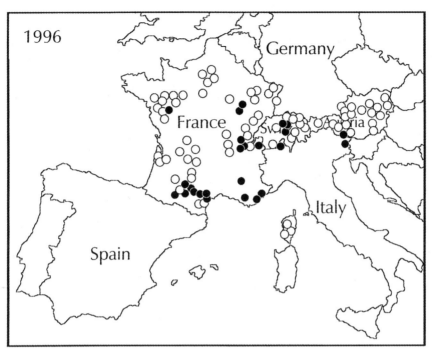

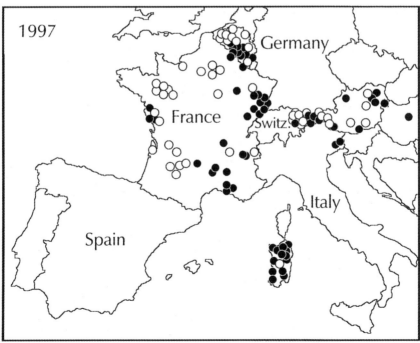

capability to withstand the dose normally used in treatments. This phenomenon is largely the result of two events: genetic variation and selection. In a population of mites the individual susceptibility to a given acaricide varies as with other characters, such as body size.

In some instances a few individuals may survive a normal pesticide dose that kills most others in the population. The possessors of this character survive the treatments and replace the susceptible individuals over time. This process, eliminating part of a population, is called selection.

A primary source of variability is constituted by mutations, i.e. changes that occur in the genes of the mite and originate modified molecules and structures. While selection takes place as a consequence of the use of the acaricide, mutations occurr independently from the exposure to an acaricide; they may be spontaneous or caused by several agents, such as ionizing radiation or mutagenic substances. Mutations can confer increased tolerance to an acaricide according to different mechanims, e.g., modification of the acaricide's site of action or enzyme changes that accelerate degradation of the acaricide.

Mechanisms that give resistance against one acaricide frequently also protect the mite against other closely related active ingredients; this phenomenon is called cross resistance. For example, the Italian strain of varroa mites resistant to fluvalinate is also resistant to the closely related pyrethroids flumethrin and acrinathrin, although the latter were never used to control varroa in Italy.

Most mutations are detrimental and produce non-working molecules; only in very rare cases they originate functional molecules modified in such a way to give increased tolerance to an acaricide. Mites with these modified structures often have a lower fitness, i.e. are slightly less viable than their susceptible counterparts: resistance has a cost. This leads to a slow decline in the frequency of the genes for resistance when the acaricide is not used. The phenomenon is usually but somewhat improperly called reversion. Preliminary data obtained in Italy indicate that, over one year, the increase of the populations of fluvalinate-resistant mites is about half of that of the susceptible mites.

Normally, resistance does not arise independently in many different geographic regions: it appears in one or a few regions and then the resistant strain(s) spread and are selected elsewhere.

In the case of V. *jacobsoni*, increased tolerance to several active ingredients, besides pyrethroids, has been observed, although these other cases of resistance were not as consequential as was resistance to fluvalinate. In particular, resistance to fluvalinate has been observed in the USA[3]; inefficacy of amitraz was reported both in Europe[2] and in the USA[4]; in 1999, resistance to coumaphos had been detected in Italy[7].

There is no reason to believe that the varroa mite cannot develop resistance against acaricides of natural origin or simple molecules (e.g., formic acid). There are hundreds of species of insects and mites which feed on plants containing natural toxins. Resistance against the simple molecule phosphine (PH$_3$) is a problem in the control of some stored product insects. In the case of the "natural acaricides" used against varroa, the selection pressure for resistance is presently low due to their limited use and variable efficacy and thus there is no immediate concern.

Persistent residues of acaricides (for example, in beeswax) have been thought to cause faster development of resistance since they act as a continuous treatment and increase selection pressure. However, this effect does not need to be invoked in the case of highly effective, widely used acaricides.

Resistance management: reducing the risk of resistance. Various tactics to slow the development of pesticide resistance in arthropods have been elaborated[1], but it is not easy to achieve significant success since not all of the factors involved in resistance can be controlled. For example, the frequency of mutations giving resistance to an acaricide is independent of the treatments; such mutations are more likely to occur in areas where the mite has more generations per year and larger populations (i.e., in Mediterranean rather than in colder climates), but we can do little to change this condition.

On the contrary, we have some control on the selection pressure; the proposed approaches fall into three main groups. These tactics have the best chance of success when they are put into practice over large areas.

First, a practice sometimes used in crop protection consists of using mixtures of two active ingredients with different modes of action (so-called "multiple attack"). If genes for resistance are initially rare, it is extremely unlikely that the same individual possesses genes for resistance to both active ingredients; resistance to just one of the active ingredients would not confer an advantage and thus selection should not take place. When new acaricides are put into use, this practice must be followed from the beginning; it is too late to resort to it when strains resistant to either active ingredient have already been selected. In the case of varroa, the multiple attack approach is unfeasible because of the scarcity of unrelated and "unresisted" active ingredients that can be combined in the same treatment.

A second tactic ("high-dose tactic"), often recommended by producers of pesticides, consists in avoiding underdoses which would make the development of resistance faster. This statement is based on three assumptions: (1) the heterozygotes (possessors of both susceptible and resistant forms of a gene) are endowed with a lower level of resistance than resistant homozygotes (possessors of only one form of a gene, in this case the resistant one); (2) initially, when the frequency of alleles (forms of a gene) for resistance is low, resistant homozygotes are extremely rare in a random mating population; (3) some individuals are not reached by the treatment and can reinvade the treated sites (e.g., varroa mites from feral swarms). A low dose would kill susceptible homozygotes (possessors of only susceptible forms of a gene) and spare a comparatively large number of resistant heterozygotes plus, of course, resistant homozygotes. In contrast, a dose high enough to kill the heterozygotes would eliminate most resistant mites; the rare resistant homozygotes surviving the treatment would be diluted by susceptible individuals immigrating from untreated areas. In the case of the varroa mite the assumption that resistant homozygotes are much rarer than heterozygotes is not true because of inbreeding (brother-sister mating), and thus the mainstay of the high-dose tactic fails. This tactic could still be valid if mutations giving a higher degree of resistance were less common or if resistance was controlled by many genes.

A third tactic ("moderation principle") might be more effective in the case of the varroa mite. A population consisting of both resistant and susceptible mites is subjected to opposite selection pressures: resistant mites are favored by treatments, while they usually lose ground slowly in the interval between treatments since they are slightly less viable (reversion). The more the selection pressure from treatments exceeds the disadvantages associated with resistance, the faster the onset of resistance. The extent to which the fitness is reduced varies in different resistant strains. In the case of the varroa mite even a decrease in the fitness in the order of a few percent per generation would produce an appreciable disadvantage over one year, since several generations of the mite take place during this period. However, we cannot expect that a 50% disadvantage over one year – like the one observed for the Italian strain of fluvalinate resistant mites – balances the selection from a treatment having 95% or higher efficacy, repeated each year: under these circumstances the resistance develops quickly. On the contrary, a significant delay can be obtained if the acaricide is used every two or more years, or the efficacy of the treatment is lower (e.g., 80%). In this case, satisfactory control of the parasite could be obtained by alternating different acaricides in successive years or combining different treatments, each one acting for a restricted period and thus with a reduced efficacy: two treatments, each one 80% effective, give an overall 96% efficacy. For example, many beekeepers prefer to carry out a treatment with products based on ethereal oils in late summer and a later treatment with oxalic acid in late fall. Treatments could be integrated with non-chemical control techniques. In this context, the selection of bee strains on which varroa populations increase more slowly could conceivably make highly effective chemical treatments unnecessary and reduce the risk of varroa becoming resistant. An added benefit of the "moderation" tactic is the reduced risk of losses, if one of the treatments becomes ineffective. To sum up: varroa control should not rely on a single, highly effective acaricide, applied repeatedly or for long periods.

Resistance management: early detection of resistance. Early detection of the presence of resistant mites is crucial to reducing colony losses. Reliable and timely detection of the presence of resistant mites can be obtained with laboratory assays, one example of which, widely used in Europe, is described here[6]. Capsules, 60 mm dia., consisting of two glass disks kept about 5 mm apart by two steel rings are prepared (Fig. 17.2). The interior of the capsules is coated with paraffin containing a known concentration of the acaricide. *Varroa* mites are taken from brood and kept for six hours in these capsules. Mites are then transferred into another capsule without acaricide where they can feed on bee larvae. After 48 hours the mites are inspected. Usually the test is carried out at a concentration expected to kill more than 99% of susceptible mites; thus survival at this concentration is an indication of the presence of resistant mites.

An evaluation of field efficacy can be obtained by carrying out back-to-back treatments with two unrelated acaricides and employing sticky bottom board inserts to quantify mite drop. The ratio of the num-

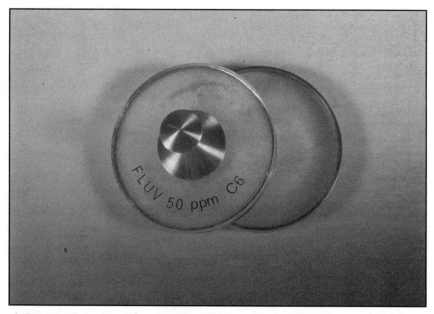

▲*Figure 17.2 Capsules used for the bioassay mentioned in the text.*

ber of mites retrieved by the first treatment to the sum retrieved by both treatments gives an indication of the relative efficacy of, or mite resistance to, the first treatment. This method was used by beekeeping experts in districts of Northern Italy between 1993 and 1995 during the spread of mites resistant to Apistan. Immediately after Apistan treatments, a sample of colonies (1-2% of the total) was treated with the varroacide preparation Perizin® (Bayer) containing the organophosphorus acaricide coumaphos. Although these surveys had some disadvantages (the results often came too late to plan the varroa control and could be influenced by reinfestation), they were useful for reducing colony losses. In addition, they provided general information on the spread of resistance. Dangerous levels of resistance built up within one year in areas where no reduction in treatment efficacy had been observed previously. There was no second warning; if adequate measures were not taken immediately, colonies were often lost. Resistance was usually detected earliest in areas with more active migratory beekeeping. There was large variation in the percentage of mites surviving Apistan treatments, both within and among apiaries. The resistant mites were often concentrated in a few colonies which without further treatments would have collapsed the following year, causing a chain of reinfestations and further collapses with disastrous consequences for beekeeping in that area.

Once resistance is detected in an area, it is important to issue appropriate warnings. Beekeepers often find it difficult to accept the idea that a very effective treatment has become unsatisfactory or to believe that a treatment is unsuccessful, even if it causes visibly high mite drop.

Summary. Treatment with synthetic acaricides will be necessary in the future to control the varroa mite. We need to develop and to put into practice strategies that reduce acaricide resistance and minimize its effects. Control of varroa should not rely upon the exclusive, repeated, or prolonged use of the few well-known acaricides that give 95% or higher efficacy. Field trials and laboratory tests should be used to understand the causes of possible failures in control and to detect the presence of resistant mites.

References cited.
1. Denholm, I. & M. W. Rowland. 1992. Tactics for managing pesticide resistance in arthropods: theory and practice. Ann. Rev. Entomol. 37: 91-112.

2. Dujin, T., V. Jovanoviç, D. Suvakov & Z. Milkoviç, 1991. Uticaj visegodisnje primene preparata na bazi amitraza na stvaranje rezis tentnii sojeva varoe (Varoa *jacobsoni*) [Effects of extended use of amitraz-based products on the formation of resistant strains of *Varroa jacobsoni*], Veterinarski Glasnik 45: 851-855. In Croatian (Latin script), with Serbian spelling.

3. Elzen, P. J., F. A Eischen, J. R. Baxter, J. Pettis, G. W. Elzen & W. T. Wilson. 1998. Fluvalinate resistance in *Varroa jacobsoni* from several geographic locations. Am. Bee J. 138: 674-676.

4. Elzen, P. J., J. R. Baxter, M. Spivak & W. T. Wilson. 1999. Amitraz resistance in *Varroa*: new discovery in North America. Am. Bee J. 139: 362.

5. Lodesani, M., M. Colombo & M. Spreafico. 1994. Ineffectiveness of

Apistan® treatment against the mite *Varroa jacobsoni* Oud. in several districts of Lombardy (Italy). Apidologie 26: 67-72.

6. **Milani, N. 1995.** The resistance of *Varroa jacobsoni* Oud. to pyrethroids: a laboratory assay. Apidologie 26: 415-429.

7. **Spreafico, M. & M. Colombo, personal communication.**

8. **Trouiller, J. 1998.** Monitoring of *Varroa jacobsoni* resistance to pyrethroids in Europe, Apidologie 29: 537-546.

Chapter 18

PARASITIC BROOD MITES NOT PRESENT IN NORTH AMERICA

Gard W. Otis
Jasna Kralj

V *arroa jacobsoni,* the best known mite parasite of honey bee brood, has changed the nature of beekeeping dramatically over the last half century as it has become introduced from Asia into Europe and the Americas. The other mite species that parasitize bee brood are still restricted in distribution to Asia. For this reason, beekeepers in western countries are poorly informed about their biology and generally unconcerned about their existence. Yet at least one species, *Tropilaelaps clareae,* is potentially more destructive to honey bees, *Apis mellifera,* than is *V. jacobsoni*[16,17,40,59,72]. In this chapter we review the biology, control, and economic importance of several species of parasitic mites known to infest honey bees (*Apis* spp.) in Asia.

Host-parasite associations. Only a few years ago, the Asian bee and bee mite situation seemed straightforward. The three Asian species of honey bees recognized before 1980 were known to be the hosts of three species of parasitic mites, each placed in its own genus[52]. Drone pupae of *Apis cerana*, the eastern hive bee, were recognized as the natural host of *V. jacobsoni*. A closely related mite, *Euvarroa sinhai*, was known to parasitize drone pupae of the dwarf honey bee, *A. florea*. A smaller mite species, *Tropilaelaps clareae*, had been collected from drone and worker brood of *A. dorsata*, the giant honey bee. However, this simple story is now known to be much more complex, owing to the recent recognition of five additional species of honey bees (reviewed by Otis[60,61]) and four species of mites. The parasite-host relationships are summarized in Table 18.1. It is now known that some bee species serve as hosts for two species of mites in the same genus, such as *V. jacobsoni*

Table 18.1 Summary of Asian parasitic mite species and their known hosts (Apis spp.). Details of these relationships are given in the text. Bee species in bold type are recent host associations of mites.

mite species	host bee species
Family Laelapidae	
Genus *Tropilaelaps* Delfinado and Baker 1961[20]	
T. clareae Delfinado and Baker 1961[19]	*A. dorsata, A. laboriosa,* **A. mellifera**
T. koenigerum Delfinado-Baker and Baker 1982[24]	*A. dorsata, A. laboriosa*
Family Varroidae	
Genus *Euvarroa* Delfinado and Baker 1974[20]	
E. sinhai Delfinado and Baker 1974[20]	*A. florea*
E. wongsirii Lekprayoon and Tangkanasing 1991[44]	*A. andreniformis*
Genus *Varroa* Oudemans 1904[62]	
V. jacobsoni Oudemans 1904, Type I	*A. cerana, A. nigrocincta?*
V. jacobsoni, Type II	*A. cerana,* **A. mellifera**
V. underwoodi Delfinado-Baker and Aggarwal 1987[23]	*A. cerana, A. nigrocincta? A.nuluensis?*
V. rindereri Guzman and Delfinado-Baker 1996[32]	*A. koschevnikovi*

and *V. underwoodi* on *A. cerana*[10] and the two species of *Tropilaelaps* mites on *A. dorsata* and *A. laboriosa*[26]. Many of the mites listed in Table 18.1 have been collected from adult bees or brood cells of other species of honey bees (for example, see Table I of Wongsiri & others[75]). However, these incidental collections are infrequent and there is no evidence that the mites reproduce on the brood of these alternate bee species.

All species of *Varroa*, *Euvarroa*, and *Tropilaelaps* have life cycles similar to that of *V. jacobsoni* (see Chapter 10). Adult female mites enter cells containing large larvae, are sealed in the cells when bees cap the brood, and produce offspring on the bee pupae. Like with honey bees, fertilized eggs develop into female mites while unfertilized eggs become males[65]. In a colony parasitized by a single female mite, her female offspring mate with their brothers and can initiate an infestation. Despite the similar biologies of these mite species, only two, *Varroa jacobsoni* and *Tropilaelaps clareae*, are known to have adopted the western honey bee, *Apis mellifera*, as a host.

Tropilaelaps mites. *T. clareae* was first collected from colonies of *A. mellifera* and from field rats in the vicinity of infested apiaries in the Phillippines[19]. The presumed association of this mite with two very different hosts, one of them an introduced species of honey bee and the other a mammal, was unfortunate because it took several more years before it was realized that the primary host was the giant honey bee, *A. dorsata*[13,42]. *T. clareae* has been collected almost everywhere that *A. dorsata* exists except Sri Lanka where a smaller species with a pear-shaped anal plate, *T. koenigerum*, occurs[24]. Both *T. clareae* and *T. koenigerum* parasitize the recently-rediscovered *A. laboriosa*, a bee species similar to *A. dorsata* that inhabits the mountainous Himalayan region of Asia[26]. Occasional collections of *Tropilaelaps* mites from *A. cerana* and *A. florea* have resulted in these bee species being listed as "hosts"[1,21,22,26,27,28] ; however, there is no evidence of reproduction by *Tropilaelaps* on brood of either of these Asian bee species.

The distribution of *T. koenigerum* is noteworthy. It is the only mite species found in association with *A. dorsata* in Sri Lanka, suggesting that it may replace *T. clareae*[24]. However, in Nepal[26] and Borneo[31], *T. koenigerum* cohabits with *T. clareae* in colonies of *A. dorsata*. Its biology is poorly known and at present there are no explanations why it is encountered less frequently than *T. clareae*. Detailed examination of brood cells in colonies of *A. dorsata* from throughout its range will probably demonstrate that *T. koenigerum* is more widely distributed than presently recognized.

Tropilaelaps clareae readily infests colonies of *A. mellifera* which have been introduced to parts of Asia where bees rear brood continuously. Through the commercial movement of *A. mellifera*, this parasitic mite can be introduced to areas where *A. dorsata* does not occur. The first confirmation that this happens was in hot regions of Afghanistan where *T. clareae* had a devastating effect on beekeeping in the 1980s[81]. More recently, *Tropilaelaps* has been reported from New Guinea[22,43] and South Korea[77]. The Korean situation is of interest because the climate there is cooler than in other areas infested by *T. clareae*. The most disturbing report was of *T. clareae* on newly-emerged adults of *A. m. scutellata* showing deformed wings and crawling in hive debris in Kenya[41]. It is surprising that there have been no further reports confirming this situation. If it proves to be true, it could have serious effects on bees and beekeeping in Africa.

Because of the difficulties of studying *A. dorsata*, most information about the life cycle of *T. clareae* comes from infested brood of *A. mellifera*. Adult mites are very active on the combs and adult bees. Female *Tropilaelaps*, and possibly a few males, invade cells of older larvae[36]. Unlike *Varroa*, these mites do not enter the brood food, and most have begun feeding on larvae by the time the cells are sealed. Some eggs may already be laid by this time in northern Thailand[68], although Woyke[86] in Vietnam reported that the earliest egg laying occurred 48-52 hours after the sealing of the cell. There is no adequate explanation for these differences. The adult mites firmly attach themselves to the prepupae with their mouthparts and feed[68]. Females swell to twice their thickness while feeding, and most egg laying is apparently associated with this feeding period[68,86]. In cells with older pupae mites become thin again and egg laying ceases[83,86].

Woyke's[83] estimate for development time of 6.0 days from egg to adult mite is considerably shorter and probably more accurate than the first estimate of 8.8 days[36]. Fan & Li[29] provided an even shorter estimate of 5 days. The egg and larval stages are very brief (0.4 and 0.6 days respectively), which may explain in part why some early researchers were unable to locate them (e.g., Atwal & Goyal[12]). The maximum number of offspring per female in worker cells is three[68] to four[83]. The fecundity has been estimated to be 1.39 offspring per reproducing mite, but when non-reproducing mites are taken into account (27%), the reproductive rate was only 1.02 offspring per mite[68]. It should be noted that both the proportion of reproducing mites (81.7-92.7%) and fecundity (1.9 offspring/mite) can be higher[84], which can result in a higher reproductive rate. Although it is nearly impossible to determine how many reproductive cycles are undertaken by individual mites, some mites removed from pupae are capable of reproducing again[88]. Mites reproduce on drones as well, but their relative contribution to the reproductive rate is not clear.

From this information it is difficult to estimate the actual rate of growth of *Tropilaelaps* populations. From the practical experience of Asian beekeepers, however, it is known that populations of *Tropilaelaps* can grow quickly. In fact, colonies of *A. mellifera* can be killed by *Tropilaelaps* within one year of infestation[42], and it is often stated that *Tropilaelaps* is a more serious pest than *V. jacobsoni* in tropical Asia[7,72]. One biological factor that differs between these mites is the length of the phoretic period–the period when mites are on adult bees after exiting one brood cell and before entering another. It has been demonstrated repeatedly that maximum longevity of *T. clareae* mites on adult bees is 2.5-3.0 days, and most live for less than two days[3,36,37,49,67,71,80,85]. Consequently, it must be concluded that the mites are usually phoretic on adult bees for two days or less, in comparison to a much longer period in *V. jacobsoni*. This shorter generation length of *T. clareae* contributes greatly to its higher population growth rate.

Over most of the range of *Tropilaelaps*, colonies of *A. mellifera* are often co-infested with *V. jacobsoni*. Both mite species are capable of reproducing in co-infested brood cells, but the incidence of mite infertility of both species is higher than in singly-infested cells. The first reports suggested that *T. clareae* suppressed reproduction by *V. jacobsoni*[17,68]. However, more detailed observations[66] indicated that reproduction by one *Varroa* mite is decreased no more by a *T. clareae* mite than by a second *Varroa* mite in a multiply-infested cell. In addition, *T. clareae* appear to infest cells randomly, with no particular attraction or repellency toward cells infested by *Varroa* mites. The greater abundance of *T. clareae* over *V. jacobsoni* in heavily infested colonies is probably an artifact of the higher reproductive rate of *Tropilaelaps*.

In cells infested by a single female *T. clareae*, male offspring mate with their sisters. Because one male can fertilize several females[89], a mother can increase her reproductive rate by producing more daughters than sons. In fact, a sex ratio of three females to every male has been reported[65,84], but one study obtained a sex ratio of 1:1[68]. A few females (2%) produce all male broods[68]. These are probably unmated females from cells in which no male offspring were produced. When they attempt to reproduce, they can lay only unfertilized eggs which develop into males. After mating with a son, they can produce a normal mixed-sex brood in a subsequent reproductive cycle.

The effects of *Tropilaelaps* on colonies of *A. mellifera* are described by Atwal & Goyal[12], Burgett & Akratanakul[16], Burgett & others[17], and Ritter & Schneider-Ritter[68]. Lightly infested brood usually complete development, but many larvae die prior to pupation if they are infested with three or more mites each[84]. The surviving adults are often smaller and exhibit deformities such as crumpled or diminutive wings, shortened abdomens, and deformed or missing legs. These damages appear at lower levels of infestation than with *Varroa*. The deformed adults are often removed by their nestmates and can be seen crawling on the ground in front of hives. Worker bees seem better able to detect capped brood cells infested with *T. clareae* than those infested by *V. jacobsoni*, and they uncap some of the parasitized cells and remove the pupae[14]. In populous colonies, discarded larvae and pupae accumulate near the hive entrance, frequently with live mites still on them. Severe infestations in which 90% of pupae are infested are possible. Up to 50% of bee larvae and numerous pupae die in severely infested colonies, resulting in an irregular brood pattern and brood cells with perforated cappings. Such colonies have dwindling amounts of brood and adult bees, and they frequently abscond.

There is relatively little information concerning *T. clareae* on its original host, *A. dorsata*. Mites are present in most colonies and infest brood cells of both drones and workers, causing deformities and mortality similar to that described for *A. mellifera* above[42,74,80]. There is indirect evidence that *A. dorsata* removes some brood that is more heavily infested, a behavior that may regulate mite populations[18]. Brood cells that remain capped after surrounding bees have emerged are usually dead and frequently infested heavily with mites[80]. Infestation can lead to weakening of the colony and secondary infestation by wax moths[42]. Unlike *A. mellifera*, *A. dorsata* can bite and injure *T. clareae* mites[15,37,65,74]. When a mite moves onto the side of the thorax or the underside of a bee, the bee grooms itself with its legs and pushes the mite towards the mouthparts. About half the mites escape detection by moving into the area between the thorax and abdomen[15]. Survival of *T. clareae* on adult *A. dorsata* workers, about 2.5 days[37], is about the same as on *A. mellifera*. Consequently, the break in the brood cycle that accompanies swarming and absconding, and the long-distance migration that occurs in many regions[69], undoubtedly cause a large reduction in mite populations[25,42]. How *Tropilaelaps* survives in swarms in unclear. Koeniger and Muzaffar[37] suggested that the mites participate in the social food exchange between bees. One of us (GWO) observed three mites between the thorax and abdomen of a queen in a small swarm of *A. dorsata*, suggesting that the queen may play a role in mite survival during swarming.

Soon after *T. clareae* was recognized as a pest of *A. mellifera* in Asia, trials with various chemicals were initiated to find effective controls. Several products, when applied properly, result in good control of *Tropilaelaps*, including fumigation with formic acid[30,35] and Folbex (chlorobenzilate)[85], dusting with powdered sulfur[12], contact with Mavrik (fluvalinate)[48], and spraying with a solution of Mitac (amitraz)[73]. Fan and Li[29] mention the wide variety of products used in China to treat mite infestations. Because many of the above treatments leave residues in honey or can cause harm to applicators, only products properly registered for use should be used for mite control.

When Woyke[80] reported that *Tropilaelaps* mites usually do not survive more than two days on adult bees, he provided the first description of biotechnical mite control methods that do not require the use of chemicals. The management systems he outlined rely on caging the queen for a period of time, depriving colonies of all brood, or a combination of these methods. These systems have been modified and refined subsequently[57,58,70,71,81,82,87]. One simple technique is to divide the colony. All brood with adhering bees is placed in a new hive, while the remaining bees and the queen remain in the original hive. The queenless colony will rear a new queen, but the resulting interruption in brood production will eliminate the *Tropilaelaps* mites. Likewise, in the queenright unit the mites also die because there is no brood to infest. At the end of four weeks, the two hives can be reunited[87]. If this procedure is done at the end of the honey flow, honey production and colony strength are not affected. Commercial beekeepers in Vietnam use biotechnical methods to control both *Tropilaelaps* and *Varroa* mites with a high degree of success[57,58].

Euvarroa mites. The two species of dwarf honey bees, *Apis florea* and *A. andreniformis*, are the natural hosts of the mite species *Euvarroa sinhai* and *E. wongsirii*, respectively. These mites reproduce only on drone brood[4,38,51,56], but can survive on adult worker bees and drones in the nest or in swarms[51,56]. All life stages except mature adult females live in capped drone cells of their hosts. *E. sinhai* has been studied in India, Sri Lanka, Iran, and Thailand. It probably occurs throughout most of the range of *A. florea*, from Vietnam westward in tropical and subtropical regions to the Persian Gulf region[61]. It would be interesting to know if it infests colonies of *A. florea* in recently-established populations in Sudan[47] and Saudi Arabia[5].

The host of *E. wongsirii*, the world's smallest honey bee *Apis andreniformis*, was not recognized as a species until 1987. Consequently, *E. wongsirii* was not collected until 1989 when it was obtained from colonies of *A. andreniformis* in peninsular Malaysia and Thailand. It probably occurs throughout the range of its host from eastern India throughout Indochina to Malaysia and western Indonesia[61], but at present there are few collection localities for this mite species.

Morphologically, *E. sinhai* and *E. wongsirii* are distinctive[44,45,51]. They are characteristically narrower in body shape than *V. jacobsoni*, but broader than *Tropilaelaps*. *E. sinhai* is about as broad as it is long, with 34-46 long hairs along the rear edge of the body shield. In contrast, *E. wongsirii* is slightly shorter and wider and has 46-54 long hairs on the posterior margin of the body. The best diagnostic feature is general body shape, which is pear-shaped in *E. sinhai* and strongly triangular in *E. wongsirii*.

The biologies of the *Euvarroa* mites are not well known, in part because it is difficult to manipulate and inspect intact colonies of their dwarf bee hosts. However, several studies of nests harvested from the wild have allowed researchers to document the life history of the mites. Adult female mites lay 2-3 eggs, as based on the ratio of the numbers of immature mites to mature females in cells[51,55]. In colonies of *A. florea*, mature mites leave the cells when the drones uncap their cells. However, if the host drone pupa dies, some of the entrapped *E. sinhai* mites are able to use their mouthparts to cut a small rectangular hole in the middle of the cell cap and exit the cell[55]. The drone cell cappings in one colony of *A. andreniformis* in Malaysia appeared to be progressively removed by the bees as the pupae matured (Fig. 6 in Morin & Otis[51]); adult and immature *E. wongsirii* mites on the drone brood appeared to be unaffected by this condition. Once emerged, the mites seem to prefer adult drones to adult worker bees[55]. Mite populations in queenright colonies never become particularly large, probably due to seasonal production of drone brood[55] and frequent absconding by their host colonies[76]. *A. florea* workers do not exhibit grooming or other responses when *E. sinhai* mites are experimentally placed on them[39]. A study in Iran showed that when brood rearing ceases in *A. florea* colonies, mites survive by feeding on adult workers for 4-10.5 months[55]. During such periods most of the mites probably live between the abdominal plates (sternites) of the bees[45] as *V. jacobsoni* does on *A. mellifera*. Euvarroa mites are rarely collected on foraging worker bees[56].

E. sinhai has had the opportunity to infest *A. mellifera* brood, as evidenced by occasional collections of this mite in debris from bottom boards of *A. mellifera* colonies in India[2,11] and Thailand[44,64]. Moreover, it has been shown experimentally that *E. sinhai* can reproduce on both worker and drone brood of *A. mellifera*[53,54]. However, neither *Euvarroa* species has been found in capped worker or drone cells in colonies of *A. mellifera*, even in areas where dwarf bee colonies live in close proximity to commercial apiaries of *A. mellifera*. When *E. sinhai* mites were placed on caged workers of *A. mellifera*, nearly half of them left the bees and wandered on the cage, suggesting that they fail to recognize the western honey bee as a suitable host[39]. There is one report of *E. sinhai* being found between the sternites of *A. cerana* drones in hives in eastern India[63]. However, there are no records of this mite infesting brood cells of this Asian bee species despite intensive inspections by numerous researchers studying *V. jacobsoni*. We doubt that either species of *Euvarroa* will become a significant problem for people managing colonies of *A. mellifera* or *A. cerana*, contrary to the suggestions of Aggarwal & Kapi[12], Mossadegh[53,54], and Delfinado-Baker & Peng[25].

Varroa mites. There are three recognized species of mites in the genus *Varroa*, all with a similar oval, crab-like body form. *Varroa jacobsoni* is the most widely distributed and best known of these, having gone in only thirty years from being almost unknown to one of the most serious pests of *Apis mellifera* worldwide. It has been reported as occurring naturally in colonies of *A. cerana* throughout most of that bee species' range.

The rediscovery of *A. koschevnikovi* in Borneo opened the possibility of an undescribed species of host-specific *Varroa* mite. One of us

(GWO) collected mites there in 1989 and observed that mites from colonies of *A. koschevnikovi* were larger than the *V. jacobsoni* mites found in colonies of *A. cerana* nearby. The suspicion that these represented an undescribed species of mite was eventually confirmed on the basis of morphological and DNA differences, and it was named *V. rindereri*[32]. It is longer and wider than *V. jacobsoni* from several different Asian populations[32]. Also, *V. rindereri* typically has more long hairs (setae) along each side of the body (average = 23) than does *V. jacobsoni* (average = 19). Its biology and distribution remain unknown. There is no information concerning its ability to successfully parasitize the brood of *A. mellifera* because colonies of *A. mellifera* are rarely maintained within the range of *A. koschevnikovi* (peninsular Malaysia, Sumatra, and Borneo[61]).

The third *Varroa* species, found in collections of mites from *A. cerana* colonies in Nepal, was named *V. underwoodi*[23]. It is considerably shorter than *V. jacobsoni*. Its most striking morphological feature is the exceptionally long setae along the sides of its body. When these long setae are included in the measurement, this smaller species is almost as wide as *V. jacobsoni* (Fig. 18.1). It is probably a parasite only of drone pupae[10].

This species is interesting from several perspectives. It has been collected, almost always in small numbers, from widely distributed regions including Nepal[23], South Korea[78,79], Borneo[33], New Guinea, Java, and Sulawesi[10]. It is more widely distributed than originally thought and rarer than most other mites parasitic on honey bee brood. Second, despite its apparent rarity, *V. underwoodi* may have a wide host range, having been collected from three honey bee species in Asia: *A. cerana*, *A. nigrocincta* in Sulawesi (although reproduction on drone brood of this species requires confirmation[10], and *A. nuluensis* (between the sternites of a worker bee in a mixed colony of *A. cerana* and *A. nuluensis*[33]). Recently it was collected in Papua, New Guinea from worker brood of *A. mellifera*, but there was no evidence of reproduction[10]. It has also been reported in brood cells of *A. mellifera* in South Korea, but no economic problems are yet reported[77]. Further studies are needed to clarify the relationship of this mite species with *A. mellifera*. Finally, the single mite specimen found on *A. nuluensis* in Borneo was larger and had fewer endopodal setae than typical *V. underwoodi* mites from Korea. Whether this represents geographical variation within this mite species or an undescribed species that parasitizes the recently discovered species *A. nuluensis* is unknown. A remarkable situation has been discovered recently by Denis Anderson in New Guinea. New Guinea had no honey bees prior to human introductions. *A. mellifera* was introduced to Papua, New Guinea (PNG) in 1948 after which it estab-

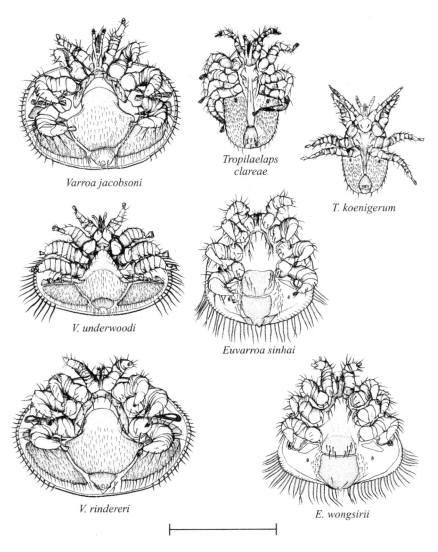

▲*Figure 18.1 The seven recognized species of mites parasitic on brood of honey bees (Apis spp.). The reference bar is 1.0 mm in length.*

lished thriving wild populations in the highlands[50]. Much later in the late 1970s, colonies of *A. cerana* containing *V. jacobsoni* mites were introduced to western New Guinea from Java from where they have spread eastward over most of the island. Interestingly, these *Varroa* mites have caused no problems in the *A. mellifera* colonies on New Guinea. Anderson observed that female mites of this New Guinean population are found in worker and drone cells of both *A. cerana* and *A. mellifera*, but reproduction occurs only on drone brood of *A. cerana*[7]. Of the 60,000 worker cells of *A. mellifera* inspected, 1064 (1.8%) contained female *Varroa* mites, but none of them was reproducing. A good report of this situation has been written by Lee[43].

This unexpected finding stimulated a series of further enquiries. One possibility is that the bees in New Guinea are resistant to *V. jacobsoni*. However, by comparing mite reproduction in genetically similar colonies of *A. mellifera* in PNG and Germany, it is evident that this is not the answer[8]. Mites reproduced readily on worker brood in Germany, but failed to reproduce on either workers or drones of *A. mellifera* in PNG. Further research has shown that there are several different populations of *Varroa* mites, including a "reproducing" strain that causes serious damage to *A. mellifera* bee colonies in Europe and North America and a "non-reproducing" strain which originally occurred in Java on *A. cerana*[8,34]. The two strains of mites can be distinguished on the basis of consistent differences in their DNA and male genitalia.

The Javanese situation is particularly interesting. *V. jacobsoni* was originally described from mites collected on Java from *A. cerana*[62]. However, before 1993 only the "non-reproducing" strain of *V. jacobsoni* existed on Java where it survived by parasitizing *A. cerana* drone brood. Recently the "reproducing" variety of mite was introduced and now can be readily collected there, but almost exclusively from colonies of *A. mellifera*[8,9]. Occasionally within the same apiary the "reproducing" strain of mites can be found in *A. mellifera* colonies next to colonies of *A. cerana* containing the "non-reproducing" strain. These observations suggest that these strains of mites are two separate but cryptic species. Because the original "*V. jacobsoni*" mites were of the "non-reproducing" PNG strain, the *Varroa* mites that now infest *A. mellifera* colonies in Europe and North America will have to be described as a new species[8]. Denis Anderson[6] has suggested the name *Varroa destructor*.

When searching for genetic solutions to the *Varroa* problem, researchers usually look first for genetic differences between bees because of the high degree of variation within *Apis mellifera*. It is now evident that when conducting such work the genetic strain of mite involved should be verified because differences in the virulence of mites could be misinterpreted as differences in resistance of the bees. Guzman & others[34] have identified three strains of "*V. jacobsoni:*" a Russian strain that reproduces on *A. mellifera* in Europe and North America, a Japanese strain from Japan that reproduces on *A. mellifera* in Brazil and Puerto Rico, and a non-reproducing Papua, New Guinea strain. Denis Anderson[6] goes even further, suggesting that the mites that have been known as "*Varroa jacobsoni*" actually belong to five different species. Yet more surprises are likely to emerge as detailed study of mites from different parts of Asia continues.

Concluding remarks. Additional parasitic species may await discovery in Asia, especially in isolated populations of bees. In addition, there are other non-parasitic mites that superficially resemble some of those depicted here (e.g., species of *Mellitiphis*, *Hypoaspis*, *Proctolaelaps*, and *Parasitus*[46]). Researchers in apiculture and mite parasitology should carefully verify the species and strain of brood mites with which they are working.

Summary. This review should enable the identification of the currently recognized mite parasites of honey bee brood. *Tropilaelaps clareae* and *Varroa jacobsoni* (*Varroa destructor*) have been responsible for the failure of beekeeping with *Apis mellifera* in Asia until the last few decades. Despite the relatively similar life histories of all the mites reviewed here, these are the only two species that have become pests of *A. mellifera*. Some species have not yet come in contact with *A. mellifera* (e.g., *V. rindereri*, *T. koenigerum*) so their potential effects are unknown. Other mites are apparently so well suited to their natural bee host that they fail to exploit *A. mellifera* as a host (e.g., the *Euvarroa* species). Additional research on some of the mite species that do not harm *A. mellifera* may further our understanding of mechanisms of resistance of *A. mellifera* to brood mites.

It seems almost certain that *T. clareae* could survive on honey bees in any region of the world where *A. mellifera* colonies rear brood throughout the year. Beekeepers in subtropical and tropical regions should be cautious about importing bees from countries where *Tropilaelaps* mites are known to occur. It is likely that this serious pest will continue to spread, largely through the movement of bees by humans.

References cited.
1. **Aggarwal, K. 1988.** Incidence of *Tropilaelaps clareae* on three *Apis* species in Hisar (India), pp. 396-403. *In* G. R. Needham, R.E. Page, Jr., M. Delfinado-Baker & C.E. Bowman [eds.], Africanized honey bees and bee mites. Halsted Press, New York.

2. **Aggarwal K. & R. P. Kapil. 1988.** Observations on the effect of queen cell construction on *Euvarroa sinhai* infestation in drone brood of *Apis florea*, pp. 404-408. *In* G. R. Needham, R.E. Page, Jr., M. Delfinado-Baker & C.E. Bowman [eds.], Africanized honey bees and bee mites. Halsted Press, New York.

3. **Akratanakul, P. 1984.** Beekeeping industry with *Apis mellifera* in Thailand, pp 222-234. *In* FAO, Proceedings, Expert consultation on beekeeping with *Apis mellifera* in tropical and subtropical Asia, 9-14 April 1984. Bangkok/Chiang Mai, Thailand.

4. **Akratanakul, P. & M. Burgett. 1976.** Euvarroa sinhai Delfinado and Baker (Acarina: Mesostigmata): a parasitic mite of *Apis florea*. J. Apic. Res 15: 11-13.

5. **Al Ghamdi, A.** *Apis florea* in Saudi Arabia. Bee World, submitted.

6. **Anderson, D. L. 1998.** personal communication.

7. **Anderson, D. L. 1994.** Non-reproduction of *Varroa jacobsoni* in *Apis mellifera* colonies in Papua, New Guinea and Indonesia. Apidologie 25: 412-421.

8. **Anderson, D. L. & S. Fuchs. 1998.** Two genetically distinct populations of *Varroa jacobsoni* with contrasting reproductive abilities on *Apis mellifera*. J. Apic. Res. 37: 6978.

9. **Anderson, D. L. & Sukarsih. 1996.** Changed *Varroa jacobsoni* reproduction in *Apis mellifera* colonies in Java. Apidologie. 27: 461-466.

10. **Anderson, D. L., R. B. Halliday & G. W. Otis. 1997.** The occurrence of *Varroa underwoodi* (Acarina: Varroidae) in Papua New Guinea and Indonesia. Apidologie 28: 143-147.

11. **Anonymous, 1987.** *Euvarroa sinhai* found in *Apis mellifera* hive debris. Bee World 68: 189.

12. Atwal, *A.* S. & N. P. Goyal. 1971. Infestation of honeybee colonies with *Tropilaelaps*, and its control. J. Apic. Res. 10: 137-142.

13. Bharadwaj, R. K. 1968. A new record of the mite *Tropilaelaps clareae* from *Apis dorsata* colonies. Bee World 49: 115.

14. Boecking, O., W. Rath & W. Drescher. 1992. *Apis mellifera* removes *Varroa jacobsoni* and *Tropilaelaps clareae* from sealed brood cells in the tropics. Am. Bee J. 132: 732-734.

15. Büchler, R., W. Drescher & I. Tornier. 1992. Grooming behaviour of *Apis cerana*, *Apis mellifera* and *Apis dorsata* and its effect on the parasitic mites *Varroa jacobsoni* and *Tropilaelaps clareae*. Exp. Appl. Acarol. 16: 313-319.

16. Burgett, M. & P. Akratanakul. 1985. *Tropilaelaps clareae*, the little known honey bee brood mite. Am. Bee J. 125: 112-114.

17. Burgett, M., P. Akratanakul & R. *A.* Morse. 1983. *Tropilaelaps clareae*: a parasite of honeybees in south-east Asia. Bee World 64: 25-28.

18. Burgett, D. M., P. *A.* Rossignol & C. Kitprasert. 1990. A model of dispersion and regulation of brood mite (*Tropilaelaps clareae*) parasitism on the giant honeybee (*Apis dorsata*). Can. J. Zool. 68: 1423-1427.

19. Delfinado, M. D. & E. W. Baker. 1961. *Tropilaelaps*, a new genus of mite from the Philippines (Laelaptidae [s. lat]: Acarina). Fieldiana Zool. 44: 53-56.

20. Delfinado, M. D. & E. W. Baker. 1974. Varroidae: a new family of mites on honeybees (Mesostigmata: Acarina). J. Washington Acad. Sci. 64: 410.

21. Delfinado-Baker, M. 1982. New records for *Tropilaelaps clareae* from colonies of *Apis cerana indica*. Am. Bee J. 122: 382.

22. Delfinado-Baker, M. & K. Aggarwal. 1987. Infestation of *Tropilaelaps clareae* and *Varroa jacobsoni* in *Apis mellifera ligustica* colonies in Papua, New Guinea. Am. Bee J. 127: 443.

23. Delfinado-Baker, M. & K. Aggarwal. 1987. A new *Varroa* (Acari: Varroidae) from the nest of *Apis cerana* (Apidae). Int. J. Acarol. 13: 233-237.

24. Delfinado-Baker, M. & E. W. Baker. 1982. A new species of *Tropilaelaps* parasitic on honey bees. Am. Bee J. 122: 416-417.

25. Delfinado-Baker, M. & C. Y. S. Peng. 1995. *Varroa jacobsoni* and *Tropilaelaps clareae*: a perspective of life history and why Asian bee-mites preferred European honey bees. Am. Bee J. 135: 415-420.

26. Delfinado-Baker, M., B. *A.* Underwood & E. W. Baker. 1985. The occurrence of *Tropilaelaps* mites in brood nests of *Apis dorsata* and *Apis laboriosa* in Nepal, with descriptions of the nymphal stages. Am. Bee J. 125: 703-706.

27. Delfinado-Baker, M., E. W. Baker & *A.* C. G. Phoon. 1989. Mites (Acari) associated with bees (Apidae) in Asia, with description of a new species. Am. Bee J. 129: 609-613.

28. Delfinado-Baker, M., W. Rath & O. Boecking. 1992. Phoretic bee mites and honeybee grooming behavior. Int. J. Acarol. 18: 315-322.

29. Fan, Z.-Y. & L.-S. Li. 1988. The distribution and damage of bee mites in China, pp. 417-419. pp. 535-540. *In* G.R. Needham, R.E. Page Jr., M. Delfinado-Baker & C.E. Bowman [eds.], Africanized honey bees and bee mites. Halsted Press, New York.

30. Garg, R., O. P. Sharma & G. S. Dogra. 1984. Formic acid: an effective acaricide against *Tropilaelaps clareae* Delfinado and Baker (Laelaptidae: Acarina) and its effect on the brood and longevity of honey bees. Am. Bee J. 124: 736-738.

31. Guzman, L.I. de 1998. personal communication.

32. Guzman, L. I. de. & M. Delfinado-Baker. 1996. A new species of *Varroa* (Acari: Varroidae) associated with *Apis koschevnikovi* (Apidae: Hymenoptera) in Borneo. Int. J. Acarol. 22: 23-27.

33. Guzman, L. I. de., T. E. Rinderer & R. R. Whiteside. 1996. A scientific note on the occurrence of *Varroa* mites on adult worker bees of *Apis nuluensis* in Borneo. Apidologie 27: 429-430.

34. Guzman L. I. de., T. E. Rinderer, I. *A.* Stelzer & D. Anderson. 1998. Congruence of RAPD and mitochondrial DNA markers in assessing *Varroa jacobsoni* genotypes. J. Apic. Res. 37: 49-51

35. Hoppe, R., W. Ritter & E. W.-C. Stephen. 1989. The control of parasitic bee mites: *Varroa jacobsoni*, *Acarapis woodi* and

Tropilaelaps clareae with formic acid. Am. Bee J. 129: 739-742.

36. **Kitprasert, C. 1984.** Biology and systematics of the parasitic bee mite, *Tropilaelaps clareae* Delfinado and Baker (Acarina: Laelapidae). MSc thesis, Kasetsart University, Thailand (Apic. Abstr. 1341/85).

37. **Koeniger N. & N. Muzaffar. 1988.** Lifespan of the parasitic honey bee mite, *Tropilaelaps clareae*, on *Apis cerana, dorsata* and *mellifera*. J. Apic. Res. 27: 207-212.

38. **Koeniger, N., G. Koeniger & M. Delfinado-Baker. 1983.** Observations on mites of the Asian honeybee species (*Apis cerana, Apis dorsata, Apis florea*). Apidologie 14: 197-204.

39. **Koeniger, N., G. Koeniger, L. I. de Guzman, C. Lekprayoon. 1993.** Survival of *Euvarroa sinhai* Delfinado and Baker (Acari, Varroidae) on workers of *Apis cerana* Fabr, *Apis florea* Fabr and *Apis mellifera* L in cages. Apidologie 24: 403-410.

40. **Koivulehto, K. 1980.** *Tropilaelaps clareae*–another mite threatening world beekeeping. Brit. Bee J. 108: 197-198.

41. **Kumar, N.R., R. Kumar, I. Mbaya & R.W. Mwangi. 1993.** *Tropilaelaps clareae* found on *Apis mellifera* in Africa. Bee World 74: 101-102.

42. **Laigo, F. M. & R. A. Morse. 1968.** The mite *Tropilaelaps clareae* in *Apis dorsata* colonies in the Philippines. Bee World 49: 116-118.

43. **Lee, B. 1995.** Mites, bees, and plagues that are and might be. Austral. Cent. Int. Agric. Res., Partners Res. for Develop. No. 8: 2-9.

44. **Lekprayoon, C. & P. Tangkanasing. 1991.** *Varroa wongsirii,* a new species of bee mite from Thailand. Int. J. Acarol. 17: 255-258.

45. **Lekprayoon, C. & P. Tangkanasing. 1993.** Comparative morphology of *Euvarroa sinhai* and *Euvarroa wongsirii*: parasites of *Apis florea* and *Apis andreniformis*, pp.427-433. *In* L.J. Connor, T. Rinderer, H.A. Sylvester & S. Wongsiri [eds.], Asian apiculture. Wicwas Press, Cheshire, CT, USA.

46. **Lindquist, E.** personal communication.

47. **Lord, W. G. & S. K. Nagi. 1987.** *Apis florea* discovered in Africa.

Bee World 68: 39-40.

48. **Lubinevski, Y., Y. Stern, Y. Slabezki, Y. Lensky, H. Ben-Yossef & U. Gerson. 1988.** Control of *Varroa jacobsoni* and *Tropilaelaps clareae* mites using Mavrik in *A. mellifera* colonies under subtropical and tropical climates. Am. Bee J. 128: 48-52.

49. **Luong, H. V., T. Q. Nguyen & D. V. Nguyen. 1993.** Biological characteristics and infestation rates of *Varroa jacobsoni* and *Tropilaelaps clareae* in *Apis mellifiera* colonies in Vietnam, pp. 556-559. *In* L.J. Connor, T. Rinderer, H.A. Sylvester & S. Wongsiri [eds.], Asian apiculture. Wicwas Press, Cheshire, CT, USA.

50. **Michener, C.D. 1963.** A further note on *Apis mellifera* in New Guinea. Bee World 44: 114.

51. **Morin, C. E. & G. W. Otis. 1993.** Observations on the morphology and biology of *Euvarroa wongsirii* (Mesostigmata: Varroidae), a parasite of *Apis andreniformis* (Hymenoptera: Apidae). Int. J. Acarol. 19: 167-172.

52. **Morse, R. A. & T. Hopper. 1985.** The illustrated encyclopedia of beekeeping. E.P. Dutton, New York.

53. **Mossadegh, M. S. 1990.** Development of *Euvarroa sinhai* (Acarina: Mesostigmata), a parasitic mite of *Apis florea*, on *A. mellifera* worker brood. Exp. Appl. Acarol. 9: 73-78.

54. **Mossadegh, M. S. 1990.** *In vitro* observations on ontogenesis of the mite, *Euvarroa sinhai* Delfinado & Baker (Acari: Varroidae), in drone brood cells of the honeybee, *Apis mellifiera* L. J. Apic. Res. 29: 230-232.

55. **Mossadegh, M. S. 1991.** Geographical distribution, levels of infestation and population density of the mite *Euvarroa sinhai* Delfinado and Baker (Acarina: Mesostigmata) in *Apis florea* F colonies in Iran. Apidologie 22: 127-134.

56. **Mossadegh, M. S. & A. B. Komeili. 1986.** *Euvarroa sinhai* Delfinado & Baker (Acarina: Mesostigmata): a parasite mite on *Apis florea* F. in Iran. Am. Bee J. 126: 684-685.

57. **Nguyen, D. V., T. Q. Nguyen, H. V. Luong & W. J. Boot. 1995.** Bio-technical manipulations used in Vietnam to control *Varroa*

jacobsoni and *Tropilaelaps clareae* in colonies of *Apis mellifera*. BeeScience 4: 11-13.

58. **Nguyen, D. V., T. Q. Nguyen, H. V. Luong & W. J. Boot. 1997.** Control of honey bee mites in Vietnam without the use of chemicals. Bee World 78: 78-83.

59. **Nyein, M. M. & C. Zmarlicki. 1982.** Control of mites in European bees in Burma. Am. Bee J. 122: 638-639.

60. **Otis, G. W. 1991.** A review of the diversity of species within *Apis*, pp. 29-49. *In* D.R. Smith. [ed.], Diversity in the genus *Apis*. Westview Press, Boulder/San Francisco/Oxford.

61. **Otis, G. W. 1996.** Distribution of recently recognized species of honey bees (Hymenoptera: Apidae; *Apis*) in Asia. J. Kansas Entomol. Soc. 69 (suppl.): 311-333.

62. **Oudemans, A. C. 1904.** Note VIII. On a new genus and species of parasitic acari. Notes Leyden Museum 24: 216-222.

63. **Panda P., J. Padhi, U. K. Nanda & N. C. Mohanty. 1989.** Record of *Varroa jacobsoni* and *Euvarroa sinhai* on *Apis cerana indica* Fabr. at Bhubaneshwar, Orissa, India. Indian Bee J. 51: 59.

64. **Rath, W. & M. Delfinado-Baker. 1990.** Analysis of *Tropilaelaps clareae* populations from the debris of *Apis dorsata* and *A. mellifera* in Thailand, pp. 86-89. *In* W. Ritter [ed.], Proceedings, Int. Symp. Recent Res. Bee Pathol., Ghent, Belgium.

65. **Rath, W., M. Delfinado-Baker & W. Drescher. 1991.** Observations on the mating behavior, sex ratio, phoresy and dispersal of *Tropilaelaps clareae* (Acari: Laelapidae). Int. J. Acarol. 17: 201-208.

66. **Rath, W., O. Boecking & W. Drescher. 1995.** The phenomena of simultaneous infestation of *Apis mellifera* in Asia with the parasitic mites *Varroa jacobsoni* Oud. and *Tropilaelaps clareae* Delfinado & Baker. Am. Bee J. 135: 125-127.

67. **Rinderer, T. E., B. P. Oldroyd, C. Lekprayoon, S. Wongsiri, C. Boonthai & R. Thapa. 1994.** Extended survival of the parasitic honey bee mite *Tropilaelaps clareae* on adult workers of *Apis mellifera* and *Apis dorsata*. J. Apic. Res. 3 3: 171-174.

68. **Ritter W. & U. Schneider-Ritter. 1988.** Differences in biology and means of controlling *Varroa jacobsoni* and *Tropilaelaps clareae*, two novel parasitic mites of *Apis mellifera*, pp. 387395. *In* G.R. Needham, R.E. Page Jr., M. Delfinado-Baker & C.E. Bowman [eds.], Africanized honey bees and bee mites. Halsted Press, New York.

69. **Ruttner, F. 1988.** Biogeography and taxonomy of honeybees. Springer, Berlin.

70. **Tangkanasing, P., S. Wongsiri & S. Vongsamanode. 1988.** Integrated control of *Varroa jacobsoni* and *Tropilaelaps clareae* in bee hives in Thailand, pp. 409-412. *In* G.R. Needham, R.E. Page Jr., M. Delfinado-Baker & C.E. Bowman [eds.], Africanized honey bees and bee mites. Halsted Press, New York.

71. **Tran, H. D., D. V. Nguyen, L. K. Nguyen, C. H. Phung, H. M. Dong & L. V. Pham. 1993.** Observations on some biological characteristics of *Tropilaelaps clareae* in Vietnam and its biotechnical control methods, pp. 560-568. *In* L.J. Connor, T. Rinderer, H.A. Sylvester & S. Wongsiri [eds.], Asian apiculture. Wicwas Press, Cheshire, CT, USA.

72. **Wongsiri, S., P. Tangkanasing & H. A. Sylvester. 1987.** Mites, pests and beekeeping with *Apis cerana* and *Apis mellifera* in Thailand. Am. Bee J. 127: 500-503.

73. **Wongsiri, S., P. Tangkanasing & S. Vongsamanode. 1987.** Effectiveness of Asuntol (coumaphos), Perizin (coumaphos), Mitac (amitraz) and powder of sulphur with naphthalene for the control of bee mites (*Varroa jacobsoni* and *Tropilaelaps clareae*) in Thailand, pp. 322-325. *In* Proceedings, 31st Int. Apic. Congr, Warsaw, Poland.

74. **Wongsiri, S., P. Tangkanasing & H. A. Sylvester. 1989.** The resistance behavior of *Apis cerana* against *Tropilaelaps clareae*, pp. 25 - 34. *In* Proceedings, 1st Asia-Pacific Conf. Entomol., Chiang Mai, Thailand.

75. **Wongsiri, S., P. Tangkanasing, C. Lekprayoon, T. E. Rinderer & H. A. Sylvester. 1994.** Biodiversity of parasitic mites of honey bees in Southeast Asia, pp. 6-13. *In* S. Wongsiri, P. Tangkanasing, C. Lekprayoon, T.E. Rinderer, H.A. Sylvester & M. Delfinado-Baker [eds.], Biodiversity of bee mites and honey bees in Thailand. Publ.

Bee Biol. Res. Unit, Chulalongkorn University (1991-1994).

76. **Wongsiri S., C. Lekprayoon, R. Thapa, K. Thirakupt, T. E. Rinderer, H. A. Sylvester, B. P. Oldroyd & U. Booncham. 1996.** Comparative biology of *Apis andreniformis* and *Apis florea* in Thailand. Bee World. 78: 23-35.

77. **Woo, K.-S. personal communication.**

78. **Woo, K.-S. 1992.** New honeybee mite *Varroa underwoodi* on *Apis cerana* in South Korea. Honeybee Science. 13: 173-174 [in Japanese].

79. **Woo, K.-S. 1992.** WARNING! The occurrence of new honeybee mite *Varroa underwoodi* from Korea. Asian Apic. Assn. Newsletter Suppl. No. 2: 5-6.

80. **Woyke, J. 1984.** Survival and prophylactic control of *Tropilaelaps clareae* infesting *A. mellifera* colonies in Afghanistan. Apidologie 15: 421-434.

81. **Woyke, J. 1985.** *Tropilaelaps clareae,* a serious pest of *Apis mellifera* in the tropics, but not dangerous for apiculture in temperate zones. Am. Bee J. 125: 497-409.

82. **Woyke, J. 1985.** Further investigations into control of the parasite bee mite *Tropilaelaps clareae* without medication. J. Apic. Res. 24: 250-254.

83. **Woyke, J. 1987.** Length of successive stages in the development of the mite *Tropilaelaps clareae* in relation to honeybee brood age. J. Apic. Res. 26: 110-114.

84. **Woyke, J. 1987.** Comparative population dynamics of *Tropilaelaps clareae* and *Varroa jacobsoni* mites on honeybees. J. Apic. Res. 26: 196-202.

85. **Woyke, J. 1987.** Length of stay of the parasitic mite *Tropilaelaps clareae* outside sealed honeybee brood cells as a basis for its effective control. J. Apic. Res. 26: 104-109.

86. **Woyke, J. 1989.** Change in shape of *Tropilaelaps clareae* females and the onset of egg laying. J. Apic. Res. 28: 196-200.

87. **Woyke, J. 1993.** Practical control method of the parasitic bee mite *Tropilaelaps clareae*. Am. Bee J. 133: 510-511.

88. **Woyke, J. 1994.** Repeated egg laying by females of the parasitic honeybee mite *Tropilaelaps clareae* Delfinado and Baker. Apidologie 25: 327-330.

89. **Woyke, J. 1994.** Mating behavior of the parasitic honeybee mite *Tropilaelaps clareae*. Exp. Appl. Acarol. 18: 723-733.

GENERAL INDEX

abdomen 58, 134, 143, 257
absconding 108, 113, 257, 259
abundance 7, 20, 119, 124, 164, 168, 255
Acarapis dorsalis 17 - 24, 30, 31, 34
Acarapis externus 17 - 24, 30, 31, 34
Acari 2, 3
acaricide (miticide)
    classification 180
    efficacy and testing 86, 87, 89, 91,
        95, 112, 163, 179, 241, 245
    for mite detection 166, 170, 171
    registration 91
    residual activity 181
    residues 186 - 191, 205, 230, 245, 257
    resistance to (see resistance)
    timing of application 163, 206, 229
    toxicity 104
acariosis 57
Acaromyces laviae 110
acephate 88
acetyl cholinesterase 187
acetylcholine 187
acinar cells 63
Actinomyces spp. 65
acute bee paralysis 67
acute toxicity 183
Aerobacter cloacae 65
Aethina tumida 187
Africa 149, 212, 254
Africanized bees 30, 57, 58, 107, 109, 122,
    153, 158, 200, 208, 210 - 212, 219, 154,
    159, 254
Afrocypholaelaps 8
age 21, 34, 62, 74, 106, 143, 185
air puffs 35
Alberta (AB) 47, 49, 93, 95, 153
alcohol 73, 74, 77, 79, 165
alleles 246
amitraz 35, 87, 88, 92, 152, 154, 166, 186,
    187, 245, 256
amoeba 66
apiary
    dispersal of mites in 36, 45, 108,
        109, 111, 134
    infestation 53, 92, 111, 150, 171,
        216, 217, 253, 259, 262
    sampling 76, 81, 82, 172
    tests 233, 234, 237, 248
apiary inspectors 46 - 49, 151, 172, 173
Apis andreniformis 9, 10, 131, 252, 258
Apis cerana 8 - 10, 21, 30, 57, 86, 131,
    134, 136, 138, 142, 143, 149, 208 -

210, 212 - 214, 252, 253, 259, 260, 262
Apis dorsata 9, 10, 30, 57, 131, 252, 254,
    255, 257, 258
Apis florea 9, 10, 131, 252 - 254, 258, 259
Apis laboriosa 9, 131, 252, 253
Apis mellifera scutellata (see Africanized bees)
Apis nigrocincta 9, 252, 260
Apis nuluensis 9, 252, 260, 261
Apis koschevnikovi 9, 132, 252, 259, 260
Apistan® 4, 24, 89, 92, 154, 155, 170,
    171, 185, 186, 241, 242, 248
Apitol® 188
Apivar® 187
Argentina 91
Arizona (AZ) 110, 121
Arkansas (AK) 46, 48, 155
ARS-Y-C-1 (bee stock) 23, 121, 123
Asia 1, 10, 30, 86, 131, 149, 209, 251 -
    255, 257, 259, 260, 263
assay 120, 186, 215, 241
Astigmata 8
Australia 21, 132, 153, 156
autumn 81, 89, 119, 186, 187, 190
Azadirachta indica (neem) 95

Bacillus alvei 65
Bacillus mesentericus 65
Bacillus mycoides 65
Bacillus subtilis 65
bacteria 34, 64 - 68
Bacterium prodigiosum 65
Bayvarol® 186
beeswax 35, 157, 172, 186 - 191, 199,
    237, 245, 256
behavior
    of *Acarapis dorsalis* and *Acarapis
        externus* 20, 21
    of *Acarapis woodi*, dispersal, 34, 35
    of *Acarapis woodi*, questing 107
    of *Apis dorsata*, hygienic 256
    of *Apis mellifera*, affecting acaricide
        movement 181
    of *Apis mellifera*, affecting mite disper-
        sal 36, 108, 136, 144, 163, 172
    of *Apis mellifera*, crawling 61, 62, 68
    of *Apis mellifera*, drifting 21, 36, 45,
        76, 106, 108, 109, 113, 136, 143,
        163, 171, 172
    of *Apis mellifera*, grooming, 5, 32,
        122, 134, 170, 181, 201, 211 -
        213, 215 - 218, 259

of *Apis mellifera*, hygienic 158, 212 - 218
of *Apis mellifera*, robbing 36, 45, 76,
        108 - 110, 113, 136, 143, 163
of *Varroa jacobsoni*, reproductive
        137, 209
of *Varroa jacobsoni*, host-seaking 173
Biak 209
bioassay 35, 123, 124, 183, 186, 242, 248
blood 17, 24, 32, 33, 58, 63, 68, 77, 93,
        134, 138, 180, 187
Borneo 259, 260
Brazil 30, 150, 210 - 212, 219, 263
breeding programs 207, 216, 218, 219
British Columbia (BC) 21, 47, 49, 93
bromopropylate 86, 188
brood, *Apis cerana* 208, 209, 213, 214
brood, *Apis dorsata* 254
brood, *Apis mellifera*
        Acarapis woodi effects on 52, 53, 58
        acaricide effects on 86, 87, 90, 92, 188
        Aethina tumida effects on 187
        Africanized bee 210 - 212
        care by worker bees 7
        cell 5, 6, 89, 131, 132, 135, 137 -
                139, 142 - 144, 154, 164, 167,
                168, 170, 172, 180, 181, 186,
                189, 191, 198 - 202, 206 - 209,
                213 - 215, 218, 235, 253 - 256,
                258 - 260, 262
        diseased 218, 231
        drone 10, 134, 137, 138, 140, 143,
                158, 164, 165, 167, 168, 170 -
                173, 198, 208 - 210, 212, 214,
                235, 258 - 260, 262
        food 63, 137, 138, 142, 253, 254
        freeze-killed 215, 217
        nest 74, 106, 142, 166, 167, 170,
                171, 189, 190, 198, 200
        pheromones 172
        rearing 112, 118, 136, 169, 170, 181,
                185, 207, 232 - 236, 241, 251,
                257, 259, 263
        worker 10, 137, 139, 140, 142, 143,
                164, 165, 167, 170, 171, 173,
                198, 199, 208 - 212, 214, 218,
                235, 247, 252, 259, 260, 262
Buckfast bees 35, 118, 120 - 123

cade oil 91
California (CA) 22, 46, 48, 50 - 53, 66,

        92, 110, 111, 152, 155
California Department of Food and
        Agriculture 50
camphor 91, 188
Canada 45, 52, 54, 58, 82, 85, 87, 92, 95,
        96, 111, 119, 120, 149, 153, 154, 156, 171
canola oil 90
capping scratcher 167
carbohydrates 7, 63
Carniolan bees 121, 123, 214
Carolina 110, 233
Caucasian bees 123
cells and tissues
        Acarapis woodi 66
        Apis mellifera 61, 63
chalkbrood 215, 217
chelicerate 2
chigger 4
China 156, 212, 213, 257
chlorobenzilate 86, 257
chronic bee paralysis 67
citral 91
cocoon 138, 142
colony strength 190, 257
Colorado (CO) 46, 48
comb
        acaricides in and on 111, 181, 189,
                190, 230, 237
        ANP 200
        as mite habitat 8, 12, 35, 254
        collecting bees from 74, 126
        drone 198, 200, 202
        Varroa jacobsoni feces on 169
        worker 199, 208
commensalism 3
compression 5
computer models and simulations 201
coumaphos 88, 89, 154, 187, 188, 245, 248
coxal plate 18
crawling 58, 60 - 63, 68, 167, 254, 256
creosote 90, 91, 190
cuticle 35, 122, 134, 202
cuticular hydrocarbons 32, 35
cymiazole 89, 188

DDT 182, 188
dead bee trap 93
debris 8, 59 - 61, 66, 68, 169, 235, 254, 259
defecation (see feces)
deformities 256

dehydration 5
Delaware (DE) 46, 48
Demodicidae 3
depopulation (colony eradication) 46, 47, 50, 51
deutonymph 4, 137, 139
dimethoate 88
diphenylcarbinol 188
dispersal 3, 8, 10, 21, 33 - 36, 58, 108, 109, 134, 136, 143, 168, 171
distribution of infested bees 74
DNA 209, 260, 262
dorsal groove 18
drones, adult *Apis cerana* 134, 138, 142, 143, 259, 262
drones, adult *Apis mellifera*
    as colony members 7
    emerging 170
    Euvarroa spp. on 258, 259
    for breeding bees 121, 123, 125, 215
    mite dispersal by 10, 33, 36, 108, 136
    rearing 109, 167, 170
    Acarapis woodi infestations in 33
    tracheae 44
drone brood foundation 168

Eastern States Agreement 156
economic injury level 11, 80 - 82
economic threshold 76, 80 - 82, 107, 112, 154, 237
ectoparasite 5
eggs
    Acarapis dorsalis 18, 20, 21
    Acarapis externus 18, 20, 21
    Acarapis woodi 21, 30, 32, 52, 58, 60, 77, 95, 106
    Apis mellifera 7
    Euvarroa, Tropilaelaps and Varroa 253, 254, 256, 258
    mite 3, 4
    Varroa jacobsoni 137 - 139, 141 - 144, 198, 208, 253
embryo 138
endoplasmic reticulum 63
endosulfan 24
England 86, 111, 118, 120
Environmental Protection Agency (EPA) 91, 154
enzyme-linked immunosorbent assay 74, 80
equilibrium position 80, 81

eradication of mites 50, 51, 54, 150, 229
Escherichia coli 65
essential oils 91, 154, 181, 189
ether roll 154, 155, 165 - 168, 171, 232, 234
eucalyptol 87, 91, 188
euchromatin 63
Europe 1, 21, 44, 53, 58, 81, 86, 87, 89, 91, 95, 105, 118, 143, 149, 153, 154, 186 - 188, 198, 200, 205, 210, 211, 216, 219, 242, 245, 247, 251, 262, 263
Euvarroa spp. 9, 10, 131, 252, 253, 258, 259, 263
Euvarroa sinhai 9, 10, 252, 258, 259, 261 (diagram)
Euvarroa wongsirii 9, 10, 252, 258, 261 (diagram)
extender patty 35, 90
exuviae 61

fall (see autumn)
feces 3, 52, 59, 64, 138, 139, 141, 168, 169
fecundity 122, 254, 255
feeding 3, 5, 8, 10, 12, 23, 33, 34, 59 - 63, 67, 68, 89, 93, 109, 135, 138, 139, 141, 142, 180, 254, 259
female (mite) 3, 5, 6, 7, 8, 10, 18, 19, 20, 30 - 33, 34, 106, 108, 119, 132 - 136, 138, 139, 141 - 144, 167, 168, 199, 206, 208, 209, 215, 218, 253 - 256, 258, 262
fenbutatin oxide 24
feral colonies 36, 157, 212
Finland 171
flight 7, 34, 53, 57, 59, 60, 62, 63, 68, 187
flight muscles 34, 53, 57, 59, 60, 62, 68
Florida (FL) 45, 46, 48, 50, 52, 88, 92, 150 - 158, 205
flumethrin 87, 95, 186, 244
fluvalinate 87, 89, 91, 150, 152 - 155, 157, 166, 170, 171, 185, 186, 205, 230, 241, 242, 244, 245, 247, 257
Folbex® 86, 87, 95, 257
foraging 8, 21, 34, 58, 74, 76, 107, 111, 112, 137, 259
Forcellinia faini 8
formamidine 186
formic acid 86, 87, 89 - 91, 93 - 95, 189, 190, 245, 257
foulbrood 108, 215, 217, 229
France 64, 106, 150, 187, 211

General Index

fumigation   89, 91, 93, 95, 180, 257
fungi 8

gasoline (petrol)   86, 166
gel matrix   89
Georgia (GA)   154, 233
Germany   190, 210, 214, 217, 262
glycogen   62, 63
grapefruit leaves   190
Great Britain   30, 50, 85, 112, 120, 121,
    234 - 236
guanine   168

Hawaii (HI)   46, 48, 153, 171
heating (thermal) treatments   110, 167, 200
hemolymph   33, 58 - 61, 63 - 68, 77
Himalayan   253
hive environment   8, 134
homeostasis   7
honey
    acaricide residues in   88, 105, 186,
        187, 189 - 191, 205, 237
    capping scratcher   167
    house   152
    importation   156
    production   51, 81, 90, 95, 107, 120,
        188, 206, 217, 218, 233, 257
    production affected by acaricides   90
    production affected by mites   52
    robbing   36, 45, 76, 108 - 110, 113,
        136, 143, 163
Honeybee Act of 1922   44
hormone   209
host range   260
humidity   7, 136, 138
hybrid bees   23, 121 - 123, 208, 211
hydrophilic   188
Hypoaspis   263
hypopharyngeal glands   34, 63, 68

Idaho (ID)   46, 48
Illinois (IL)   46, 48, 152
immunity   119
imported bee stock   45, 106
in vitro rearing of mites   11
Indiana (IN)   46, 48
inbreeding by mites   139, 141, 142, 246
India   8, 10, 30, 86, 258

Indochina   258
Indonesia   209
infestation   5, 11, 24, 35, 45
    affected by honey flow   106
    of Acarapis dorsalis   22,23
    of Acarapis externis   23
    of Acarapis woodi   30, 43, 48 - 50,
        52, 53, 57, 58, 60 - 64, 66, 67, 74
        - 77, 79 - 81, 90, 106, 108, 109,
        112, 113, 117, 119, 121, 122, 126
    of Euvarroa sinhai   10
    of Tropilaelaps   253
    of Varroa jacobsoni   23, 142, 163,
        166, 167, 171 - 173, 206, 209 -
        211, 213, 214, 216 - 219, 234,
        235, 238, 241, 256
injury   17, 43, 59, 61, 179, 187, 191
instrumental insemination   125
integrated pest management (IPM)   80, 8
    2, 112, 158
integument   4, 5
intensity   119, 208
Iowa (IA)   46, 48
Iran   10, 258, 259
Ireland   118
Irian Jaya   209
Isle of Wight   30, 36, 43, 85, 118
Israel   88, 237
Italian bees   109
Italy   87, 150, 210, 241, 244, 245, 248

Japan   131, 149, 210, 263
Java   209, 260, 262
juvenile hormone   208

Kansas (KS)   46, 48, 90
Kentucky (KY)   46, 48, 153, 170
Korea   254, 260
K-wing   43, 44, 58

Larrea tridentata   90
larva   4, 20, 137, 138, 172, 198, 200, 206,
    208, 209, 215
lethal concentration   183
lethal dose   157, 183, 184
lethal exposure time   183
Liebefeld applicator   94
life cycle   4, 20, 29, 32, 34 - 36, 57, 67,

164, 253, 254
life history   20, 132, 143, 197, 258
life stages   20, 31, 258
lipophilic molecule   186 - 188
Lombardy   241
longevity   20, 23, 33, 34, 255
Louisiana (LA)   23, 45, 46, 48, 50, 122
Maine (ME)   152, 153
Malaysia   10, 258, 260
male (mites)   7, 21, 33, 34, 143, 254, 256
mangrove   8
Manitoba (MB)   47, 49, 92, 153
Maryland (MD)   46, 48, 88
Massachusetts (MA)   46, 48, 53
mating   32, 33, 123, 125, 136, 137, 139,
    141, 142, 144
Mavrik®   152, 153, 257
melanin   60
Melittiphis alvearis   8
menthol   5, 24, 85, 87 - 93, 95, 188
Mesostigmata   8
metabolism   5, 60 - 62, 181, 182, 189
metamorphosis   4
methanol   86
methyl salicylate   86, 87
Mexico   45, 64, 87 - 89, 106, 107, 109,
    111, 112, 122, 150, 153, 154, 156,
    211, 212
Michigan (MI)   46, 48, 152
Micrococcus flavus   65
Micrococcus luteus   65
Micrococcus pyrogenes var. albus   65
Micrococcus radiatus   65
migration   158, 257
migratory beekeepers   45
Minnesota (MN)   46, 48, 53, 219
Mississippi (MS)   46, 48, 152
Missouri (MO)   46, 48
Mitac®   88, 257
mitefall   167, 170, 171
miticide (see acaricide)
Miticur®   187
mitochondria   62
models   124, 198, 201, 234, 237
molt   138, 139, 141, 183
Montana (MT)   46, 48, 155
mortality   18, 23, 53, 58, 87, 89, 90, 92, 94,
    121, 122, 139, 142 - 144, 186, 187, 207,
    230, 231, 256
mouthparts   2, 33, 77, 134, 135, 141, 212,
    254, 256, 258

myofibrils   62

Nassenheider Verdunster   94
Nebraska (NE)   46, 48, 88, 152
neck   17, 18
nectar   7, 34, 36, 58, 66, 91, 106, 109,
    111, 112, 136
Neocypholaelaps   8
Nepal   260
nerve   60, 63, 68, 182, 185, 187
Nevada (NV)   46, 48
New Brunswick (NB)   47, 49
New Hampshire (NH)   46, 48
New Jersey (NJ)   46, 48
New Mexico (NM)   46, 48, 110
New York (NY)   21, 45, 46, 48, 92, 152
New Zealand   21, 22, 24, 132, 153, 156
nitrobenzene   86, 87
nocturnal dispersal   34
non-reproduction by Varroa jacobsoni
    210, 214, 218, 255, 262, 263
North Carolina (NC)   61, 62
North Dakota (ND)   45, 46, 48
nosema disease   62, 66, 229
Nova Scotia (NS)   47, 49, 153
nucleus hive (nuc)   22, 63, 93, 106
nurse bees   106, 207
nutrition   206, 209
nymph   20

octopamine   187
Ohio (OH)   46, 48, 152
Ontario (ON)   47, 49, 82, 94, 123 - 125
Opiliones   3
Oregon (OR)   18, 22, 46, 48
organophosphate   187
ovaries   143
overwintering   52, 53, 90
oviposition   32, 137, 208
oxalic acid   154, 190, 247
oxygen   59 - 63, 68

Pacific Northwest   107
package bees   92, 156, 157, 163, 185, 233,
    234
Papua New Guinea   10, 131, 209, 260 - 263
Paraguay   149
patchouli oil   91

pathogenicity   54
pathogen   59, 64, 67, 68
Pennsylvania (PA)   46, 48, 152
peretrimes   137
Perizin®   187
Persian Gulf   258
petroleum jelly   169
pheromone   7, 172
phoretic   8, 132, 135, 136, 143, 199, 202, 207, 213, 255
pine oil   87, 91
pleural hairs   32
Poland   211
pollen   7, 8, 58, 187, 210
pollination   51, 95, 107, 152, 153, 155 - 157, 179
post-capping duration   211, 212, 218
potassium nitrate   86, 188
powdered sugar   181
prepupae   254
prevalence   18, 22, 36, 58, 89, 91, 111, 119, 126, 164, 165
Prince Edward Island (PEI)   47, 49, 153
probit analysis   183
Proctolaelaps   263
propodeum   18
Prostigmata   8
proteins   138
Proteus mirabilis   65
prothoracic trachea   33, 60, 61
protonymph   4, 137, 138
Province Quebec (PQ)   47, 49
Pseudacarapis indoapis   8
Pseudomonas apiseptica   67
Pseudomones fluorescens   65
Puerto Rico   8, 210, 263
pupa   167, 168, 207 - 209, 213, 215, 216, 251, 252, 254 - 256, 258
pyrethroid   150, 185, 186, 241

quarantine   43, 45, 50, 51, 54, 120, 156
Quebec (see Province Quebec)
queen bee   7, 10, 33, 44, 52, 58, 89, 90, 92, 93, 106, 109, 117, 121, 123, 125, 156, 157, 185, 188, 199, 257
queen cell   10, 93, 106, 109
queenless   257

regulations   50 - 52, 91, 153, 155, 156

reproduction
    in *Acarapis externus*   18, 34
    in *Acarapis dorsalis*   18, 34
    in *Acarapis woodi*   23, 34, 74, 89, 95, 109, 110
    in *Apis mellifera*   113
    in mites in general   3, 4, 8, 12
    in *Tropilaelaps*   253, 255, 256
    in *Varroa destructor*   262
    in *Varroa jacobsoni*   132, 135, 137 - 141, 143, 144, 151, 171, 199 - 201, 206 - 212, 214, 218, 219, 253, 255, 262
    in *Varroa underwoodi*   253, 260
resistance
    in *Acarapis woodi*, to acaricides   31
    in *Apis mellifera*, to *Acarapis woodi*   11, 29, 32, 35, 66, 92, 95, 111, 117 - 126
    in *Apis mellifera*, to *Varroa jacobsoni*   11, 23, 95, 163, 197, 205 - 207, 210 - 212, 215 - 219, 262, 263
    in mites, to acaricides   4
    in *Varroa jacobsoni*, to acaricides   2, 4, 91, 150, 154, 155, 163, 181, 186, 187, 191, 197, 205, 230, 236 - 238, 241, 242, 244 - 249
respiratory structure   5
Russia   210, 263

safrol   86
saltpeter   86, 88
sampling
    accuracy   74, 82, 164, 166, 167, 169, 171, 173
    hives   22, 50, 66, 73, 74, 79, 80, 112, 119, 122, 164 - 169, 172, 173, 229, 232 - 235, 248
    pooled (apiary)   76, 81, 82
    sequential   75, 76, 82
    subsamples   170
Santa Catarina   210
Sarcina aurantiaca   65
Sarcina flava   65
Sarcina lutes   65
sarcoplasm   62
Saskatchewan (SK)   47, 49, 58, 92
Saudi Arabia   258
Scandinavia   21
scavenger   8

sclerites 5, 134
sclerotized *Varroa jacobsoni* 134, 170
Scotland 60, 66, 111
scutellum 18
scutoscutellar groove 18
scutum 18
season 59, 75, 164, 165, 169, 170, 173, 199, 207, 218, 232 - 236
Section 3 154, 187
semen 215
seminal receptacles 209, 218
sensitivity 5, 76, 139, 164, 166 - 171, 173, 189, 232
septicemia 66
setae 134, 260
small hive beetle (see *Aethina tumida*)
smoker fuel 166, 191
spiracle 18, 30, 32, 122
soapy water 165
South America 2, 11, 21, 156
South Carolina (SC) 47, 49, 152
South Dakota (SD) 45, 152
spermatheca 141
spermatogenesis 141
spermatozoa 136, 139, 141, 209, 218
spider mites 3
Spiroplasma melliferum 66, 67
spiroplasmas 66, 68
spring 22, 36, 52, 66, 74, 80, 81, 87, 89, 91, 106, 112, 152, 155, 167, 170, 181, 186, 187
Sri Lanka 10, 253, 258
Starline bees 217
sticky board 169 - 171, 173, 191, 232, 234
Streptococcus faecalis 65
Streptococcus liquefaciens 65
stress 58, 107, 108, 113, 233
stylets 20, 33
subtropical 8, 258, 263
Sulawesi 260
sulfur 86
Sumatra 260
summer 22, 34, 36, 60, 66, 67, 74, 86, 92, 167, 170, 207, 235, 247
supersedure 33
survival 7, 10, 29, 35, 36, 52, 131, 134, 206, 216, 218, 219, 244, 257 - 259, 263
susceptibility (see also resistance) 86, 118, 119, 122, 123, 185, 186, 202, 211, 232, 244, 246, 247

swarming 36, 108, 109, 118, 136, 143, 166, 212, 235, 236, 246, 257
Switzerland 21, 106
symbiont 3
synergistic effects 107
synergists 181, 182
systemic 89, 187, 188

talcum powder 181
Tarsonemus woodi 30, 43
temperature 7, 62, 73, 110, 139, 142, 168, 181, 189, 190, 200
Tennessee (TN) 47, 49
tentorial pits 18
terpineol 87, 91
Texas (TX) 45, 47, 49, 53, 88, 90, 109, 158
Thailand 10, 258
thoracic salivary glands 57
thorax 4, 7, 30 - 32, 44, 57, 59, 64, 66, 77, 78
treatment threshold 11, 81, 94, 107, 231 - 234, 236 - 238
thymol 91, 188
tibia 20
time of year (see season)
tobacco 90, 166
tolerance 119, 155, 191, 206, 244
trachea (tracheal tubes) 4, 18, 24, 30 - 33, 44, 53, 57 - 61, 63 - 65, 68, 76 - 79, 111
transpiration 5
trapping method 198
trichlohexyltin hydroxide 24
tritonymph 4
trophallaxis (food sharing) 180, 187, 188
tropics 8, 153, 208, 211, 255, 258, 263
Tropilaelaps spp. 9, 10, 131, 251 - 258, 263
Tropilaelaps clareae 9, 10, 11, 251 - 257, 261 (diagram), 263
Tropilaelaps koenigerum 9, 252, 253, 254, 261 (diagram), 263
trucking bee hives 45, 109, 110
Tunisia 211, 212
tyrosine 60

unfertilized 4, 138, 209, 253, 256
United Kingdom 30, 165
United States (USA) 120, 121, 123, 152, 153, 156, 180, 187, 188, 190
Uruguay 211

USA Department of Agriculture (USDA)
   45, 50, 88, 90, 96, 120, 121, 151, 152, 173
USDA Animal Plant Health Inspection
   Service (APHIS)   50, 151, 152, 156
USSR   21
Utah (UT)   47, 49

vapor   5, 24, 86, 94, 166, 190
Varroa destructor   10, 262, 263
Varroa jacobsoni   261 (diagram)
Varroa rindereri   9, 252, 260, 261 (diagram), 263
Varroa underwoodi   9, 252, 253, 260, 261
   (diagram)
vegetable oil   35, 88, 90, 93, 95, 96
vegetable shortening   2, 90, 169
Veracruz   95
vermiculite   188
Vermont (VT)   47, 49
vibration   35
Vietnam   254, 257, 258
Virginia (VA)   47, 49
virulence   11, 23, 118, 263
viruses   11, 59, 66 - 68, 111
virus-like particles   66

Washington (WA)   47, 49, 110, 152
water   3, 5, 7, 78, 79, 110, 134, 169, 187,
   188, 190
wax (see beeswax)
wax moths   256
wind   190
wing   12, 18, 19, 35, 44, 58, 63
winter   29, 30, 36, 53, 54, 58, 74, 81, 85,
   91, 107, 108, 110, 112, 134, 135, 156,
   170, 199, 207, 208, 234, 235
wintergreen oil   86, 90
Wisconsin (WI)   47, 49, 150 - 152
worker bee   10, 20, 35, 44, 52, 62, 74, 89,
   93, 119, 122, 125, 126, 136 - 140, 142
   - 144, 164, 165, 167, 170 - 173, 198 -
   200, 208 - 214, 218, 235, 252, 254,
   258 - 260, 262
Wyoming (WY)   47, 49

Yapen   209
yeast   64, 110
Yugoslavia   121